Stepping Off the Edge

Anne McConnell

STEPPING OFF
THE EDGE

DALKEY ARCHIVE PRESS
Dallas / Dublin

CIP Data available on request.

Chapter 4 appeared in different form as "Writing the Impossibility
of Relation: Marguerite Duras's *La maladie de la mort*, Maggie
Nelson's *Bluets*, and Lydia Davis's *The End of the Story*" in *Comparative
Literature Studies* 55.3 (2018).

Partially funded by a grant from West Virginia State University, with
additional support from the West Virginia Humanities Council

www.dalkeyarchive.com
Dallas / Dublin

Printed on permanent/durable acid-free paper.

TABLE OF CONTENTS

Stepping Off the Edge

INTRODUCTION

In the Afterword to "Canicula di Anna" in *Plainwater*, Anne Carson asks the reader, "what is so terrible about stepping off the end of a story?" (88) "Stepping off the end of a story" might mean a variety of things; in this context, Carson points to a textual moment, the end, and our unwillingness to let it arrive and therefore accept our dismissal from the text. We seek the end, the closure to the story, at the same time that we put it off, lingering along the edges of the cliff, knowing that the end means we will be cast out, dislocated at the moment of completion. We might seek other ways to fill the silence that follows the story, finding a means to perpetuate the story beyond its seeming departure: "Because you would always like to know a little more. Not exactly more story. Not necessarily, on the other hand, an exegesis. Just something to go on with" (88). But, why? What if, instead, we step off? Carson seems to suggest that the intimacy we desire with a text might require an outsider's gaze, even if our alienation becomes the only basis for intimacy. After all, the end is inevitable. Yet, in shifting our attention to what can take place at the margins, somewhere just off the edge of a text, we see that the inevitability of closure perhaps becomes its impossibility. The end points to something else—an invitation, a demand, to keep reading, to keep writing, aware of our dismissal and inspired by the promise of a perpetually open text.

Carson further describes the experience of the end of the story: "But there is a moment of uncovering, and of covering, which happens very fast and you seem to be losing track of something. It is almost as if you hear a key turn in the lock. Which side of the door are you on? You do not know. Which side am I on?" (89) Carson interrogates the boundary marking inside from outside—not to erase it or to deny its existence, but, rather, to trouble our relation to it and our attempts to locate it. The moment of uncovering *is* the moment of covering; the end announces closure at the same time that it reveals the impossibility of closure. Once the story ends, we have no place in the story and therefore cannot experience its closure—except perhaps from the outside, on the other side of the door. When Carson does indeed nudge us off the end of the story, it is not in order that we might find fulfillment, understanding, or closure. Instead, stepping off might actually serve as an alternate means of perpetuating the end, of causing the end to recur and to initiate a different kind of approach. The end thus becomes a locus of play in Carson's work—a place where she reflects upon the various ways one might step off the edge, putting the end into question, while also affirming the value of exclusion, of dismissing ourselves from the story in order to sneak around back. At the end of the afterword to "Canicula di Anna," after she has asked us to contemplate stepping off the end of the story, Carson assures us:

> I find I do have something to give you. Not the mysterious, intimate and consoling data you would have wished, but something to go on with, and in all likelihood the best I can do. It is simply the fact, as you go down the stairs and walk in dark streets, as you see forms, as you marry or speak sharply or wait for a train, as you begin imagination, as you look at every mark, simply the fact of my eyes in your back. (90)

What Carson says she will give us does not fill in the silences of the story, creating intimacy and understanding; instead, what she gives will allow the story to seep into the outside, the space of our dismissal. As Adam Phillips suggests in his review of *Plainwater*, "[…] for Carson, ends are always edges, there is no closure; there is only translation or flight."

For many writers, the end represents a moment of contestation[1]—one where the closure of the text opens onto that which exceeds closure and refuses incorporation. And that's one way of framing the interest many contemporary writers have in playing with endings and edges. Of course, as Frank Kermode examines in *The Sense of an Ending*, an interest in the question of ending and closure is not unique to contemporary literature and perhaps broadly reflects "a need in the moment of existence to belong, to be related to a beginning and an end" (4). Fortunately, as Kermode points out, "It is not expected of critics as it is of poets that they should help us to make sense of our lives; they are bound only to attempt to the lesser feat of making sense of the ways we try to make sense of our lives" (3). Kermode's far-ranging study looks at the question of endings and closure in literature as a means of sense-making; he concludes his discussion by analyzing the work of Camus and Sartre, where he observes the complexities of closure in texts that remain skeptical about beginnings and ends, drawing attention to the fictions we construct and try to distinguish from an extra-fictional reality. Barbara Herrnstein Smith takes up the study of literary closure as well, focusing on poetry and the ways that poems end. Like Kermode, she begins her study with a few initial remarks about what seems to be a general desire for closure:

> It would seem that in the common land of ordinary events—where many experiences are fragmentary, interrupted, fortuitously con- nected, and determined by causes beyond our agency or comprehension—we create or seek out "enclosures": structures that are highly organized, separated as if by an implicit frame from a background of relative disorder or ran- domness, and integral or complete. (2)

Smith goes on to examine the ways that the last lines of

poems work to gratify the reader's experience by resolving tensions and fulfilling expectations; to provide closure and affirm the poem's structure; to create a sense of integrity and wholeness. In her analysis of twentieth-century poetry, Smith discusses the aesthetics of anti-closure and concludes her study with a few poems by E. E. Cummings and William Carlos Williams. Though both poets tend toward anti-closure, Smith argues that their poems necessarily offer some degree of closure—syntactically and thematically in the case of Cummings, and, for Williams, simply because the poem stops. The literal conclusion of the poem, no matter how seemingly arbitrary, forces us to consider the poem as a whole (256, 258).

Kermode and Smith published their books about endings in the late sixties, and in many ways foreshadowed a prolific critical discussion of and literary engagement with the artifice of closure and the supposed boundaries separating text from *hors-texte*.[2] Derrida famously deconstructs the assumptions upon which Emmanuel Kant built his critiques, and specifically takes aim at the assumption that a "frame" could somehow be distinguished from a "text proper."[3] De Man demonstrates the fallacies of New Criticism, revealing the dependence of that critical approach upon a definitive boundary between "inside" and "outside," despite the necessity of readerly intervention when trying to disentangle contradictory meanings.[4] And I would argue that since then a good deal of literature has taken interest in questions of ending, closure, and boundary-making. While I do not want to over-emphasize a narrative approach to literary history and criticism, suggesting a sort of linear progression over time that apparently would lead to a particular "end," it is hard to ignore the way that the writing of the last few decades—criticism, fiction, and everything in between—zeroes in on the question of what happens when we reach an "end" and explores what it might be like to write in excess of that end. And we arrive at some basic questions: To what extent do ends provide closure? How might texts remain "open," despite arriving at a final word? How do our readings of texts arrive at, facilitate, or avoid the end? How do writers flesh out a sort of *hors-texte*, composing in the marginal space of the *parergon*, as a mode of interrogating textual ends, edges, and hierarchies?

The works I have chosen for this study span nearly four decades, beginning with the 1980s and continuing into contemporary literature. Over that period of time, critics have attempted to identify particular literary movements, trends, and critical approaches, often with the use of words like "post," "beyond," "after," and even "post-post," in the case of Jeffrey T. Nealon's chosen label for the various literary and cultural trends that develop after postmodernism.[5] While one might wonder how anything can come after the "modern," or the present moment, (or, even more confusingly, what would come after whatever comes after the modern, in the case of post-postmodernism), Brian McHale assures us that the term "postmodernism" refers not to what comes after the modern, but to what comes after the modernist movement (*Postmodernist Fiction* 5). That makes sense, of course, although I prefer to maintain the sense of excess implied in the less sensical interpretation of the term "postmodern." In that way, the postmodern echoes what John Barth famously refers to as "The Literature of Exhaustion," as a means of identifying and discussing works that start with the assumption of "the used-upness of certain forms or exhaustion of certain possibilities" (19). What do we write after everything has already been written—when the moment has come and gone, and we arrive late, *post*erior to the main event? And, then, when our late arrival has passed as well, what comes next? David Rudrum and Nicholas Stavris collected a number of essays on that last topic in *Supplanting the Postmodern*. The essays in the second part of the book, including Nealon's on post-postmodernism, attempt to identify literary trends that follow the end of post-modernism, and, as is presumably expected of them, do their best to coin a term, proposing names such as: "hypermodernism," "performatism," "digimodernism," "metamodernism," and "renewalism." My point here is to demonstrate the way that, in recent decades, critics have tended to frame literature in terms of an "after-thought"—as coming *after*, arriving *late*, attempting to return after time away, and as needing to figure out what to do after there's no more to be done.[6] And, lest that seem depressing, as Barth demonstrates in his discussion of the work of Jorge Luis Borges in "The Literature of Exhaustion," the recognition of a certain type of end, or exhaustion, can indeed foster a particularly rich space for writing, even if, and perhaps because, that space remains excessive and marginal.[7]

The interest in closure, textual endings, and exhausted possibility does not stop with writing, but also extends to the ways that particular approaches to reading close or open a text. The work of deconstruction clearly targets attempts to stabilize and close texts, demonstrating the way the epistemological structures of those texts collapse under close scrutiny. And, aside from the critical practice of deconstruction, writers like Maurice Blanchot and Roland Barthes take a particular interest in approaches to reading, with regard to the question of closure. Barthes famously undermines the authority of the author in his essay, "The Death of the Author," and privileges the reader, upon whom the multiple writings of a given text fall. Barthes also clarifies, however, that we should not replace a mythic Author with a mythic Reader, for: "the reader is a man without history, without biography, without psychology; he is only that someone who holds gathered into a single field all the paths of which the text is constituted" (147). Blanchot, for his part, discusses the act of reading in *The Infinite Conversation*, comparing reading to the resurrection of Lazarus from the tomb:

> But what does this Lazarus saved and raised from the dead that you hold out to me have to do with what is lying there and makes you draw back, the anonymous corruption of the tomb, the lost Lazarus who already smells bad and not the one restored to life by a force that

> is no doubt admirable, but that is precisely
> a force and that comes in this decision from
> death itself? (36)

In reading, we resurrect the dead, bringing the work to life, light, and understanding; but what we have resurrected conceals what we cannot possibly resurrect. Reading, from that perspective, becomes an act of closure, in the sense that it sends away what it seeks, precisely in its effort to illuminate and understand.

Perhaps for that reason, critics ranging from Susan Sontag to Jonathan Culler argue "against" or "beyond" interpretation, promoting a different kind of engagement with a text—one that avoids what Culler calls "the conscious or unconscious persistence of the notion that a critical approach must justify itself by its interpretive results" (7). Again, we see the question of what to do when we reach the death of interpretation—here, precipitated by the enterprise of New Criticism—and how we might read from a different position, rather than imposing ourselves, extracting meanings, and stripping resources to the point of exhaustion. Culler proposes some ideas for how we might do this, as do many other critics, like Stanley Fish, who focuses on the reader's interaction with the text. And while certain trends in contemporary literature—in order to distance themselves from the undecidability and uncertainty of reading and writing commonly associated with postmodernism—attempt to re-establish a monist system that limits a reader's interpretive conclusions, as Raoul Eshelman explains in his discussion of "performatism," in particular, the reader remains aware that "the author [...] imposes a certain solution on us using dogmatic, ritual, or some other coercive means" (118).[8] In other words, the reader must choose to accept and believe in what she realizes is a construct, and, according to Eshelman, often does so, since it is preferable to the chaos and multiplicity of the alternative. The reader resurrects Lazarus and chooses to enjoy his company, even if she knows he's not really there. While this sort of reading does indeed close the text, that closure recognizes the uncontrollable openness that necessitates such a readerly decision.[9]

For the purposes of this study, I will make a different choice, drawing attention to constructs of closure at the ends and edges of texts, and exploring the ways that those texts invite us to witness and participate in the movement of contestation involved in the "closure" of a text. In other words, as a reader, I plan to regard the Lazarus whom I have necessarily resurrected in the act of reading with a sidelong glance, especially since the particular texts that interest me fit with what Barthes calls a "writerly text" in *S/Z* and Lyn Hejinian calls an "open text" in her essay, "The Rejection of Closure" (*S/Z* 4, "The Rejection of Closure" 42). In both cases, we are talking about texts that leave space, rather than closing it off. Hejinian writes, "The 'open text' often emphasizes or foregrounds process, either the process of the original composition or of subsequent compositions by readers, and thus resists the cultural tendencies that seek to identify and fix material and turn it into a product;

that is, it resists reduction and commodification" (43). If the text leaves space for continual re-reading, then the text never arrives at closure, rejecting its identification as a "completed" work. Therefore, even if, as Barbara Hernnstein Smith argues, a poem necessarily ends when the writing stops, that really only represents one type of closure (something that Smith surely would not deny). Interestingly, many writers who play with issues of closure and the possibility of writing beyond the end of a text butt up against the material limitations of textuality and explicitly recognize the point that Smith makes about the literal end of a poem. Borges, for example, imagines a labyrinth-book called *The Garden of Forking Paths*, where the fictional author, Ts'ui Pên, attempts to develop all of the possible branching narratives of a particular story, rather than limiting the book to a single narrative path. While Ts'ui Pên's project aspires to multiplicity, and even infinitude, he can't possibly realize his project, its never-ending premise failing at the point where Ts'ui Pên puts his pen down; in addition, we discover that what he leaves behind is understood as "a contradictory jumble of irresolute drafts" (Borges 124).

Borges's fictions and essays demonstrate an obsessive preoccupation with the possibility and/or impossibility of defying the material limits of a text. He imagines a 602nd night in *1001 Nights* where Scheherezade tells her own story, which, theoretically, would send her back to the first night and engage her in an endless cycle of storytelling ("The Garden of Forking Paths" 125). He writes a story about an "aleph," which contains infinite

time and space in a single hiding spot under the stairs
of a friend's house ("The Aleph" 280). But, ultimately
(and probably ironically), Borges says he prefers the traditional detective story, due to the fact that "it cannot
be understood without a beginning, middle, or end"
(*Selected Non-Fictions* 499). Though Borges's work pre-
dates the texts discussed in this book, his fascination
with ends and endlessness, textual boundaries and their
transgression, foregrounds the various ways that more
contemporary writers meditate upon and engage with
those issues. As we saw with the passage from Anne
Carson's *Plainwater*, the question of what happens when
we step off the edge of a text presumes a sort of boundary, a demarcation of "inside" and "outside," at the same
time as it draws attention to the permeability of that
boundary, the persistence of the text beyond the text,
and the marginal space of dismissal and exteriority. With
this in mind, I would like to look at a few different ways
to frame the play of endings and edges in contemporary
literature.

Continuing with Carson's reflection on the problems and paradoxes of edges, ends, and endlessness, we
can turn to "The Anthropology of Water," a work that
recounts the speaker's pilgrimage to Compostela.[10] In
the introduction to the piece, the speaker admits, "I like
the people in Kafka's parables. They don't know how to
ask the simplest question" (119). Of course, the inability to ask the simplest question, here, means that the
story continues in its labyrinthine meanderings while
the protagonist becomes more and more lost. We might

imagine the simplest question to be something like, "What's the quickest way out of here?" or "How do I get from here all the way over there?" The simplest question hypothetically provides understanding and closure—something that would solve the problem or provide the answer. From an outside perspective, and according to the speaker's father, the question might seem "as obvious as a door in water," but this does not change the difficulty of happening on that door once immersed (119). In Jennifer K. Dick's essay, "The Pilgrim and the Anthropologist," she examines and questions the notion of an obvious "water door" that would provide an exit and closure:

> But where is that door? If we pass through it, are we submerged, unable to breathe, seeing through eyes whose view is skewed, seeking clarity and the oxygen which will allow us to live? Or are we at the start underwater and the door is opening back out, the text is the oxygen, and life above us, beyond the surface? (64)

While the door itself might seem obvious, it does not provide access, since we are always positioned outside of, or unable to see, to soak up, the answer to the question we pose—no matter which side of the door we are on. Dick concludes that "Carson's reader simply must let go, flow under, breathe in the aquatic literary shifts, the pain of inhaling the impossible, or reaching across it into whatever connections emerge" (64).

After commenting on Kafka's protagonists and their search to discover the simplest question, Carson's

speaker in "The Anthropology of Water" describes her
own attempts to navigate the labyrinth of her father's
increasingly debilitating dementia. Feeling like a "locked
person," she meets "a pious man who knew how to ask
questions" (122). The man invites her to join him on the
pilgrimage to Compostela, posing the particular question: "How can you see your life unless you leave it?"
(122). That question points again to the importance
of departure, and even exile, as a means of approaching something from the outside, at a distance. From
that point of view, though, the man's question implicitly points to another: How can you see your life *if* you
leave it? Carson's use of the journey as a metaphor for
(the impossibility of) self-discovery again evokes Kafka's
protagonists, in the sense that she seems to be positing
that the fulfillment of the journey, or the arrival at a destination, ruins or collapses the journey. In other words,
the journey necessarily remains incomplete, despite the
pilgrim's equally necessary "belief that a question can
travel into an answer as water into thirst" (122). Kafka's
protagonists don't discover the simplest question, and
neither does Carson's speaker. She departs with much
hope—"Look I will change everything, all the meanings!"
(123)—and eventually concludes, "Just as no mountain
ends at the top, so no pilgrim stops in Santiago" (183).
As readers of Carson's work, we enact the pilgrimage
undertaken by the speaker in "The Anthropology of
Water," seeking "a road that is supposed to take you
to the very end of things, if you keep going" (184).
Logically, if such a road requires that we keep going,

then we will never reach the very end of things. In that way, each act of reading "has the same structure, a question mark" (148).

Carson's particular reflection on the impossibility of closure offers a number of insights worth pursuing. First, "The Anthropology of Water" identifies the desire for closure, and the way that desire propels us forward. The "end game" of a text promises a final word, a last page, and even invites us to consider that we will have the answers to our questions. As Peter Brooks writes in *Reading for the Plot*, "only the end can determine final meaning" (22). Yet, we eventually find ourselves wandering, particularly in a text that functions by way of digression, delay, and a sense of aimlessness. Christine Montalbetti and Nathalie Piégay-Gros argue that digression, in texts, "is frequently considered a transgression. [...] Digression, on a first read, is heterogeneity, deconstruction; it undermines the principle of coherence" (9).[11] Ross Chambers uses the term "loiterature" to refer to texts that feature digression. He writes:

> It may seem paradoxical that a literature of hanging out does not, and can't, stand still. But its art lies not in not moving but in moving without going anywhere in particular, and indeed in moving without knowing—or maybe pretending not to know—where it's going. What makes it loiterly is that it moves, but without advancing. (10)

While, for the speaker in "The Anthropology of Water" and certainly for Kafka's characters, endless wandering feels like a sort of curse that prevents us from getting the answers and closure we seek, Chambers explains that one can take pleasure in literary loitering. Rather than feeling oppressed by the demand to arrive in a certain place at a certain time, to take a clear, direct path to a pre-determined destination, we can simply "go with the flow," relaxed and distracted. While that seems pleasurable enough, Chambers argues that loitering and digression do indeed confront certain limits and problems: "But if there's pleasure in digression, all the warnings about slippery slopes and open floodgates are nevertheless appropriate. Digression happens because it can happen, but it escalates because what can happen, once it escapes control, will go on happening" (13). At some point, loitering becomes excessive and must be contained, at the risk of the loss of the work. Chambers describes the moment of contestation here—he refers to Blanchot's notion of *désœuvrement*, in particular—or, a sort of confrontation of the infinite digression and deferral of the work with the limits of the text (14). In this way, the delay of closure becomes the demand of closure, which then becomes the impossibility of closure—since the work is "undone" at the moment it comes to a close.

The end of a text represents a particular edge off of which we might step, but not the only one. In texts that resist linearity and teleology, ends and edges can occur just about anywhere, and often do when we start considering different modes of framing, footnoting, and "paratexting," in general.[12] Brian McHale identifies the "postmodernist *split text*" as "two or more texts arranged in parallel, to be read simultaneously, to the degree that is possible" (191, emphasis in original). He goes on to explain that, "Whenever a text is split into the text proper and gloss, whether marginal or in footnotes, questions arise about the relation between the two parallel texts" (191). Using the examples of *Pale Fire* and *The Third Policemen*, McHale describes the way that such novels "flout the convention" of distinguishing text from gloss, inverting assumptions about the hierarchy between the parallel texts and disrupting presumed boundaries between a text proper and its excess (191). In that way, egregious footnoting and endnoting move and blur the supposed edge of the text, encouraging us to consider how we know what belongs to the text (*ergon*) and what supplements it (*parergon*). For Chambers, footnoting and glossing relates to his notion of digression, and he explains how these "supplemental" texts exemplify "the etcetera principle":

> For the word *etcetera* has the function of conferring formal exhaustiveness and closure on any inventory—but it signals simultaneously that the inventory, as it stands, is in need of supplementation precisely because it is not complete. The closing gesture turns out in this way to be a marker of lack and vice versa. (86)

From this perspective, footnoting points to a failure of closure and completion; and, while we might traditionally see such texts as "side-notes," not totally necessary to the text proper, Chambers explains that their existence undermines the ability of the text proper to come to close, to say it all. Furthermore, he notes, one footnote, or extra-textual digression of any sort, points to the possibility of more—whether that means another footnote, or a footnote to a footnote. Therefore, it's not just that we can no longer distinguish text proper from whatever exists outside or after it, but that we become aware that there is always more room for another gloss, delaying and making impossible the closure of the text.

Those sorts of ruptures point to the way that texts seep beyond the limits that supposedly contain them, and also force a re-evaluation of what we traditionally refer to as "context." In *Framing the Sign*, Jonathan Culler warns against this term though: "But the notion of context frequently oversimplifies rather than enriches discussion, since the opposition between an act and its context seems to presume that the context is given and determines the meaning of an act" (xiv). Thus, if we perceive a renewed interest in and awareness of issues of context in contemporary literature and criticism, it is important to recognize the way that, as Culler writes, "context is not fundamentally different from what it contextualizes" (xiv). Again, that perspective reinforces the permeability of the border presumably separating text and context and troubles our efforts to find the "edge" of the text, bringing our attention to the play of multiple discourses in every act of reading and writing—evoking what Julia Kristeva demonstrates about textual interaction: "every signifying practice is a field of transpositions of various signifying systems (an inter-textuality)" (60). This critical interest, exhibited by Kristeva, Culler, and

many others, also takes shape in contemporary literature that pushes against naïve assumptions about textual
containment. As noted earlier, the "writerly" or "open"
text solicits the participation of the reader, implicitly or
explicitly, and asks us to consider our role, within our
own discursive contexts, in producing the text. In the
most explicit examples, the process of textual production
literally relies on the reader's (or viewer's) participation,
and the text develops in response to a reader's feedback
or activity. Valeria Luiselli's novel, *The Story of My Teeth*,
which I will discuss in Chapter 1, demonstrates this
kind of interaction between writer and reader, as her
conversations with a group of factory workers in Mexico
about her developing novel influence the unfolding of
the narrative. Aside from such very literal incorporation of the readers' response, other works simply draw
attention to acts of reading and writing, and how they
condition the development and understanding of a text.
According to Linda Hutcheon, in fiction, that particular
interest "has taken the form of overt textual emphasis on
the narrating 'I' and the reading 'you'" (76). As figures
of writer and reader within the text, the narrator and
narratee clearly point to our own activity, and to the
contextual factors of our interaction; that emphasis recognizes the diegetic levels of the text, at the same time as
it implies a sort of migratory movement back and forth
over the border. In *Fiction Now*, Warren Motte writes,
"[…] We are always divided when we read fiction. We
are *outside*, but we are also *inside*; we are *here*, but we are
also *there*—and vice versa, as it were" (4).

Again, the particular vein of contemporary literature that interests me seeks to avoid re-instating what Barthes calls the mythic Author or the mythic Reader; but, in challenging the definitive boundaries of texts and textuality, it also avoids pretending that we can write and read texts in some equally mythic, closed-off space. And, for that reason, we see a tendency to play with all of those myths, pointing to an extra-textual reality where individuals experience the world, and read and write books, and also pointing to the complexity of discursive contexts involved in the writing and reading of texts (and in the construction of the individual). Linda Hutcheon relates this to a surge in what she calls "historiographic metafiction," or "well-known and popular novels which are both intensely self-reflective and yet paradoxically also lay claim to historical events and personages" (5). One could also point to the re-emergence of autobiographical writing that incorporates a strong sense of skepticism about its status as "autobiography," focusing on what it might mean to write one's own life. This would include the genre of "autofiction," exemplified by writers like Serge Doubrovsky, Hervé Guibert and Annie Ernaux; hybrid texts, such as the "poem-essays" of writers such as Claudia Rankine, Anne Carson, and Maggie Nelson; and the autobiographical meditations of Roland Barthes, Paul Auster, and Gérard Genette. In any case, the blurring of text and context, and the insistence upon the complexities of that relation, further draws attention to the tricky job of locating the ends and edges of any text. In addition, it seems to result in the hybridization of texts and the disintegration of traditional generic boundaries.

Another way to think about the edges of texts concerns issues of de-centering and dispersal, often associated with postmodernism but clearly persisting into more recent literature. Hutcheon argues:

> Part of [postmodernism's] questioning involves an energizing rethinking of margins and edges, of what does not fit in the humanly constructed notion of center. Such interrogations of the impulse to sameness (or single otherness) and homogeneity, unity and certainty, make room for a consideration of the different and the heterogeneous, the hybrid and the provisional. (42)

In "Structure, Sign, and Play in the Discourse of the Human Sciences," Derrida exposes and dismantles the role of the center in various structures that frame our understanding of the world. In doing so, he pushes critical and literary discussion to the margins, drawing attention to issues of heterogeneity, difference, and liminality. Clearly, literature can explore marginality and de-centeredness in a variety of ways—whether we're talking about the literal margins of the text, as discussed above; literature's relationship to and representation of issues of cultural marginalization; and/or to the undermining of what Lyotard calls "meta-narratives," or the overarching conceptual systems we use to understand and order the world (generally revolving around some "center") (xxiii-xxiv). All of these issues arise throughout

my study of the edges of literature, though I am particularly interested in what it might mean to write and
read at the margins of the text, putting that boundary
into question and also affirming it in some ways. Many
of the texts I will discuss explore the question of writing
outside of the possibility of writing, from a marginal
position where the work comes to an end as it simultaneously falls apart, and where we experience closure
at the moment of our ousting. Several of the narrators
and speakers are often trying to tell a story which, for
one reason or another, puts them outside of the telling. Other texts feel pieced-together, collage-like, from
the scraps of a story that has ended and remains out
of reach. And most of the texts deal with various types
of end, like death, the failure of relation and intimacy,
and even the end or edge of the world. Those textual
concerns interrogate centeredness on many fronts and
relate to Hutcheon's description of an interest in heterogeneity, difference, and provisionality. And, as Hutcheon
clarifies later in her analysis, that interest does not simply replace the center with the marginal: "It does not
invert the valuing of centers into that of peripheries and
borders, as much as *use* that paradoxical doubled positioning to critique the inside from both the outside and
the inside" (69). That "doubled positioning" points to
a sort of duality that might allow us to write and read
from two positions and also implies the split to which
Motte refers—both here and there, *inside* and *outside*,
never static or stable in either position.

In *Stepping off the Edge*, I consider the way that specific works of literature explore the various issues of edges and endings discussed above. The texts I have chosen engage literal and material questions of closure, like the delineation of text and *hors-texte*, or the way that a narrative arrives at a particular end or conclusion; at the same time, they reflect on the ways we experience and write about endings and edges in our lives—the end of a life, or the sense that we are approaching the end of the world in one way or another, for example. The texts in this study remain skeptical about the firmness or stability of textual edges and ends, drawing attention to what escapes closure. And, for this reason, they also tend to shift our perspective to the margins of the text, considering what it might mean to write from a position of otherness, or even exclusion.

Since each of the chapters of *Stepping off the Edge* attempts to foster a conversation between multiple texts, I have split the chapters into sub-sections, in order to allow readers to navigate the chapters more easily and to jump into different sections of a chapter if desired. In other words, the book contains a relatively small number of long chapters, and I have organized these chapters in such a way that they can be approached as a whole, or in parts. In keeping with the themes and concerns addressed in the book, I have attempted to compose a structure where the chapter topics, and the works chosen to demonstrate those topics, feel distinct from one another and also invite the reader to consider other ways we might piece the works and topics together, creating new conversations about the broader issue of edges and ends. In other words, the conversations between texts take place not only within chapters, but also between chapters. I have chosen a set of writers and works I believe encourage such conversations, because they share a set of interests and questions—most importantly, for the purposes of this study, a preoccupation with issues of closure, textual margins, and the limits and boundaries of a work of literature.

CHAPTER 1:
LOCATING, RELOCATING, DISLO-CATING THE EDGE OF THE TEXT

Writers, artists, and critics from the past several decades have taken a keen interest in the permeability and instability of a text or artwork's boundaries, demonstrating, for example, the complexity of trying to define the "inside" or "outside" of a work. In Jacques Derrida's deconstruction of Emanuel Kant's efforts to distinguish *ergon* from *parergon*, he puts into question the notion that one might easily identify a "work proper" and therefore differentiate it from anything external: "What is the place of the frame. Does it have a place. Where does it begin. Where does it end. What is its inner limit. Outer. And the surface between the two limits" (26). Derrida's analysis reveals the impossibility of locating such limits and further challenges the hierarchical understanding of "inside" and "outside," suggesting that a framing device might serve an integral function in a work, despite its seeming exteriority or supplementarity. While Derrida exposes the problems of claiming definitive borders for an artwork or text, he does not dismiss the operation of framing: "There is no natural frame. There *is* framing, but the frame *does not exist*" (39, italics in original). Perhaps it is for this reason that many contemporary writers play with framing devices—footnotes, appendices, critical notes, prologues, or anything else we might consider *hors texte*—as a means of exploring the way that the act of framing can shift the text in multiple directions, drawing attention to the endless possibilities of re-reading, re-writing, and revision. Framing, by definition, provides a certain perspective or way of looking; in that way, it limits our focus and asks us to see or read from a particular position. At the same time, when a text emphasizes the act of framing, and the possibility of exchanging one frame for another, it points to that which exceeds the frame and leaves the text open to further re-framings.

Anne Carson's *Autobiography of Red* and Valeria Luiselli's *The Story of my Teeth* ask us to occupy the frame in a sense—not as a means of getting somewhere else, but as a textual site that makes explicit the various acts of reading and writing that cause a text to morph, slip, and unfold in different ways. Of course, the question of what constitutes the frame, as noted by Derrida, remains open; but the act of framing and the deliberate crafting of a sort of "extra-textual" space in both works clearly emphasizes the importance of textual margins. In addition, Carson and Luiselli's works question, more specifically, the notion of closure and the sense that a text's limits define and stabilize it. Their interest in the *hors-texte* demonstrates the way that framing material enacts different, and sometimes contradictory, readings of a text, and also points to the inevitable revision and re-writing of a text every time we pick it up.[13] Our acts of reading represent, in some ways, acts of writing, in the sense that our position in relation to the work—the frame(s) that we occupy in a given reading—shifts and changes the work, despite any impression of textual closure. Rather than trying to control and stabilize the text, Carson and Luiselli compose what Roland Barthes calls a "writerly text"—one which invites the reader's participation in writing and re-writing, thus making her or him "a producer of a text" (4). In addition, both *Autobiography of Red* and *The Story of My Teeth*, in terms of narrative, focus on protagonists who frame and re-frame their own experiences, appropriating, or recycling, their "life stories" as a means of shifting what and how those stories signify. In this way, Carson and Luiselli draw our attention to the issue of framing both "within" and "outside of" what one might call the main narrative, emphasizing the crossing and blurring of supposed textual borders, and inviting an exchange between "text proper" and "*hors texte*."

Anne Carson's *Autobiography of Red*

In *Autobiography of Red*, Carson offers a re-writing of Stesichoros's *Geryoneis*, framing it with: her own critical commentary and playfully-translated fragments of the Greek poet; allusions to more recent poets like Emily Dickinson and Gertrude Stein; and various appendices about Stesichoros's legendary blinding by Helen. The multiple framings in which Carson engages in her own telling of Geryon's story evoke what Brian McHale calls the tendency of "postmodernist long poems to burst through their textual enclosures and overrun their boundaries, in the most literal ways" (*Obligation* 16). For McHale, that sense of textual "overflow" serves as a means to question textual limits, and challenges the definition of "intrinsic" and "extrinsic." Carson, for her part, demonstrates how a sparse collection of fragments from a marginally-known Greek poet is not some sort of dead end, but offers an opportunity, or an opening, for more writing. She implicitly offers her own work up for the same sort of revisionary process, inviting us to follow her lead and "keep shaking the box"—whether the box contains fragments of Stesichoros's poem or her own. Carson's positioning of the "extra-textual" material before and after "A Romance" (the novel in verse) points to its liminality and the way that a liminal position might provide a site for seeing, or reading, at a distance. In addition, Carson's protagonist, Geryon, occupies the margins, asking us to consider how composing a story might require us to oust ourselves from the telling, to take the dive off the edge and into the volcano, emerging as one who has seen from an unimaginable outside. *Autobiography of Red* plays with endings and boundaries, making them impossible to locate or pin down, while simultaneously asking us to step off the end of the story, creating closure by recognizing its impossibility.

One of the most striking features of *Autobiography of Red* is its resistance to any attempt to identify a "text proper." The text brings attention to the complexity of beginnings and ends, or textual "edges," and interrogates common hierarchical distinctions between a central text and framing, or extra-textual, material. For that reason, the reader often feels as if she or he is continually stepping off some sort of an edge, not quite sure whether or not we find ourselves "inside" or "outside" of the text. While some critics dismiss the various poetic fragments, appendices, and interviews in *Autobiography of Red* as unnecessary and even detracting from the "central" coming-of-age story of Geryon, others have provided insightful analyses into the importance of the "extra-textual" material and the way the different pieces of Carson's work interact.[14] I will follow the lead of that second group of critics, focusing specifically on Carson's crafting of an *hors-texte* as a means of putting textual boundaries into question and also of encouraging us to occupy the margins of a text, as a place of reading rather than a secondary place of entrance into a privileged space.

Carson explicitly positions the sections preceding "A Romance" as exterior to the dominant narrative, referring

to the first section as a "proemium" and later sections as
"appendices" (6). In this way, she does not cast the various sections as part of an integrated whole, or even deny
the marginality of sections that seem to fulfill a supplementary role. At the same time, Carson's consideration
of marginality, and of the act of "appending," asks us
to think about the way an "appendage" might ground
or unground a text, sometimes as a radical gesture. In
"Red Meat: What Difference Did Stesichoros Make?",
the proemium and initiating text in *Autobiography of
Red*, Carson briefly outlines Stesichoros's place in literary history, explaining the way in which he broke from
Homeric tradition and the "fixed diction" associated
with that tradition (4)[15]. She specifically draws attention to Stesichoros's use of adjectives and the way he
"released being" by disrupting traditional couplings of
nouns and descriptors (5). Before providing examples
of Stesichoros's transgressive couplings, Carson offers
an understanding of what adjectives do and why they
matter, implicitly addressing the notion that adjectives
serve a sort of secondary, decorative function:

> Adjectives come from somewhere else. The
> word *adjective* (*epitheton* in Greek) is itself an
> adjective meaning "placed on top," "added,"
> "appended," "imported," "foreign." Adjectives
> seem fairly innocent additions but look again.
> These small imported mechanisms are in
> charge of attaching everything in the world to
> its place in particularity. They are the latches
> of being. (4)

Carson's description emphasizes the exteriority of adjectives, as they "come from somewhere else" and are "foreign"; yet, from that position, they transform the general into the particular, creating a specific "latch" for a noun. Again, she refuses to elevate outsidership by claiming its integration or insider status; instead she seems to suggest that, from the outside, an adjective can latch a noun in a way that disrupts easy conceptualizations and the reduction of objects into general categories. Carson explains that Stesichoros "began to undo the latches," refusing to depend upon traditional epic descriptions, and instead introduced uncommon adjective-noun couplings. According to Carson, as a result of that radical use of adjectives, of *appending* nouns with strange and foreign descriptors, "All the substances in the world went floating up" (5).

The word "appended" in the passage above also encourages us to question the traditional understanding of an appendix—something we might dismiss, like an adjective, as a largely unnecessary, albeit helpful and informative, add-on. In other words, we can read the text without it. If, however, we apply Carson's understanding of Stesichoros's revolutionary use of adjectives to her own text, we need to consider the appendices, and other extra-textual material, as different ways of latching Geryon's story to its "place in particularity." The appendices are necessarily external to that story, but they also lean on and press up against the story in a way that shifts and releases it, challenging our lesser readerly instincts to let it settle into a comfortable position that makes it available for "epic consumption" (4). Carson *foregrounds* Geryon's story with appendices, causing us to consider which parts of the text constitute the "add-on," and which occupy a primary position. Or, perhaps more likely, Carson's unusual ordering of the text's parts points to disorder, or the arbitrariness of the order we impose as a means of creating hierarchies and boundaries that provide the comfortable illusion of an inside, or clearly delineated primary text. Clearly, she's interrogating common assumptions about framing devices, whether we are talking linguistically about adjectives or in terms of textual structures. In addition, from a structural standpoint, beginning the text with appendices externalizes "A Romance," in the sense that the main narrative is positioned *after* what we commonly think of as the "last word" of the text. We must step off the edge in order to begin reading, residing in the marginal space of appenditure.[16]

Carson notes that the other "difference" Stesichoros made was to uproot the traditional mythic telling of Herakles' Tenth Labor by writing a long poem from the perspective of Geryon, the vanquished red monster whom Herakles kills. Carson portrays the significance of that shift in perspective by turning to the well-known legend that Helen blinded Stesichoros when he followed the Homeric tradition of using unflattering epithets to describe her. According to the legend (addressed in the three appendices to *Autobiography of Red*), in an attempt to appease Helen, Stesichoros followed his negative portrayal of her with a *Palinode* that rejected the claim that she went to Troy with Paris, instigating the Trojan

War. In doing so, Stesichoros uprooted "an adjectival tradition of whoredom" attached to Helen, releasing her from that particular latch and undoing common narrative understandings of the Trojan War—those tied to female sexuality and betrayal (5). As Ian Rae explores in his essay on *Autobiography of Red*, "Dazzling Hybrids," Stesichoros's story in the *Palinode* proposes that a sort of ghost or image of Helen joins with Paris and goes to Troy, while the real Helen actually travels to Egypt to avoid the war. Stesichoros's version of the Helen story "never supplanted Homer's version, but it created a rival interpretation well-known throughout antiquity" (28). Stesichoros's alternate narrative is significant not only because it suggests the multiplicity of narrative paths through a story and challenges the notion that one particular telling has ownership over the "truth," but also because it shifts the blame from Helen's supposed seduction and treachery to our misogynistic cultural understandings of "woman" and the way those understandings cause us to see Helen on the ship to Troy—despite the fact that she is actually in Egypt. Returning to Stesichoros's portrayal of Herakles' Tenth Labor from Geryon's perspective, illuminating his "red boy's life and his little dog," we can think about the way that that shift in perspective parallels what happens to Helen's story with the *Palinode*. As Carson explains, "If Stesichoros had been a more conventional poet he might have taken the point of view of Herakles and framed a thrilling account of the victory of culture over monstrosity" (6). In other words, presenting the Tenth

Labor from the perspective of Herakles would reaffirm our binary understandings of "us" and "the other," falling into a sort of conventional logic that privileges the triumph of the familiar. Stesichoros takes on Geryon's perspective, however, not only creating empathy for the "monster," but also challenging the logic that casts him out, as something that needs to be vanquished. Perhaps just as the *Palinode* draws attention to our cultural imaginings of woman, so the *Geryoneis* asks us to consider how we define "monsters" and "others," condemning them to the outside in order to prop up and maintain familiar power structures.

Rae points out that Stesichoros's *Palinode* "called [Helen's] vilification into question," but he also argues that Carson "is not content with a simple reversal of value judgments" (28). Instead, in "Appendix C: Clearing Up the Question of Stesichoros's Blinding by Helen," Carson provides a series of syllogisms which, in their circularity, demonstrate the impossibility of clearing up that question, or, really, any other. The appendix starts out in a seemingly simple manner: "Either Stesichoros was a blind man or he was not" (18). One or the other is true, right? Stuart J. Murray, in his essay, "The Autobiographical Self," describes the syllogisms of "Appendix C" in these terms: "all ostensible truths because they are logical binaries, presumably exhaustive and presumably obedient to the law of noncontradiction" (106). Of course, one does not have to get very far into the list of syllogisms before realizing that the logical binaries begin to fall apart, creating a circular, muddy mess of statements that

demonstrate the impossibility of coming to any conclusions about Stesichoros's supposed blinding. Murray
continues, "In a wider context, then, Carson unmoors
the underlying conditions of intelligibility, throwing
into question the power of signification, the reliability
by which words name things, and the fragility of the
social conventions that would uphold both the authority to name and the authority of the name" (106). The
"unmooring" that Murray mentions here seems to relate
back to the unlatching performed by Stesichoros, both
in his use of adjectives and in his approaches to narrative. The operation of latching and unlatching emphasizes the way in which "words bounce," to use Carson's
Gertrude Stein-inspired expression, shifting and slipping
in different directions, and ultimately putting into question any claims that logic or language might pin something down for us, making it available for comprehension. The simplest question, in this case, clearly unfolds
into a multiplicity of questions, opening a matter, rather
than closing it.

In the end, while Carson's proemium and appendices largely focus on Stesichoros's work, she clearly takes
an appropriative approach to the Greek poet, telling
his story in a way that creates an edge from which we
might jump into her own version of Geryon's tale. From
the perspective of a contemporary poet and a translator who seems to enjoy taking scandalous liberties with
her translations, the fact that the "papyrus scraps [...]
withhold as much as they tell" perhaps feels more like
an opportunity than a problem (6). Carson writes, "[...]

the fragments of the *Geryoneis* itself read as if Stesichoros had composed a substantial narrative poem then ripped it to pieces and buried the pieces in a box with some song lyrics and lecture notes and scraps of meat" (6-7). When dealing with the scraps, Carson exhorts us to "keep shaking the box," since we can always shake a little more, and, in effect, compose a different poem depending on the way the way the pieces fall out. Carson herself manages to shake the box in a way that produces the coming-of-age story of a gay teenager who is trying to figure out how to live in a world that marginalizes him, and, in the fashion of a *Künstlerroman*, how to tell the story of that marginal life. Just as Stesichoros revised the story of Helen's treachery and the story of Herakles' victory over monstrosity, Carson revises Stesichoros's sparse collection of fragments, placing the ancient monster in the modern world and allowing his story to become a sort of meditation on exteriority, outsidership, and art. As Rae aptly explains, "Stesichoros's 'master-text' undergoes the same overhaul to which the lyricist subjected his epic predecessors" (27). Carson is not interested in putting together what has been lost; rather she radically challenges attempts to reconstitute, put together, discover, translate, and/or re-write in view of a supposed whole. Her text questions the possibility, and even desirability, of the whole and of closure.

Carson's translations of Stesichoros's fragments mirror her revisionary approach to Geryon's story and demonstrate her willingness to take liberties with what we normally think of as the "original text." As Rae notes, her translation "becomes an act of composing elements from different epochs and speech genres, rather than an exercise in maintaining a uniform identity for the text across languages and periods" (24). Some of Carson's liberties involve the insertion of modern institutions and objects into the translated fragment, like a "ticking red taxi" or the "coil of the hot plate," and some reflect the particular angle she will take on the telling of Geyon's story, emphasizing his sexual relationship with Herakles (10). For Carson, translation represents not only a practice, but also a mode of thought and of writing. Carson's earlier translation of Mimnermos in *Plainwater* foreshadowed what she would eventually do with Stesichoros's fragments, and her later translation of Sophocles' *Antigone*, which she entitled *Antigonick*, demonstrates a sustained interest in the possibilities of radical re-contextualization that translation can offer. In her description of adjectives in *Autobiography of Red*, as we saw above, Carson emphasizes their exteriority and foreignness; something comes in "from the outside" and disrupts the way we have situated or understood a particular concept. Translation obviously introduces a foreign element as well, and, much like a noun and an adjective rub up against one another, so can two (or more) languages, creating a sort of friction, as well as a palpable feeling of distance, or space. In an interview with Kevin McNeilly, Carson speaks to her interest in translation:

> I like the space between languages because it's a
> place of error or mistakenness, or saying things
> less well than you would like, or not being able

to say them at all. And that's useful I think for
writing because it's always good to put yourself
off balance, to be dislodged form the compla-
cency in which you normally go at perceiving
the world and saying what you've perceived.

That "dislodging" echoes Carson's description of adjectives and points to her interest in error—which, in this
case, can mean the persistent possibility (inevitability)
of mistranslation and also the sense of wandering, or
groping, involved in the act of translation. Carson does
not attempt to erase the act of translation or its foreignness from the text; instead, the translation enables her
to draw the text out, into marginality and strangeness.[17]

At the end of Carson's translations of fragments from
the *Geryoneis*, she does provide a list of "Total Things
Known About Geryon" in order to establish the "facts"
of his story, gleaned from the fragments and other
ancient texts. When writing and translating, Carson
does not dismiss the importance of facts, criticizing, in
an interview with John D'Agata, writers who lazily turn
inward, refusing to interact with the facts of the world—
"gifts," as she calls them: "A gift shouldn't turn back into
the self and stop there. That's why facts are so important,
because a fact is something already given. It's a gift from
the world or from wherever you found it. And then you
take that gift and you do something with it, and you
give it again to the world or to some person, and that
keeps it going" (17). In other words, the facts serve as a
jumping-off point; they offer something valuable, and
though they don't determine what we do with them,

they do demand our attention. Interestingly, the list of "Total Things Known about Geryon" re-appears in "A Romance," as Geryon himself begins to write his autobiography. The word "things" is replaced with "facts" in this instance, emphasizing the sense that he has a collection of "given information" and that he can approach that information as an interpreter, an interrogator, and a translator. Translation, in the broad sense that Carson's work seems to endorse, would imply the opportunity to re-write and subvert, while interacting with the facts of the matter. Geryon follows the list of facts with, "QUESTIONS Why did Herakles kill Geryon?" and offers three possible answers, based on what we know of Herakles and his Labors (37). Of course, on a logical level, none of this makes much sense, as it resembles the moment in *Don Quixote* when the eponymous hero and his sidekick read about their adventures in a book. Still, we see Geryon interacting with a collection of outside facts and using them as a jumping-off point for his own writing of that story—recycling, subverting, and appropriating the "given" material, and demonstrating the way a story, and maybe even the construction of an identity, can always be re-initiated, regardless of the appearance of closure.

As noted above, "A Romance" starts at the tail end of three appendices, asking us to begin at the end, so to speak. That circularity takes on additional meaning once we realize that Geryon's plunge into Icchantikas, the volcano he visits with Herakles and Ancash at the end of the narrative, in a sense allows him to tell his story—as

one who has seen. But that story, the one Geryon constructs over the course of the text—in sculpture, writing, and photographs—does not appear to be the story
that we read, especially since "A Romance" functions
through a third-person narrative perspective. What,
then, does the word "autobiography" mean, in light
of the fact that *Autobiography of Red* is not, properly
speaking, autobiographical? A number of critics have
attempted to address that question, and Murray's essay,
"The Autobiographical Self: Phenomenology and the
Limits of Narrative Self-Possession," more or less takes
it as its subject. Murray writes:

> Although the novel is called autobiography,
> this titular term is itself unclear, its meaning
> unstable, because the novel is ostensibly less
> the autobiography of its author than the auto-
> biography of its main character, Geryon, and
> about the world in which he dwells; it is the
> autobiography "of red," no less than the auto-
> biography of the reader who writes his or her
> own life into its pages; and, more generally
> still, it is the autobiography of autobiographi-
> cal writing itself. (102)

To me, this last possibility—that *Autobiography of Red*
refers to the subject of the book, rather than the form
or genre—is the most compelling. From that perspective, the novel's title refers to Geryon's composition of
his autobiography, which also implies the composition
of his life and his varied efforts to figure out how to
tell or represent that life (if it is even possible). For the

purposes of this paper, I would like to explore the way that that composition—those compositions—involve a sort of stepping off of the edge into a marginal space where ideals like representability, closure, and self-discovery become dislodged. While Geryon's narrative at times feels like a journey towards "self-discovery," we would be mistaken, like the pilgrim-speaker of Carson's "The Anthropology of Water," if we understood his story as an affirmation that such a journey empowers him to "change everything, all the meanings!" (123). Instead, we might see his story in light of the directive/question posed by the pilgrim's travel companion: "How can you see your life unless you leave it?" (122).

Geryon begins his autobiography in an effort to protect his inner world from external threats, and he takes solace in the notion that a firm boundary separates "outside" from "inside." The day after Geryon first experiences sexual abuse by his brother, we learn: "That was also the day he began his autobiography. In this work Geryon set down all inside things / particularly his own heroism / and early death much to the despair of the community. He coolly omitted / all outside things" (28). At this point, Geryon does not yet read or write, so we can imagine that the act of beginning his autobiography refers to his conscious decision to take control over the way his story is told and to start crafting a narrative that emphasizes a preferred vision of himself. Geryon's autobiography seems to interact with the previously-established "facts" of his life, though we already see that he intends to portray those facts in a revisionary way—highlighting his

heroism and presenting his death as a tragedy mourned
by all. Significantly, Geryon depicts himself as a val-
ued part of the community, which clearly contrasts his
experience as a boy in a world that casts him out. For
Geryon, the world is harsh and unaccepting, as demonstrated by his experience of the "alien terrain" of his
school, where he hides in the bushes, "until someone
inside notice[s] and [comes] out to show him the way"
(24, 25). The delineation of outside and inside, in this
case, marks Geryon's lack of access, which becomes
emblematic of his marginal experience throughout "A
Romance." And while his alienation and exclusion certainly cause pain and heartbreak, they also provide a
degree of freedom from the limiting structures of the
world. Geryon turns inward, cutting off the world; in
doing so, he can unlatch his story from the "facts," and
he can release his life from the pressures and restrictions
of conformity. In some ways, this struggle—because it
is not always easy to reside on the "outside"—characterizes Geryon's coming of age. He learns to appropriate
his outsider status and to occupy the margins by choice.

Geryon's mother, though blind to the abuses taking
place in her home, offers support and warmth to her red,
winged son. She provides a sort of safe space for Geryon,
in a world that she seems to understand alienates and
excludes him. Geryon's mother encourages his work
on his autobiography, which at first takes the form of
sculpture and then evolves into writing. When Geryon's
teacher sees the beginnings of the autobiography—"Total Facts Known About Geryon" and the question about

why Herakles killed him—she asks Geryon's mother, "*Where does he get his ideas*" and "*Does he ever write anything with a happy ending?*" (38, italics in original). The teacher's criticism of the sadness and negativity of Geryon's autobiography, and implicit criticism of him as an individual, provokes him to revise his story into something more pleasing: "*New Ending. / All over the world the beautiful red breezes went on blowing hand / in hand*" (38, italics in original). The teacher reins in Geryon's artistic impulses, bringing him back to the convention of telling a "normal" story with a happy ending. She reprimands not only Geryon's writing, but also questions the value of his introspection and self-questioning. The teacher's action introduces a pattern of interventions that work to keep Geryon—to use one of the basic metaphors of the text—from untethering his wings and taking flight outside of the conventional forces that ground him. Edith Hall writes, "The recurrent imagery of flying is intimately linked with Geryon's delighted discovery of his autonomous selfhood" (222). While I am not convinced that Geryon arrives at such a discovery, which implies a sort of affirmation of selfhood that I don't think Carson provides, Hall provides several interesting examples throughout Geryon's narrative that illuminate the linkage of flight imagery and Geryon's appropriation of his own story. Geryon slowly begins to rebel against the dictates of people like the teacher, though Herakles in many ways also keeps Geryon tethered to the world that excludes him.

When Geryon and Herakles meet, they have an

immediate connection—"one of those moments that is the opposite of blindness," describes the speaker, with an expression that evokes Stesichoros and the proemium (39). Of course, "the opposite of blindness" recalls and contrasts this moment with Stesichoros's blinding. As Geordie Miller notes in "Shifting Ground," we can read the description as ironic, knowing that Herakles will eventually vanquish Geryon at some level: "Geryon's desire for Herakles is thus predicated on his blindness to Herakles' dominant position, as fixed by the coding of myth." Herakles' dominance arises from his age and experience, and from the fact that he wants and needs less from the relationship than Geryon does. While not necessarily a "bad guy," Herakles' mildly doltish personality and privileged, empowered perspective limit and restrict Geryon, functioning in a similar way to the teacher who forces Geryon back into convention. In the end, Herakles' lack of complexity proves problematic and marks the incompatibility of the pair, foreshadowing the way that Herakles will tether Geryon's flight. For Geryon, the younger and more introspective of the pair, the "sex question" looms in the air, as something that attracts him but also provokes fear (44). He seems to fear that Herakles, who describes himself as "someone who will never be satisfied," constantly wants and thinks about sex (44). In other words, Herakles, Geryon assumes, wants the answer, or consummation, and doesn't particularly value the act of thoughtful questioning. That gap leaves Herakles and Geryon "as two cuts lie parallel in the same flesh"—a gap that I would argue persists throughout their relationship, despite Geryon's deep attachment to and love for Herakles (45). When the two go out to graffiti various buildings and tunnels around town, Herakles complains, "All of your designs are about captivity, it depresses me" (55). That comment mirrors the teacher's criticism of Geryon's autobiography and demonstrates the way that Herakles tries to control Geryon's marginal artistic expression, asking him to do something "more cheerful" (55).

As "someone who will never be satisfied," when Herakles breaks it off with Geryon, it comes as no surprise (to the reader)—though, we probably cringe when Herakles casually hints to Geryon: "*Think you should be getting back?*" (62). Herakles casts Geryon out of his grandmother's house, and out of his life, seemingly unaware and unconcerned that "Geryon's heart and lungs were a black crust" (62). Herakles later divulges the meaning he has extracted from the relationship and his decision to end it: "Freedom is what I want for you Geryon we're true friends you know that's why / I want you to be free" (74). Understandably, Geryon doesn't experience this comment as Herakles intends it, rejecting its premise, but it's worth considering that Herakles does offer Geryon a sort of freedom by leaving him. Geryon will no longer feel pressured to conform to Herakles' demand that he operate according to a set of privileged norms. Many critics have noted that Geryon's relationship to Herakles coincides with the evolution of Geryon's autobiography from writing to photography, and therefore has a positive or nourishing effect on

the artistic process. Miller argues that Geryon's transi-
tion to photography releases "Geryon from the shackles
of the linguistic code" and sees Geryon's "relinquished
speech" in favor of the photographic image as a sign of
progress. I agree that Geryon's evolution to photography
announces or unfolds into a breaking free from certain
constraints, but I would suggest that those constraints
concern all conventional representational modes, including traditional photography. And that break takes place
over the rest of the novel, rather than right at the moment
he shifts into photography. Miller mentions, as a sign of
Geryon's positive development away from the restraints of
language, the exchange between Geryon and his mother
at the point when he has decided to take pictures as a
replacement for talking. At first, Geryon's mother, probably a little exasperated but still willing to play along,
responds to Geryon's attempts to communicate via clicks
of the shutter with a "half laugh" (40). By the next
chapter, though, Geryon's silence feels much heavier
and decidedly un-playful. "'How does distance look?'
is a simple direct question. It extends from a spaceless
/ within to the edge / of what can be loved" (43). The
loss of words in this scene has no replacement; no photo
fills in the chasm separating Geryon from his mother,
which challenges the idea that photography somehow
solves the problems of speech. Interestingly, the question "How does distance look?" emphasizes the issue of
visual representation, and the possibility of representing
the abstract. That question—the artistic expression of
distance, of the "spaceless within" pushed all the way

to the edge—propels Geryon towards a more radical expression of his experience, outside of a conventional approach to writing or photography.

In many ways, Geryon's photographic work actually turns back to language, playing with the relation of words and images as a means of releasing images and objects from conventional ways of thinking. After the account of Herakles' break up with Geryon, we find the first example of an image matched with a title: "In Geryon's autobiography / this page has a photograph of some red rabbit giggle tied with a white ribbon. / He has titled it 'Jealous of My Little Sensations'" (62). In "Toward a Photography of Love," E.L. MacCallum argues, "The synaesethetic paradox of a photograph of a rabbit giggle foregrounds the text's concern with the way representation works and with the limits of photographic representation." MacCallum's point can help us to see the way the "rabbit giggle" photograph communicates with the question of capturing a visual image of distance. Taking a picture of a sound—a strange sound, at that—parallels the notion of trying to *see* a felt gap, or distance, between two people, in the sense that both cases demonstrate a reflection on the way something non-visual might look. MacCallum asserts that Carson's text "unfixes vision as the privileged and singular medium of the photograph, suggesting that we rethink photography as a synaesthesia of touch and sight, or sound and sight, much as written language is." Part of Geryon's development as a photographer/autobiographer involves his exploration of the possibilities of his work to push

against the constraints of traditional representational art
and to approach his project from the marginal position
he occupies. Later in "A Romance," Geryon remembers
a seventh-grade science project that made him question
his own sanity, forced to confront the fact that others
didn't seem to experience the world in the same way
he did: "It was the year he began to wonder about the
noise that colors make" (84). While Geryon never really
questions, for example, the sound of "the silver light of
stars crashing against / the window screen," he came to
realize, "Most of those he interviewed for the science
project had to admit they did not hear / the cries of the
roses / being burned alive in the noonday sun" (84). The
science teacher, presumably in a sarcastic tone, quips,
"*You should be / interviewing roses not people*," ridiculing
the premise of Geryon's project (and his experience of
the world) and mirroring the actions of Geryon's first
teacher. Geryon, though, misunderstands the teacher's
comment as a genuine suggestion and ends up concluding his project with "a photograph of his mother's rose-
bush under the kitchen window. / Four of the roses were
on fire. / They stood up straight and pure on the stalk,
gripping the dark like prophets / and howling colos-
sal intimacies / from the back of their fused throats"
(84). While we might see this photograph as an early
suggestion of what Geryon's photography will eventually explore—especially considering the importance
of synaesthesia noted by MacCallum—it is important
to remark that Geryon remembers this experience in
a moment of "despair" and the suspects that "Perhaps

he was mad" (84). The young Geryon does not seem to recognize the ridicule of the science teacher, but the older Geryon now understands that story as possible evidence for his insanity and disconnect with the rest of the world. Interestingly, Geryon's suffering results not from the experience of hearing blades of grass or howling roses, or even from his efforts to capture that synaesthetic experience through a visual image, but, rather, from the awareness that such experiences aren't acceptable or "normal"; they mark his outsidership and strangeness.

Throughout the novel, Geryon experiences his otherness, emblematized by his wings and red coloring, as painfully alienating and isolating. During his relationship with Herakles, the physical pain of his wings intensifies: "His wings were struggling. They tore against each other on his shoulders / like the little mindless red animals they were. / With a piece of wooden plank he'd found in the basement Geryon made a back brace / and lashed the wings tight" (53). We don't really see Geryon's relationship with his wings begin to change until much later in the narrative, after he has spent an evening with a group of philosophers and ends up with a free plate of sandwiches. While the philosophers manage to live up to the expectation of a certain degree of insufferableness, Geryon also notes that "Jokes make them happy" and, as a result of the evening, finds that "for a moment the frailest leaves of life contained him in a widening happiness" (97). Geryon returns back to his hotel room and photographs himself, naked on the bed: "The fantastic fingerwork of his wings is outspread on the bed like a black lace / map of South America" (97). While anyone looking at this photo would immediately notice the extended, intricate wings of the young man, Geryon provides the title "No Tail!", recalling an earlier conversation with the philosophers, but also as a sort of joke of his own, undermining the tendency to reduce and other him on account of his wings. "No Tail!" becomes a tongue-in-cheek pronouncement of his "normalcy," due to his lack of a foreign appendage—a title and pronouncement that draw attention to the parallel image of the wings and the way the presence (or absence) of an appendage destabilizes our perceptions. Here, the play of title and image shows the way that visual and linguistic modes interact in productive and illuminating ways—in this case, through irony and subversion of expectation.

Though Geryon displays his wings in the autobiographical portrait, he continues to keep them lashed and hidden at this point, experiencing them as a burden that marks his difference with the world. When Ancash discovers Geryon's wings, he provides a new framework and narrative through which Geryon might see the presence of his wings. According to a legend common in the mountains north of Huaraz, the "*Yazcol Yazmac* [...] *saw the inside of the volcano*," and flew up and out, returning "*as red people with wings*"; they are referred to as "*the Ones who Went and Saw and Came Back*" (128, italics in original). As Miller points out, "Ancash here provides Geryon with an empowering mythic identity and autobiographical purpose apart from his subordinate role in the classical Herakles story." Up until this point, Geryon's wings—and more specifically the presumed demand to lash and hide them—have supported a narrative of otherness and disempowerment. And while Geryon's wings will always mark his difference, that appendage, released, might serve to re-contextualize him and his story, transforming a narrative of defeat and subjugation into one of possibility and privileged access. In this way, Geryon's outsider status paradoxically opens onto the possibility that he might penetrate the inaccessible "inside," and, like the "lava man" of the 1923 eruption of the volcano in Herakles' hometown, he will be able to say: "I *am molten matter returned from the core of earth to tell you interior things*" (59).

Geryon has made a lifelong project of documenting the "interior things" he seeks to protect from the harsh outside world—through sculpture, writing, and photography. As Jennings points out, the image of the volcano serves as a metaphor for Geryon's self-expression: "An image of a boundary between interior and exterior, a normally placid surface punctuated by intense bursts from its core, it mirrors the pressure that builds within Geryon himself, his interior always threatening, or promising, to surface" (932-933). While that basic metaphor, along with the metaphor of wings and flight, might feel a bit on the nose, Carson's text complicates the transportational aspect of metaphor by offering unexpected and paradoxical arrival points. Yes, Geryon uses his wings to ascend from the limiting conventions of the world that keep him down; and, yes, the quiet and timid red boy who protects "inside things" promises

eventually to erupt in one way or another. But the metaphors do not function as a simple, stable exchange. As
Monique Tschofen argues in "First I Must Tell About
Seeing," metaphor "is dynamic, introducing motion into
stasis and duration into flux, just as it fragments experiences and then reconnects them in new ways. And
even more importantly, metaphor is liberating" (48).
Tschofen asserts that Carson uses metaphor in a way
that parallels Stesichoros's use of adjectives, bringing
our attention to the freeing effect of making unexpected
connections. Carson, unsurprisingly, doesn't settle for
an easy metaphor; she focuses on the complexities of
transport or exchange—the flight, where it takes us, and
how it cuts and swerves, eluding our grasp.

The arrival point of Carson's flight and volcano metaphors involves Geryon's step off the edge, which challenges, I believe, any attempt to read his narrative as
one of self-discovery or self-realization. It is important
to note that Geryon's final gesture of his autobiography involves handing the camera off, in some sense recognizing the impossibility of capturing the experience
of leaping into and flying out of Icchantikus: "It is a
photograph he never took, no one here took it" (145).
Therefore, Geryon's flight does not lead to a trium-
phant self-expression of the "inside things" threatening
to erupt. Instead, it seems to suggest that the only way
to tell his story, to tell of "inside things"—whether that
refers to his own inside things, or the inaccessible inside
of the volcano—paradoxically requires a relinquishing
of the tools of representation, including cameras and

words. While Geryon "flicks Record" himself, he soon becomes the object rather than the taker of the photo: "He peers down / at the heart of Icchantikus / dumping all its photons out of her ancient eye and he / smiles for / the camera: 'The Only Secret People Keep'" (145). Geryon confronts the absolutely unrepresentable; yet unlike Orpheus, a fellow Greek figure who makes a similar plunge, Geryon seems to have no delusions about bringing the invisible into the world of sight. Instead, he seeks a record of his experience—as one who stepped off the edge, One Who Went and Saw and Came Back—and smiles in this moment of turning away. One might see this as the *undoing* of self-expression, in the sense that the arrival point of Geryon's story involves his confrontation with the impossibility of representing his experience and composing the self through that representation. Though Geryon, like the *Yazcol Yazmac*, might be an eyewitness, he cannot *bear* witness, in the sense that he cannot tell of his experience. Geryon's smile marks his complicity in the "Secret"—the invisible, immortality, or whatever we might associate with the impossible depths of the volcano—even if it remains a secret to him, resisting revelation and representation.[18]

As is the case in each of the last eight chapters of "A Romance," the chapter detailing Geryon's preparations to step off the edge and into the volcano describes the process and context of the photograph. MacCallum observes: "Carson seems not to give us the photographs as visual objects, nor, I would argue, does she really give us the verbal representation of a visual image, in part because she is depicting the moment of representing, not the content of representation." Though our first instinct might be to value and privilege the final art object, Carson's "photograph chapters" document the process of art and, as MacCallum notes, do not demonstrate much of an interest in describing the actual image. Each photograph chapter begins with a one-line description of the photograph—"It is a close-up photograph of Geryon's left pant leg just below the knee," for example—and then goes into the complexities of the particular context surrounding the taking of the photo (137). The attention to surroundings, and to the way a moment or image is latched to a particular context, supports Carson's continual emphasis on what we might at first dismiss as "appending" or supplementary material. The description of the context highlights the role of language in evoking what doesn't appear in the photograph, pointing to the play of text and image in both Geryon's and Carson's work. In addition, the near absence of the actual object or product of art mirrors the way that *Autobiography of Red* focuses on the composition of an autobiography rather than presenting an actual autobiography. We can get to the autobiography, or the photograph, from the outside, seeing it from a distance through the description of its process and external characteristics. We never have a hold of it, though.

Geryon takes flight into the volcano in order to emerge a storyteller with an impossible story to tell, and no camera or words to tell it. He has, in a sense, stepped off the edge of the possible story, entering a sort of distance that allows for an outsider's gaze. "How can you see your life unless you leave it?" (*Plainwater* 122). It seems that, by the end of the text, Geryon has managed a kind of departure, even if he returns from the volcano to walk the streets of Huaraz with Ancash and Herakles, "quarrelling all day" (146). His plunge into the volcano points to his decision to occupy the margins, in a space where one might not be able to compose a self, snapping the picture at the moment of revelation, but, instead, can enjoy the experience of an outsider's gaze. Geryon's journey has led him not to a destination, but to a place of wandering and exteriority, unburdened by the felt obligation to affirm and reside within a set of arbitrary limits. As readers, we find ourselves in a parallel position, stepping off the edge of "A Romance" only to wander into another outside—a closing interview with "S," who might best be described as Stesichoros channeling Gertrude Stein, or the other way around.[19] Regardless, Carson deliberately muddies our exit, drawing attention to the artifice and arbitrariness of closure, suggesting that there's always room for another door out, another frame that might re-cast our understanding of the preceding pages. And that's the point—an invitation, a demand, to keep reading, to keep writing, aware of our dismissal and inspired by the promise of a perpetually open text.

Valeria Luiselli's *The Story of My Teeth*

When writing her 2015 novel, *The Story of My Teeth*, Valeria Luiselli approached her work as a sort of reciprocal ethnography, sending excerpts of her developing novel to factory workers at the Grupo Jumex juice factory, recording their discussions, and incorporating their feedback as she continued to write. Luiselli's novel takes the Jumex factory as its setting and subject, perhaps especially because it borders and supports the Galería Jumex, an important collection of contemporary art in Ecatepec, Mexico. Luiselli explains in her afterword, "There is, naturally, a gap between the two worlds: gallery and factory; artists and workers; artwork and juice. How could I link the two distant but neighboring worlds, and could literature play a mediating role?" (191) In this way, Luiselli's novel is interested in exploring boundaries that separate seemingly different worlds, and this exploration goes well beyond the line separating gallery from factory. She tests and prods other borders as well—story and history, fiction and reality, original work and translation, authorship and collaboration—and uses literature as a means of investigation, questioning and, as she says, mediating. Luiselli's novel reflects upon the ways in which various types of collaboration—including that with the workers and with the translator—might further take literature out of the borders that traditionally define it and open up new ways of thinking about textuality and authorship. Luiselli engages such questions by providing multiple frames that become an integral part of the story—the story of the protagonist, Highway, and the story of the composition of the novel.

Like *Autobiography of Red*, *The Story of My Teeth* continually morphs as a result of the multiple re-framings of the narrative. Brian McHale's description of postmodernist long poems that "burst through their textual enclosures and overrun their boundaries" seems to apply to Luiselli's novel as well, since she follows Highway's narrative with several additional sections, including a series of images, an afterword, and, in the translation, a timeline with references to the novel and historical events. Luiselli also peppers the margins of the text with epigraphs from writers and philosophers, fortune-cookie sayings, and provocative sub-titles, and her novel implicitly asks us to spend some time there, rather than looking for the door "in." Luiselli plays with her novel's framework in ways that disrupt our readerly progress through the narrative, since they tend to send us back to reassess, reconsider, and question what we have read up to that point. In addition, like Carson's, Luiselli's engagement of the frame draws attention to the conventional textual boundaries that Derrida deconstructs in "Parergon"— boundaries that seek to assure us of, for example, an "inside" and an "outside" of the text, and also a beginning and an end. Luiselli thus works to unsettle the text and to make sure the reader never takes root in anything solid or closed; we begin to realize that the novel will shift and elude our attempts to grasp it every time we sit down to read. While Carson, in *Autobiography of*

Red, provides a proemium and appendices before we get to "A Romance," and therefore ushers us into the text precisely by drawing attention to issues of framing and textual boundaries, Luiselli submerges us in the narrative from the beginning and only later does she begin to chip away at the borders that define and stabilize it. In this way, Luiselli's novel seems to take some degree of pleasure in pulling the rug out, so to speak, though the playful quality of the framing and re-framing does not detract from the intellectual seriousness of the gesture.

Most of *The Story of My Teeth* is told from the first-person perspective of a quirky, but seemingly trustworthy, auctioneer and collector, Gustavo "Highway" Sánchez Sánchez. While Highway's narrative clearly demonstrates a flair for storytelling and an appreciation for a good yarn, we most likely buy what he's selling, at least on the whole. In "Book I: The Story (Beginning, Middle, and End)" Highway tells us the story of his life, which also happens to be the story of his teeth, since he tends to see his life, and the lives of others, through his obsession with teeth. We learn about Highway's youth, his picaresque meanderings as a young adult, and his eventual success as an auctioneer, culminating in his purchase of Marilyn Monroe's teeth, with which he replaces his own set of teeth, "as wide as shovels, each pointing in a different direction" (8). Toward the end of the first book Highway tells us about an "intensive initiation course" where he learns the Yushimoto method of auctioneering (19). According to the Yushimoto method, "there are four types of auctions: circular, elliptical,

parabolic, and hyperbolic" (19). Basically, the different
kinds of auctions pertain to the degree to which an auctioneer deviates from what one might theoretically call
the basic material object, unadorned by language, narrative, or anything else that might alter one's perception
of its value. We also learn that Highway adds another
category to the Yushimoto method, called the allegoric
method, which, he explains "does not depend upon contingent or material variables" (20). In other words, the
allegoric method is not limited or tied to an object, or to
any claim to an objective reality, in a definitive way. The
auctioneer, in a sense, sells the *story* of an object, since
the story provides value and meaning to an object that
might otherwise disappear into a vast sea of objects that
blur one into another. Highway explains, "I wasn't just a
lowly seller of objects but, first and foremost, a lover and
collector of good stories, which is the only honest way of
modifying the value of an object" (23). Highway latches
a story onto on object in a way that parallels Carson's
description of adjectives: "small imported mechanisms
[…] in charge of attaching everything in the world to
its place in particularity. They are the latches of being"
(*Autobiography of Red* 4). Highway uses language to
modify and unground; he disrupts conventional ways
of seeing an object by providing that object with a story
that particularizes and defamiliarizes it.

The auctioneering methods that Highway describes
in Book I provide the framework for his narrative.
Book II bears the title "The Hyperbolics," which we
now can identify as the auctioneering method that, not

surprisingly, engages in hyperbole more than any of the other three Yushimoto methods. It's here that we begin to perceive the novel's playful engagement of framing devices—in this instance, the use of what Gerard Genette calls a "paratext," which refers here to the titles of Books I-VII in the novel (3).[20] Since Highway's narrative proceeds from Book I into Book II in a way that feels continuous—in terms of chronology, narrative style, and narrative voice—we most likely don't perceive any shift in our narrator's reliability, to the extent that reliability is a matter of "truth-telling." Yet, the title of Book II frames this section of Highway's narrative as hyperbolic, deviating from the supposed truth of the events he recounts, and perhaps attempting to add value to those events through storytelling. Of course, one might rightly argue that any narrative does that, but the framing of Highway's narrative specifically plays with identifying the sections of his story in terms of their relation to some sort of objective reality. Most of Book II focuses on an auction Highway holds with a local priest, Father Luigi, where the two hatch a plan to sell objects to elderly parishioners at Father Luigi's church—a group that the priest describes as "advanced in years, but solvent" (36). Highway decides to put his own former teeth up for auction using the "hyperbolic method," giving them interesting backstories that clearly deviate from any objective reality. As he explains, "This meant that the stories I would tell about the lots would all be based on facts that were, occasionally, exaggerated or, to put it another way, *better illuminated*" (37, emphasis in original). Highway specifically claims that each tooth once belonged to a different famous writer, including Virginia Woolf, Michel de Montaigne, Jorge Luis Borges, and Plato. Highway's use of "hyperbolics" in the auction recounted in Book II clearly provides one way of understanding the title of Book II. But it is also important to consider this section of Highway's first-person narrative through the lens, or framework, of hyperbolics. To what extent does Highway's story of this period of life seek to "modify value" through the use of hyperbole? To be clear, I would not argue that Book II announces a shift from "true story" to "hyperbolic story," but that the framework asks us to reassess our own trust in Highway's narrative and to ask ourselves if we are playing audience to a sort of auction.

We can understand Luiselli's playfulness with the novel's book titles in a variety of ways, especially when, later in the text, we learn from a second narrator that Highway's description of his life story seems to have "added value" to the less impressive realities of his life— perhaps especially in the sections labeled with auction-eering terms that designate a significant departure from a more objective reality. But Highway's, and likely Luiselli's, take on storytelling insists not so much on the fabrication or falsification of some "real" or objective thing, but more on the possibility of actually elevating some thing, or event, or person, through story, creating new meanings and value by providing new context. The hyperbolics and parabolics do not simply function as extraneous supplements or add-ons, referring back to the "true story"; instead, the story, like an object on the docket at an auction, requires a storyteller to transform it, freeing it from the limitations of "truth" or "reality." And for Highway, as he explains, doing so "is the only honest way of modifying the value of an object" (23).

Interestingly, as noted above, Book I bears the title of "The Story (Beginning, Middle, and End)," and Highway explicitly notes, "As any other story, this one begins with the Beginning; and then comes the Middle, and then the End. The rest, as a friend of mine always says, is literature: hyperbolics, parabolics, circulars, allegorics, and elliptics" (3). While the reader does not at this point know the specific meanings of these terms as they are defined in Highway's auctioneering world, we get the gist of what he's saying: storytelling involves the artful crafting of a story, and thus takes certain liberties with the "truth." What mostly likely surprises us, however, is that Highway announces, "End of story," roughly twenty pages into the novel (26). Book II, or "Hyperbolics," then begins, as a section of the novel identified as "outside" or "after" the story, even though, in terms of the narrative, it appears continuous with Book I. As we saw in *Autobiography of Red*, *The Story of My Teeth* subverts the notion of closure, of textual ends that tie everything together and announce a final product. The bulk of *The Story of My Teeth* follows the pronouncement, "End of Story," much in the same way that the "novel in verse" of *Autobiography of Red* follows a set of appendices. Luiselli asks us to step off the edge, like Carson, prodding us to think about what constitutes the end of a story, and what sort of a text throws closure into question, making it into an opportunity or invitation for more writing.

The headings of the sections of *The Story of My Teeth* challenge any sort of static relationship into which we might fall with the text, and with Highway's narrative in particular. In addition to the headings, each section of the text includes an epigraph from a well-known thinker, like Bertrand Russell or Gottlob Frege, on the philosophy of language and signification. For example, a quotation from Saul Kripke provides the epigraphic entrance into "Book III: The Parabolics" with an imperative: "Call something a rigid designator if in every possible world it designates the same object..." (69). In his reading of Luiselli's novel, Alex McElroy argues, "The passages are startling besides Sànchez's ribald first-person voice, but they serve to wed together the novel's theoretical underpinnings with Sànchez's lewd, everyday sagacity. Luiselli wants readers to see that Sànchez's auctioneering pursuits are of high intellectual value." From this perspective, the epigraphs encourage us to consider Highway's narrative within the context of academics, linguistics, and philosophy, even if his language and style starkly contrast the density, and sometimes humorous circularity, of much philosophical writing (including that cited in the epigraphs). When placed beside serious critical thought on the functioning of signification, McElroy points out, "Sànchez's techniques seem less fraudulent than semiotic." In other words, Luiselli provides epigraphs that frame her narrator in a particular way, inviting us to see him not as a manipulator who exploits the vulnerability of his audience, but as a thinker who takes interest in the ways we might modify and even determine the world around us with the language we use and the stories we tell. While most of the epigraphs demonstrate a desire to clarify the system that allows naming and signification to function, Highway prefers to work outside the system, using language to free an object from any concrete, predetermined meaning. For Highway, language and narrative can appropriate objects and transform them into something new. That philosophy recalls Stesichoros's latching of nouns onto unfamiliar adjectives, as well as Carson's appropriative approach to textual objects—the way in which revision and translation can shift and unlatch a text or narrative; it also suggests the literary inventiveness with which Highway approaches his work.

The best example of Highway's philosophy of language comes late in his narrative, when he tries to convince a young writer named Voragine—the eventual second narrator of *The Story of My Teeth*—of the relevance and importance of language and storytelling. Voragine suffers from a fear of irrelevance, explaining, "There are already too many things—[...] too many books, too many opinions. Anything I do will only add to the great pile of trash every person leaves behind" (102). Highway says that, as an auctioneer, he understands exactly what Voragine describes, but also that he approaches the trash pile of human output from a different perspective. As an auctioneer, Highway doesn't seek to make anything new; instead, he renovates pre-existing objects through language. He explains, "You see, I'm like those people who scavenge in your garbage. But with pedigree. I expurgate; I find. I aromatize, clean, and disinfect. I recycle" (106). Highway's description evokes a sort of Duchampian project of elevating an ordinary object to art by shifting the frame through which we see it. Rather than adding another thing to the trash pile, Highway adds value to the trash, transforming it into something other than trash. Though one would probably argue that Highway's "philosophy of art" invests far more in the masterful practice of a craft, or *techne*, the parallel with Duchamp illuminates the way the artist's role involves the shifting of contexts and frameworks.

After spending some time with Voragine, Highway convinces the young writer to help him steal a number of artworks from the Jumex art gallery, and then explains how he plans to sell the artworks in an auction:

> The series would be called "Allegorics of Ecatepec," and would recycle our new collected objects by telling stories that used collected names of my friends and acquaintances from the neighborhood—giving due credits to the artists who had made the works and using the catalogue we had requisitioned as our guide. (123)

When Voragine reminds Highway that using the artists' real names would reveal that they had stolen the artworks, Highway agrees and then asserts that they can "modify" the names to protect themselves. After all, for

Highway, the possibilities for naming and identifying the objects are open and endless, since their value comes precisely from the artistic act of naming and identifying, and how that framing process can modify an object. Voragine makes the practical point that the artworks would lose their value, since the artists' names identify the objects as valuable works of art (assuming, for example, that a random prosthetic leg, outside of the context of a museum and without the signature of Abraham Cruzvillegas, would not have much artistic value). Again, though, Highway sees no problem with modifying the artists' names and rejects the notion that the value of the objects depends absolutely upon that specific contextual element. A different framework might even raise the value of an object, since, for Highway, value has little to do with a conventional notion of truth or factuality. With that notion in mind, Highway creates an "allegoric" for each of the stolen artworks, telling a compelling a tale, and weaving together various references to his favorite writers. He modifies the artists' names simply by adding the name "Sànchez" to the actual name—Abraham Cruzvillegas Sànchez, for example. While the addition of "Sànchez," in practical terms, does little to hide the identity of the stolen artworks, Highway inscribes *himself* into the artwork, as a sort of collaborator with the artist; it also points to the way we might see the work as continually unfolding and in process, rather than as static, closed, and tied to a single origin. There's always room for more writing.

Highway's approach to appropriating art objects

parallels the way that he appropriates the names and stories of literary figures that populate his narrative. On one level, like the epigraphs we saw above, the references to writers from Michel de Montaigne to Enrique Vila-Matas form a stark contrast with the conversational, brusque tone of Highway's narrative. Interestingly, however, Highway refers us to a familiar name but then latches that name onto an unfamiliar, invented story, therefore complicating the operation of the reference. When he refers us, for example, to Virginia Woolf, we follow his reference but then arrive to see a strange lady who maybe only looked like Virginia Woolf from a distance. In a review in *The Rumpus*, Anita Felicelli notes that the novel encourages us to ask, "What does it do to these literary names, to remove them from the comfort and familiarity of their own stories—to decontextualize them—and place them in stories that are not their own?" I think we understand that the Virginia Woolf in Highway's narrative is indeed the Virginia Woolf we know, at the same time as Highway constructs a story for the writer that takes her out of what we know and places her somewhere else. He recycles the name and personage, not getting rid of the object, but rather modifying it through storytelling. According to Highway's dentocentric story, Virginia Woolf's "emotional ills were due to an excess of bacteria around the roots of her teeth" (57). Other literary figures appear in the text with a story that completely detaches them from their "literary identity": Mr. Cortázar, a neighbor from Highway's youth, leaves the family his green armchair after dying of tetanus; Rubén Darío owns the local newspaper stand; Darío's wife happens to be having an affair with Mr. Unamuno, "a pigeon-chested old codger who had a program on public radio" (9). In this way, numerous famous and less famous figures of the world of art and literature appear in the pages of Luiselli's novel, at the same time that those figures never really appear anywhere in her novel—at least not before they are recycled into something unfamiliar, or unlatched, to use Carson's term, from our conventional ways of understanding and framing them.

In Book VI, the narrative perspective abruptly shifts to Voragine, who re-tells and adds to the story told by Highway. While the change in narrator likely surprises the reader, who has spent the last five books and the most of the novel with Highway, we might also note that Voragine has appeared throughout the pages of Highway's narrative, even if we have not perceived his presence in the writing. In Book IV, Voragine tells Highway, "I'd be happy to write your dental autobiography," after the latter proposes that they make a sort of exchange (111). Highway would like Voragine to transcribe his autobiography—and insists upon the distinction of autobiography and biography, making sure Voragine recognizes his place as transcriber, rather than teller—and, in return, Highway will share his insights about and connections in Ecatepec, allowing Voragine to "become a real artist" (109). The two agree to the plan, and, soon afterward, Highway's narrative comes to a conclusion, at which point Voragine emerges from his role as transcriber to take over the narrative. While the words of the first five books belong ostensibly to Highway, the fact that they come through the pen of Voragine causes at least some degree of reconsideration of those books. Learning about Voragine's transcription provides a new context for Highway's narrative and brings our attention to a sort of ghostwriter who has been hiding behind the writing.

Before considering the way in which the story changes with the new narrative framework, it is important to consider Voragine himself, a young writer who tries to make ends meet by giving tours of *relingos* in Mexico City. He describes a *relingo* walk to Highway as "A walk around the gaps, sir, around vacant lots, spaces without owners or fixed use [...]" (102). Luiselli's interest in the *relingos* of Mexico City arises in a number of places, including her essay collection, *Sidewalks*. In one essay, "Relingos: The Cartography of Empty Spaces," she focuses on the relationship of *relingos* to writing. After considering and rejecting a few different possibilities for that relationship, she concludes, "A writer is a person who distributes silences and empty spaces. Writing: making relingos" (*Sidewalks* 78). From this perspective, the writer doesn't fill in space, create bridges, or recover the gaps; she makes, and perhaps maintains, the gaps. In an interview in *BOMB Magazine*, Luiselli discusses the *relingos* of Mexico City and points out "how there are still a few of these gaps left, and how important they are to the city. How, without them, there's no room for imagining anything." In *The Story of My Teeth*, Voragine's work as a guide for relingo walks suggests his role in Highway's narrative. As a (ghost)writer, Voragine provides the empty space within which Highway inscribes his story, not filling it up with something concrete and definitive, but perhaps creating more space through the imaginative and playful procedures of hyperbolics, allegorics, and parabolics. When Voragine explains to Highway the meaning of *relingo*, Highway humorously opens his at-the-time toothless mouth and asks, "Empty spaces like this one?" (102). In other words, Highway speaks from a sort of gap, one of those "spaces without owners or fixed use," enacting the imaginative use of that space, at the same time that he rejects ownership and thus any claim to having filled in the gap. In this way, Highway and Voragine both function as distributors and navigators of empty space and issue a sort of invitation for imaginative play.

One of the questions that arises, however, is whether or not Voragine's appended narrative to Highway's own account seeks to ground Highway's story in some more stable or objective version of events. At first glance, Voragine's narrative does seem to announce "here's what really happened" from the beginning, as it describes Highway in decidedly unromantic terms: "Indeed: the little hair he had was permanently sticking up heavenward; he had scrawny, veined legs, and a rounded, bulging belly. He had lost his beloved false teeth, so that such an ordinary thing as speaking was, if not impossible, a constant battle against humiliation" (149). Our suave, charming hero becomes a defeated, frail man who has lost what little he had, which apparently did not amount to what he claimed: "Despite all his training and innate talent for the art of auctioneering, when he returned to Mexico, Highway had, in fact, little luck in the profession" (152). According to Voragine, Highway never garners the appreciation his talents merit, except maybe later in his life when he becomes a sort of performance artist at a local bar. At that point in his life and the evolution of his auctioneering philosophy, Highway's auctions no longer require objects—just stories, provided by the auctioneer, who sometimes removes the dentures from his mouth in order to perform a strange form of ventriloquism as part of the spectacle: "He would hold [his dentures] between his fingers, like the castanets used for flamenco dancing and, depending on the occasion, make them speak or chant and tell fascinating stories of the lost objects that had once formed part of his collectibles" (157). Voragine reveals that Highway begins all of his final performances "in roughly the same way," with a claim to his status as the "best auctioneer in the world," and mention of his abilities to imitate Janis Joplin, balance an egg upright on a flat surface, analyze fortune cookies, count in Japanese, and float on his back (158). That information throws us back to the beginning of the text, where we can verify that, yes, Highway's narrative, in Book I, begins in the same way. And, if we had any question about whether, as readers, we are playing audience to an auction of sorts, Voragine's description of Highway's performance would seem to provide confirmation. The question then becomes: What is Highway trying to sell to us?

Whether Highway's final moments of artistry represent the sad decline of a broken man or the great achievement of a man who finally has a space and audience for the performance of his allegorics depends upon the framework through which we see Highway's life. While Voragine's narrative offers a sobering dose of realism to Highway's story, Highway has already encouraged us to approach claims to "reality" and "truth" with skepticism, since they lack imagination and creativity, which, in a very real way, modify the value of an object, or, in this case, a life story. The addition of Voragine's narrative certainly shifts the way we see Highway's first-person narrative, but I think the reader still probably chooses Highway's compelling, thoughtful, and joyfully consumable version of his own story. That is what he's selling. In the end, Highway's narrative has value as story, which, following his own way of thinking, adds value to what in some ways seems to be a difficult and unrewarding life. Luiselli's novel, therefore, provides Voragine's account as a sort of "corrective narrative," theoretically meant to counter and clarify any inconsistencies or misinformation provided by Highway's first person-narrative; but her novel sets up that corrective narrative in a way that dismisses it before it has arrived. Like Highway's audience members, we have most likely been "enthralled by the spectacle," enamored by a floating set of dentures, an empty mouth, a *relingo* (157). By the time Voragine takes over the narrative, we can only feign interest in his efforts to re-latch Highway's story onto the limits and difficulties his life has imposed. Like Carson, Luiselli plays with the notion of revisionary narratives and perspectival shifts that unground and destabilize conventional storytelling; but the revisionary narrative in Luiselli's novel serves a function that contrasts with what we saw in *The Autobiography of Red*, where the telling of Herakles' Tenth Labor from Geryon's perspective challenges the conventional narrative told from the perspective of the empowered victor. In the case of *The Story of My Teeth*, Voragine's narrative revises the story Highway has already provided (a story which itself could be understood as a revision), yet his revision attempts to re-capture what Highway has released from the constraints of convention and the limits of a supposed objective reality. Voragine's "corrective narrative," through a lens that privileges "truth," might in other contexts emerge as the favored perspective; in this context, however, such a lens has already been dismantled. Highway's narrative is not one of self-discovery or self-revelation; like Geryon, Highway journeys to a point that challenges the ideal of arrival. The handing off of Highway's narrative to Voragine parallels the moment that Geryon hands off the camera: Voragine does not bring Highway's story to light; instead it emphasizes the moment of turning away, or the realization that revelations of "truth" shed little light. Voragine, like Carson's pilgrim, aspires to greatness—"Look I will change everything, all the meanings!" (123)—and ends up providing a revisionary tale based on outmoded ideals.

Significantly, Voragine does not have the last say in the text, which includes a series of photographs, Luiselli's afterword, and, in the English translation, an extra book composed by the translator, Christina MacSweeney. Each of these sections puts into question a definitive ending to the book, since they straddle the diegetic levels of the text, participating both in the fictional narrative and an extra-textual "reality"—the "real-life" Ecatepec represented in the appended photographs and inhabited by the workers who helped Luiselli to compose her novel. Luiselli explains in her afterword that two of the Jumex factory workers who participated in the book discussions also joined her in taking pictures of the city and artworks, which, she writes, "enabled me, virtually at least, to move around and explore the places I was writing about" (193). The local workers functioned as tour guides for Luiselli, providing access to an unfamiliar space—seemingly in the fashion of Highway as he taught Voragine the ins and outs of Ecatepec. The photographs include images of the Ecatepec junkyard, the Jumex gallery artworks referenced in Highway's narrative, and an urban castle-like structure labeled "Highway's House" (163). As we saw with Geryon's photographs, the photographs' titles interact with the images in a playful and complex way. In *The Story of My Teeth*, this interaction demonstrates a sort of play between the diegetic levels of the text: the actual factory workers took pictures of locations in the city of Ecatepec, yet the photograph titles encourage us to see the photos through the framework of the narrative—as Highway's house, as the works of art he encountered in the gallery, or as the junkyard where he obtained objects to collect, recycle, and auction. The photographs therefore become part of the story—rather than an extraneous appendage—as do the workers who took the pictures; one of the workers, El Perro, actually appears in Highway's narrative as well. Therefore, Luiselli's novel subverts any attempt to draw a boundary line between the seeming end of the narrative and the *post-texts* following that narrative; she pulls the narrative into the extra-textual space, and vice versa, interrogating the assumption of definitive textual edges and endings.

MacSweeney's extra book in the English translation, titled "Chronologics," works in a similar way to the photographs, since she composes a timeline that includes historical events, such as the "Centennial of the first-edition publication of Rubén Darío's *Azul*" and "Massive Earthquake under Mexico City leaves at least ten thousand people dead," and also events belonging to Highway's narrative, such as "Highway buys Marilyn Monroe's teeth in an auction in Miami" (182, 186). MacSweeney chooses historical events that have some sort of tie to Highway's narrative, although the historical account sometimes contrasts with the recycled account that Highway provides. For example, MacSweeney's historical reference to Darío marks the 1888 publication of the poet's collection of poems, *Azul*, and, in Highway's narrative, as noted above, Darío is re-contextualized as the owner of a Pachuca newspaper stand in the 1950's—a detail also noted in MacSweeney's timeline, meaning that the seemingly irreconcilable historical and narrative versions of Darío both appear in the translator's chronology.

MacSweeney follows Luiselli's lead in playing with the
boundaries of the text, asking us to embrace the possibility that, for example, Darío can be two things at
once, depending on the context in which we place him.
MacSweeney's active participation in the composition of
the text also asks us to reconsider the role of the translator. In interviews, Luiselli has described her relationship
with her translator as a collaborative exchange, explaining that the translation will sometimes inspire her to
go back and rewrite the original.[21] And in the afterword, she discusses the way in which MacSweeney's role
in the composition of the English version of the text
"both destabilizes the obsolete dictum of the translator's
invisibility and suggests a new way of engaging with
translation" (195). MacSweeney's translation, including
her "Chronologics," provides another contextual layer, or
framework, that shifts the way we read the novel. While
all translations necessarily offer a new linguistic and cultural framework, MacSweeney's translation brings explicit
attention to this shift, rather than, as Luiselli notes, seeking erasure, or trying to function as an imperceptible window through which we can reach the original. As we saw
in Carson's approach to translation, MacSweeney actively
modifies the text, not only adding to it, but also inviting
us to read the text through the specific lens of translation. In addition, considering translation as an additional level of composition—a continuation or perpetuation of the writing process—provides the sense that we
can "keep shaking the box" to see how the pieces may
fall out as we shift linguistic and cultural frameworks.

As mentioned several times above, Luiselli includes an afterword at the conclusion of *The Story of My Teeth*, which again re-frames the text, this time in terms of the collaborative writing of the novel. The process of composition becomes very much a part of the book—not in the sense that Luiselli attempts to resurrect a conventional notion of authorship and authorial presence, but rather in the sense that, as she noted in an interview in *The White Review*, "the procedures leave very clear traces in the work." Luiselli's approach emphasizes the *making of the thing*, which echoes what Lyn Hejinian says about the way an open text brings attention to process.[22] In this particular case, Luiselli's emphasis on process points to the multiplicity of authorial voices, the blurring of the diegetic levels of the text, and the seemingly continuous process of composition that never, even in the publication of the book, aims at closure. Like DuChamp, Luiselli plays with the notion of authorial signature, rejecting traditional notions of authorship at the same time that she brings our attention to the way that various signatures can shift and complicate contextual meanings. In *The Story of My Teeth*, those signatures, or traces of authorship and process, point back to multiple, shifting origins, resulting from the procedure Luiselli used to write her novel—sharing drafts of her work in installments to the factory workers at Grupo Jumex, and developing the narrative based on their discussions. In the afterword, she writes that the feedback and conversations of the workers "directed the course of the narrative" and also prompted her to reflect upon questions of value and meaning in the art world from a different perspective (194). The factory workers also provided local details, personal anecdotes, and photographs that Luiselli incorporated into the novel. In this way, the participation of the workers determined the unfolding and the fleshing out of *The Story of My Teeth*, prompting us to consider Luiselli's role as a "lover and collector of good stories," as her novel's narrator describes himself, rather than a traditionally-conceived author (23). And, if we see Luiselli in this way, we need to see the authorial voice in the afterword in a nuanced way—inscribed in the margins, commenting upon the preceding text, but as part of the composition, holding the teeth of the story "like the castanets used for flamenco dancing," and leaving a *relingo*, open for imaginative play (157).

In the afterword, Luiselli actually refers to her process as a "reverse Duchampian procedure," taking Duchamp's innovative ideas a step further by posing new questions that push against some of the seeming assumptions of Duchamp's gesture. What if an art object can be elevated by taking it out of the museum and putting it into the world, conversing with the factory workers at the margins of the Jumex gallery rather than only those who enter the sacred space of the museum? To what extent does art require that sacred space, or framework, and if it doesn't, then how and where do we locate its value and identity as art? When Highways extracts artworks from the gallery and injects them into a different, *hors-museum* context, he poses such questions. And Luiselli clearly enacts a similar extraction with the composition of her novel, challenging the conventional hermeticism of the writing process by eliciting the participation of the workers at the factory—individuals who literally and figuratively reside outside of the space of the gallery. She explains in the last line of the afterword, "This book began as a collaboration, and I like to think of it as an ongoing one, where every new layer modifies the content completely" (195). Luiselli closes her text with a paradoxical nod to its non-closure, and to the possibility of "new layers" that might offer a different framework that radically rewrites the novel.[23] That notion of layering evokes a passage from Luiselli's first novel, *Faces in the Crowd*: "A horizontal novel, told vertically. A novel that has to be told from the outside in order to be read from within" (61). While the horizontal novel comes to an end—from the perspective of its linear progression from first page to last—the vertical novel remains, open to additional layers. In that way, we step off the end of the text aware of the last page, yet nudged off with a reminder that the possibility of writing persists.

CHAPTER 2:
TANGIBLE GHOSTS:
WRITING AFTER LIFE

In "Portrait of an Invisible Man," *Nox*, and *Jane: A Murder*, Paul Auster, Anne Carson, and Maggie Nelson respectively all address a similar subject: the death of a loved one, and how to write about that death. Perhaps more significantly, and distinctively, these writers approach their subject from a position of marginality and exclusion—because of a lack of relations or intimacy with the lost loved one, and the paradox of feeling a sense of loss for someone or something that was never present, known, or accessible. To be sure, even the term "loved one" becomes problematic, since it implies the presence of one to be loved. Writing about someone who has died necessarily means writing after and in excess of the end of the life the writer seeks to portray; it seeks to recuperate or revive what has been lost in the form of writing, despite the impossibility of such a project. As Sarah Webster Goodwin and Elisabeth Bronfen point out in *Death and Representation*, "Perhaps the most obvious thing about death is that it is always only represented. There is no knowing death, no experiencing it and then returning to write about it, no intrinsic grounds for authority in the discourse surrounding it" (4). Clearly, we can't write about our own death, but it would seem our ignorance also precludes us from writing about another's death—in the sense that a definitive exclusion from our subject matter creates the possibility for writing in the first place. Beyond that first problem, as Goodwin and Bronfen go on to note, "Representation presupposes an original presence, and in the case of death, that is clearly paradoxical. In any representation of death, it is strikingly an absence that is at stake, so that the presentation is itself at a remove from what is figured" (7). Carson, Nelson, and Auster bring that remove to the forefront in their works, emphasizing their distance from what and whom they attempt to represent—a sort of doubled distance that results from the absence of, or absent relation with, the living person, before he or she died. Thus, the absence at stake reflects not only the necessary condition of representing death, but also the invisibility or inaccessibility of a particular life.

In the case of Carson's *Nox* and Auster's "Portrait of an Invisible Man," the exclusion of the writer reflects the shadowy character of the figure she or he wishes to describe, whereas, in *Jane: A Murder*, Nelson writes about a family member who died before she was born. In addition, the secrecy and silence surrounding all

three individuals—the father in "Portrait," the brother
in *Nox*, and Jane in the book of the same name—makes
it difficult for the writers to piece together, after the
fact, any narrative or understanding of the lives about
which others refuse to speak. Yet, as noted above, the
specific difficulty faced by the writers in these books can
be understood as a redoubling, and therefore illumination, of the problems any writer confronts when trying
to represent and retrieve life, through writing, upon the
death of a loved one. Both Nelson and Auster mention Peter Handke's *A Sorrow Beyond Dreams* as an earlier work that grapples with many of the questions that
motivate their own writing.[24] In it, Handke responds
to his mother's suicide by writing about her life, and
her failing mental health, noting, "I had better get to
work before the need to write about her, which I felt so
strongly at her funeral, dies away and I fall back into
the dull speechlessness with which I reacted to the news
of her suicide" (3). Though the "horror" that Handke
feels certainly attests to the way his mother's suicide
affected him personally, he tells his mother's story at
a distance, keeping the focus on her: "As usual, when
engaged in literary work, I am alienated from myself
and transformed into an object, a remembering and for-
mulating machine. [...] [L]ike an outside investigator,
though in a different way, I would like to present this
VOLUNTARY DEATH as an exemplary case" (5). For
Handke, writing puts him at a remove and allows for an
investigational approach to an intimate, heartbreaking
subject. We never really know much about Handke's

relationship with his mother or whether or not he felt close to her, since that's not his goal. Instead, he wants to transform the particular into the general, presenting his mother's story as an "exemplary case," and perhaps dulling the pain of personal loss by erasing the individuality or particularity of his mother's life—ironically by inscribing the specific details of her life before they are lost forever.

I mention Handke's portrait of his mother because it introduces a number of themes and questions that arise in *Nox*, "Portrait of an Invisible Man," and *Jane*. What does it mean to write about someone who has died— perhaps especially because the portrait no longer has a referent? How can one make visible (or avoid attempting to make visible) something or someone who was never *there*? What is the value of getting "the facts" down, and how do those facts capture or relate to the life to which they are tied? How does one write after or outside of a life, and still have something to say about that life? Roland Barthes's writing about his mother and her death feels pertinent here as well, as it provides an illuminating lens for what Carson, Auster, and Nelson address in their later works. *Camera Lucida* and *Mourning Diary* offer a strange and compelling balance of Barthes's interest in the complexities of signification and language, specifically in relation to death, and the expression of his devastating personal loss and grief after the death of his mother. While Barthes dedicates himself to the medium of photography in *Camera Lucida*, it is important to note that the famous Winter Garden Photograph of his mother never actually appears in the book, unlike many of the other photographs he discusses. In other words, Barthes provides a written portrait as a stand-in for the photographic portrait, partially as a means of protecting the "sacredness" of the photograph in his own subjective experience: "I cannot reproduce the Winter Garden Photograph. It exists only for me. For you, it would be nothing but an indifferent picture, one of the thousand manifestations of the 'ordinary' […]" (73). In some ways, at least in terms of the actual image, Barthes seems to want to avoid what Handke seeks in his portrait of his mother—an appropriation and reduction of the mother into a general category. Barthes's protectiveness of the image also serves to delineate *studium* and *punctum*, the latter of which emphasizes the intensely personal, incommunicable relation to the photograph, and implicitly, its referent (Barthes's mother, in this case). From one point of view, Barthes's decision to leave the photograph out, and thus to provide a written discussion without a referent, emphasizes the relation of both photography and writing to absence and death.

In an interview with Guy Manderey, collected in *The Grain of a Voice*, Barthes describes the relation of photography to death: "It's true that a photograph is a witness, but a witness of something that is no more. Even if the person in the picture is still alive, it's a moment of this subject's existence that is photographed, and this moment is gone" (356). In some ways this quotation seems to defy what we see in *Camera Lucida*, where Barthes's examination and discussion of the Winter

Garden Photo arise out of his unexpected discovery of an image where he truly recognizes his mother, announcing, "I found it" (67). He then proceeds to analyze the portrait as a means of getting at why, with this particular photograph, he finds himself "overwhelmed by the truth of the image" (76). Barthes's meditation on photography goes hand in hand with an exploration of the experience of grief and loss. In the end, Barthes's analysis of the Winter Garden Photograph emerges from a process of seeking to find what he has lost. While the photograph obviously cannot replace or resurrect his mother, he writes, "in Photography, *the thing has been there*" (76). Barthes's mother has died, but he has proof that she existed—because he has found her in a photograph. That desire for proof, for something that affirms a past presence, in the face of a definitive, endless absence propels all three books that I will consider in this chapter. And that search, for Carson, Auster, and Nelson, in contrast to Barthes who shared a very close relationship with his mother, is complicated by the uncertain existence for which they want to find proof.

Before turning to those three works, I would like to return briefly to the question of writing, since Barthes, of course, discusses a different medium in *Camera Lucida*—one which, he argues, is distinct from other forms of representation, precisely because "the referent adheres," or, in other words, cannot be detached from the artifice of a photograph (6). And perhaps for a similar reason, Carson, Auster, and Nelson discuss at length their relation to various objects and images that indexically signify the existence of the individual about whom they write. The faded handwriting of letters and journal entries, dated photographs, and even personal toiletries become grounding objects, assurances of existence and life, when that life feels so irretrievably distant and inaccessible. Yet, as Barthes contends, those markers of presence always simultaneously mark the loss of that presence. And writing, as Barthes seems to suggest in *Mourning Diary* and throughout his oeuvre, attests to that absence. Barthes writes, in *Mourning Diary*, about a consistent, particularly painful revelation about his mother: "the realization that *she no longer exists, she no longer exists*, totally and forever. This is a flat condition, utterly unadjectival—dizzying because *meaningless* (without any possible interpretation)" (78). Language cannot make sense of or provide a means for interpreting the fact that "she no longer exists"; it can, instead, repeat the expression, performing the infinite process of deferral that it fails to capture through adjectival description or signification. In addition, according to Barthes's contemporary, Maurice Blanchot, in "Literature and the Right to Death," language enacts the "she no longer exists," because it negates what it names:

> Hölderlin, Mallarmé, and all poets whose theme is the essence of poetry have felt that the act of naming is disquieting and marvelous. A word may give me its meaning, but first it suppresses it. For me to be able to say, "This woman" I must somehow take her flesh and blood reality away from her, cause her to

be absent, annihilate her. The word gives me the being, but it gives it to me deprived of being. The word is the absence of that being, its nothingness, what is left of it when it has lost being—the very fact that it does not exist. (379)

When we write, we name; and when we name, we negate (since naming destroys the particular in favor of the concept).[25] Without wandering too far from the specific focus of the present chapter, I would like to draw attention to the way in which Carson, Auster, and Nelson all meditate upon the act of the naming and the way in which writing necessarily makes absent what it describes. The role of death and absence in the act of writing both subverts and upholds the writer's aim to portray the life of an individual who has died. In its obligation to negate and its failure to resurrect, writing brings forward "the very fact that [that life] does not exist."

Paul Auster's "Portrait of an Invisible Man"

Paul Auster begins "Portrait of an Invisible Man," the first section of *The Invention of Solitude*, with the end of a life, writing specifically in response to the sudden death of his father.[26] While this end is, of course, definitive, Auster's urge to write, before it's too late—much like Handke—points to the fear of a sort of second death: "I thought: my father is gone. If I do not act quickly, his entire life will vanish along with him" (4).[27] Auster makes a distinction here between his father and his father's life, hoping that he might salvage the life his father composed by providing a record of that life, despite the death of the man. Auster's stated project might at first seem to suggest his confidence in the ability of writing to preserve and make present, but we soon learn that his sense of urgency and compulsion to write arise from the shadowy, barely visible character of his father—the sense that his father was never really there, that he had always already vanished.

> Even before his death he had been absent, and long ago the people closest to him had to accept this absence, to treat it as the fundamental quality of his being. Now that he was gone, it would not be difficult for the world to absorb the fact that he was gone forever. The nature of his life had prepared the world for his death—had been a kind of death by anticipation—and if and when he was remembered, it would be dimly, no more than dimly. (4)

Auster further complicates the moment of death in this passage by suggesting that his father's death became the defining feature of his life; he remained absent to everyone around him, as a sort of specter foreshadowing the eventual death of his body. Therefore, Auster's writing project seeks to stave off death in a sense, by capturing and recording a life before it has vanished, but that project must deal with the fundamental irony of trying to represent and preserve the life of someone who, in some ways, was already dead even before he died. It doesn't take long for Auster, "To recognize, right from the start, that the essence of this project is failure" (18).

Auster's composition of a portrait takes invisibility and unrepresentability as its starting point. In the portrayal of an invisible man, presumably, the subject won't appear; but we can perhaps see the lines of composition and the questions that arise when we seek to tell the story of another person's life. In an interview published in *Yale French Studies*, Auster explains:

> I never thought of this book as an autobiography—not even as a biography. But I was very conscious of what I was trying to do, which was to write a kind of meditation on how you might write a biography. Or, more importantly, how and if anyone can talk about someone else: what you know about other people. This is really what it's about. It's not just about my father. (180)

From this point of view, the failure, or impossibility, of Auster's project points to larger questions of narrative

and representation—questions that loom especially
large when the subject, Auster's father, remains so inaccessible and elusive. Portraiture here becomes a mode
of seeking or attempting to hold in place, even if just
for a moment, something that has eluded the grasp for
decades; but, as noted above, that seeking always folds
in on and becomes about itself, about the way writing
and portraiture address and perpetuate absence.

Auster's meditation on his father's life and death concerns the question of how one might write about a person
who is not there, without attempting to make him appear
or become visible—even if the desire to do so in some
sense motivates the writing. Early in the text, Auster confronts objects in his father's home that offer evidence of
life, specifically in the residue of daily rituals, at the same
time as they evoke death or absence. Auster mentions
the stubble left in a recently used razor, stashed bottles
of hair coloring, condoms kept in sock and underwear
drawers, and "a closetful of clothes silently waiting to be
worn again by a man who will not be coming back to
open the door" (8). And while the objects seem indexically to signify the father's presence—his life before it
ended—they also strike Auster in their meagingless-
ness, in the sense that they signify nothing. "Things are
inert: they have meaning only in function of the life
that makes use of them. When that life ends, the things
change, even though they remain the same. They are
there and yet not there: tangible ghosts, condemned
to survive in a world they no longer belong to" (8).
Auster's experience of the ghostly quality of his father's

objects resembles Barthes's description of the childhood photograph of his mother. Like the Winter Garden Photograph, the objects put Auster in a position of recollecting something or someone he never experienced the first time. In a literal sense, Auster's lack of intimacy with his father means that he was never familiar with his father's daily life and rituals, which perhaps contributes to Auster's sense that he is now invading his father's privacy: "I felt like an intruder, a burglar ransacking the secret places of a man's mind" (9). Therefore, the objects don't provide a means for recollecting the relationship he had with his father, but, rather, serve as indicators of what he never knew or experienced—a recollection of absence, in a sense.

Laura Barrett points out in her essay, "Framing the Past": "[…] the Winter Garden photograph does not reflect Barthes's recollection, since it was taken long before he was born. The photograph is neither document nor *aide-mémoir*, neither trace nor metonym; instead, it is metaphoric, like poetry (specifically, as Barthes notes, a Haiku) than recording in its ineffability" (88). In Auster's case, though, his exclusion from what his father's objects theoretically recollect speaks to his distant relationship with his father, and also his father's spectral character. Auster mentions later in "Portrait of an Invisible Man" that his father purchased new clothing after splitting up with his wife, attempting to infuse style and color into his wardrobe, to make himself visible in a sense. Auster writes, "But in spite of these efforts, he never looked quite at home in these costumes. They were not an integral part of his personality. It made you think of a little boy dressed up by his parents" (56). For this reason, the clothes hanging in Auster's father's closet point not to the presence of the man who wore them, but to the absent man whose invisibility became more obvious when he tried to make himself visible. Auster ultimately decides to keep some of his father's things, even if, as signifiers, they sort of float, untethered to a specific meaning, use, or individual. Perhaps, he thinks, the objects will remind him of his father, despite the complexities of recollecting an invisible man. "But all of this is no more than an illusion of intimacy. I have already appropriated these things. My father has vanished from them, has become invisible again" (69). Auster seems to realize that he can't wear his father's watch without making it *his* watch, and perhaps in the same vein, he can't tell his father's story without making it *his* story. The appropriation just happens; it comes with the act of naming, the act of writing.

While sifting through his father's things, Auster also finds a pile of photographs and a blank photo album, titled, "This is Our Life: The Austers" (11). The empty album reaffirms the sense of difficulty or impossibility in Auster's search for something tangible that would document his father's life, at the same time as it seems to work as a sort of invitation, much like the blank piece of paper that lies before A. in "The Book of Memory," the second half of *The Invention of Solitude*. Interestingly though, there *are* photographs—just not in the album. "Someone, probably my mother, had gone to the trouble of ordering this album, but no one had bothered to fill it" (11). Therefore, the documents, or evidence, exist, even though they lack the framework and contextualization that an album might provide. Auster tells us he obsesses over the photographs, for the first time feeling as if his father were in front of him—a collection of visual, and *visible*, images that he can scrutinize. He explains:

> Discovering these images was important to me because they seemed to reaffirm my father's physical presence in the world, to give me the illusion that he was still there. The fact that many of these pictures were ones I had never seen before, especially the ones of his youth, gave me the odd sensation that I was meeting him for the first time, that a part of him was only just beginning to exist. I had lost my father. But at the same time, I had also found him. (12)

Auster admits that "most of these pictures did not tell me anything new," but, using similar language to Barthes in *Camera Lucida*, he still finds them helpful, as physical documentation of a man whose existence was, in some sense, always in question (12). Though Auster experiences a sense of fulfillment from the photos, and even feels as if he has "found" his father for the first time, the narrative soon returns to the previous themes of invisibility and solitude, evasion and impenetrability. The pictures provide the satisfying illusion of presence—satisfying until the illusion falls apart, and Auster must confront the question of what a photograph of an invisible man can actually depict. In the end, as Auster tells us, "My father's capacity for evasion was limitless," suggesting that, if anything, the picture might capture the moment of turning away, of the refusal to be present (13). The representation of that refusal soon emerges, when Auster describes a trick photo taken of his father in Atlantic City. By overlaying a series of images where Auster's father sits at different seats at a table, the photograph appears to depict a singular moment in time—and thus five men, yet each the same man, sitting together. Auster explains, "There are five of him there, and yet the nature of the trick photography denies the possibility of eye contact among the various selves. Each one is condemned to go on staring into space, as if under the gaze of the others, but seeing nothing, never able to see anything. It is a picture of death, a portrait of an invisible man" (29).

I would therefore like to return to the importance of the blank album, not as a place where the father and family's life might take shape, but as a place where Auster grapples with the refusal of the story he's trying to tell. As I noted, the image of the album resembles the blank page, and it also resembles the various notebooks that appear throughout Auster's fiction and other writings. Dennis Barone lists the many notebooks in his introduction to *Beyond the Red Notebook*, a collection of critical essays on Auster's work, pointing to their significance at the same time that he contends, "Trying to pin the red notebook down is even more difficult than claiming once and for all that Hawthorne's scarlet letter 'A' is this or that" (2). Regardless of what the notebook may *mean*, we can say that the notebook suggests the process of notetaking and documentation, and it perhaps even points to the anxiety associated with the ephemerality of the thoughts and occurrences of our life—the sense that they might vanish if we don't get them down in writing. Clearly, that notion ties into Auster's motivation for writing his father's story, and even his approach to the story of his father's life by sifting through a collection of documents and facts, trying to make sense of them and to provide the context missing in the unorganized, album-less mass of pictures. In the face of his father's silence—both the silence of a man who refused to be known during his life and the absolute silence of his death—Auster notes, "At the very least, I want to put down the facts, to offer them as straightforwardly as possible and let them say whatever they have to say. But even the facts do not always tell the truth" (18). Writing here becomes a sort of case file, evidence compiled by a detective-writer looking for an explanation by way of the facts; yet, writing also confronts the slippery, sometimes deceptive nature of the facts, and maybe even its own inability to make them make sense.

Not long after Auster resolves to get the facts down, he admits, "[...] the farther I go the more certain I am that the path toward my object does not exist. I have to invent the road with each step, and this means that I can never be sure of where I am" (30). Auster portrays, at this moment, writing as a sort of movement without a path or clear destination, which contrasts a more detective-like approach, where writing might serve the process of discovery and ultimately lead to a satisfying conclusion that reveals the path tying all the pieces together. He notes, "Just because you wander in the desert, it does not mean there is a promised land," using language that recalls his critical work on Franz Kafka and Edmond Jabès (30).[28] In "Pages for Kafka," Auster writes:

> He is never going anywhere. And yet he is always going. Invisible to himself, he gives himself up to the drift of his own body, as if he could follow the trail of what refuses to lead him. And by the blindness of the way he has chosen, against himself, in spite of himself, with its veerings, detours, and circlings back, his step, always one step in front of nowhere, invents the road he has taken. (23)

The specific language of inventing the path or road arises in the passage here and the passage cited above from "The Portrait of an Invisible Man," identifying the writer's process as a sort of directionless, endless wandering. Inventing, in this case, does not suggest empowered artistic creation, rather it points to the uncertainty of proceeding blindly without a path, and to the sense that any direction the writer takes is largely arbitrary, reflecting, more than anything else, his or her groping around in the dark. As Pascal Bruckner argues in "The Heir Intestate," "Wandering, in Auster, has this original aspect: rather than pitting the individual against a cold, hostile world, it forces him to confront himself and the scattered fragments of his existence" (29-30). As I noted earlier, Auster's portrait of his father continually folds back upon his own process of trying to sketch his father's life—and, as Bruckner points out, the way his own identity and existence come into question in his effort to write about his invisible father. Auster describes Kafka as "invisible to himself," which brings attention to the way the writing process involves the disappearance of the writer, as a wanderer in the dark. And, of course, in exposing the invisibility and absence of his father, Auster implies his own invisibility, in the sense that he emerges as origin-less, without father. That lack of origin ties into Bruckner's argument that Auster's writing avoids conventional autobiographical writing, devoted to the revelation and *visibility* of the self, with a sort of refusal: "he dissolves this self, declares it a non-entity" (31). Thus, Auster proceeds to write about his invisible father, as an invisible man himself.[29]

Auster delves into the complexities of his father's secret backstory, writing, "if I am to understand anything, I must penetrate this image of darkness, that I must enter the absolute darkness of earth" (32). Despite his skepticism of "the facts" and his characterization of writing as a sort of aimless groping in the dark, Auster walks us through the story of his father's past, focusing on the events surrounding the murder of his father's father, by his father's mother. Auster knew of the story for many years, but after his father's death he takes an investigative approach to the story, collecting and pouring over old newspaper articles about the murder and subsequent legal proceedings. While the crime was solved long ago, the relation of the crime to his father's life has remained unexamined, largely as a result of the secrecy surrounding the events. Auster seems to wonder if, unlike the photographs that end up affirming the invisibility of his father, maybe these documents, the newspaper articles, can provide an explanation for that invisibility, and, in a sense, can make his father emerge from the shadows. Auster writes, "I do not think they explain everything, but there is no question that they explain a great deal. A boy cannot live through this kind of thing without being affected by it as a man" (36). And, after reading through Auster's summary and commentary upon the newspaper articles detailing his grandfather's murder, we surely agree with that assessment—yes, the documents do seem to "explain a great deal." Yet, *what* exactly do they explain? The end of Auster's grandmother's trial, and the last newspaper article dedicated to the story, marked the beginning of silence, the family moving east in order to start anew, out of the public eye—invisible. Therefore, Auster must insert himself, as writer and son, into the narrative, forging paths between the story of family trauma and the man who, as an adult, receded into the background, out of sight.

Auster begins that process with a degree of confidence, since, with "the few things [my father] did mention, I was able to form a fairly good idea of the climate in which the family lived" (49). Auster discusses the "nomadism" of the family, as they moved from place to place to avoid landlords and creditors (49); the relationship of his father and his four brothers, in addition to his father's marginalization as the youngest child; the unpredictability of his father's mother and of the family's existence in general; and the way his father's uncertain, constantly changing situation as a child seemed to manifest itself in his adulthood. Auster describes his father's hyper-practicality and extreme thriftiness, and, perhaps unsurprisingly, his disapproval of his son's career as a poet: "In his eyes, you became part of the world by working. By definition, work was something that brought in money. If it did not bring in money, it was not work. Writing, therefore, was not work, especially the writing of poetry" (61). All of this makes sense, given Auster's father's childhood experience with poverty and uncertainty; the past provides a more-or-less self-evident explanation for the present. But, Auster notes, those predictable outcomes would sometimes confront baffling inconsistencies. For example, despite the hard line Auster's father took on the writing of poetry as a profession, he would go to the public library to read his son's recently published work in a literary magazine. Auster writes:

> The rampant, totally mystifying force of contradiction. I understand now that each fact is nullified by the next fact, that each thought engenders an equal and opposite thought. Impossible to say anything without reservation: he was good, or he was bad; he was this, or he was that. All of them are true. At times I have the feeling that I am writing about three or

four different men, each one distinct, each one
a contradiction of all the others. Fragments.
Or the anecdote as a form of knowledge. (62)

In such moments of contradiction, Auster realizes that
the facts of his father's life seem to produce different
men, like the men sitting around the table in the trick
photograph, a single man dispersed into many. No matter the amount of facts, objects, and photographs Auster
can accumulate, the result remains fragmentary, or
incomplete. Everything becomes anecdotal—reflective
of a single experience or moment that might or might
not relate to some unknowable, invisible "whole" story.

Towards the end of "A Portrait of an Invisible Man,"
Auster finds himself trying to avoid the closure of the
text, suggesting that his writing has, in a sense, managed
to defer the end of his father's life, or at least the demand
that he must confront and accept that end. He writes:

I want to postpone the moment of ending, and
in this way delude myself into thinking that I
have only just begun, that the better part of
my story still lies ahead. No matter how use-
less these words might seem to be, they have
nevertheless stood between me and a silence
that continues to terrify me. When I step into
this silence, it will mean that my father has
vanished forever. (65)

As long as Auster continues to write, he doesn't have to
face the silence, or the absolute invisibility of a man who
has vanished forever. The irony, though, is that Auster
has realized the impossibility of coming to an end, in

sense that he knows he can't "complete" or close the story. Whatever he has to say, whatever he writes, will never say it all; it remains anecdotal and contradictory, and, therefore, any textual ending he provides necessarily leaves a remainder, or unincorporated excess. As he tries to come to a close, Auster mentions Maurice Blanchot's *L'arrêt de mort*, where the narrator has goals that are similar to Auster's in "Portrait"—specifically, a desire "to put an end to it all" by telling the story of a series of events involving a ghostly, barely visible figure (*L'arrêt* 131). Blanchot's narrator comes to a similar realization that the ending of the text marks the impossibility of closure, of naming and identifying what we want to make visible and known. He tells us (and Auster quotes), "What is extraordinary begins at the moment I stop," suggesting that the failure of writing to provide closure, announced by the closing words of the text, opens onto the "extraordinary" (63)—that which exceeds what writing can do. Therefore, Auster's comment that his father will vanish forever perhaps takes on a double meaning: at the end of the book, he will experience the fact of his father's death, without the sense of deferral that writing offers; and, at the end of the book, his father's invisibility, his vanishing act, persists, in excess of the text.[30]

Auster ends the piece with an image of his own son, lying asleep in his crib. "To end with this" (69). As Auster meditates upon what it means to conclude his portrait of his invisible father, he fixes upon the image of his son, wondering what his son "will make of these pages" (69). The portrait of Auster's father, if it ever appeared, vanishes as the text concludes, and the image of the son comes into focus. Clearly, the image of the son evokes the way that ends open onto beginnings, and puts side-by-side Auster's experience as the son of a distant, inaccessible father and his experience as a father, to a son he imagines reading "these pages" where he attempts to conjure an invisible man—a grandfather the boy will never know and to whom he will only have access through "these pages." The depiction of Auster's son at the end also converses with the Kierkegaard passage that he cites just above it: "he who is willing to work gives birth to his own father" (69). On its face, that passage seems to suggest that the "work" traced in "Portrait" might give birth to Auster's father, in the sense that it transforms his father's life into a visible, material object. At the same time, the specific work of Auster's "Portrait" would seem to point to the impossibility of trying to make visible a man who hid from sight and refused to be known. For that reason, it becomes important to complicate the Kierkegaard passage and the image of the son within the context of "Portrait." We have to ask ourselves to what extent the "work" of writing and understanding might turn away the thing (or individual) it attempts to depict. Throughout "Portrait," Auster continually finds himself at a loss, aware of the contradiction of portraying invisibility. As the father vanishes, the son remains (both Auster and *his* son); they *surv*ive, living beyond the death of Auster's father. In some sense, Auster and his son signify the unincorporated excess of the father's life—that which defies an attempt at closure, or a final word. Auster's decision to end the text with an image of his son evokes a sense of hope and possibility, which strangely arises out of the failure to bring his father to light, and the inability to arrive at closure, through writing, in his death.

Anne Carson's *Nox*

Interestingly, in first pages of Anne Carson's *Nox*, she cites a passage by Hecataeus, who describes the mythic phoenix, encasing his dead father in an egg in order to carry him to Egypt and to bury him there.[31] The image of the father's corpse enshrined in a symbol of fertility and birth resembles what we see at the end of Auster's "Portrait," with the citation of Kierkegaard. The work of grief, in both cases, is tied up in the ability to survive, to give birth to the father precisely in burying him. In reference to the egg, Carson writes, "The phoenix mourns by shaping, weighing, testing, hollowing, plugging, and carrying toward the light" (1.1).[32] The phoenix grieves the death of his father and prepares for the journey to bury him in a sort of flurry of activity, measuring and interrogating, ensuring the stability of the material object in which he will carry the absence of the father. Dealing with the physicality of the egg seems to help with the mourning. At the same time, Carson wonders if the phoenix's work, the productivity of his grief, brings attention to what his activity misses:

> And in the shadows that flash over him as he makes his way from Arabia to Egypt maybe he comes to see the immensity of the mechanism in which he is caught, the immense fragility of his own flying—composed as it is of these ceaselessly passing shadows carried backward

by the very motion that devours them, his
motion, his asking. (1.1)

The forward motion of the phoenix's flight, the activity
of his grief, cannot produce closure; closure, even when
seemingly ensured by an expertly composed, well-sealed
egg, escapes the activity of the phoenix, as the "ceaselessly passing shadows" move backwards, a testament to
what exceeds (and supports) the phoenix's activity.

Carson relates the activity of the phoenix to that of
the historian, or "One who asks about things—about
their dimensions, weight, location, moods, names, holi-
ness, smell" (1.1). Like the phoenix, the historian collects
information, through careful prodding, and constructs
something as a way of dealing with and encasing the past.
Carson adds, "But the asking is not idle. It is when you
are asking about something that you realize you yourself
have survived it. And so you must carry it, or fashion
it into a thing that carries itself" (1.1). The historian
operates from the outside, as one who has survived and
therefore can speak and ask questions about the past; the
weight of the past relies on the historian to hoist it upon
his or her shoulders, or to produce a story, an understanding, that would no longer require any hoisting. In
any case, the asking, the carrying, the manufacturing
all point to a sort of productivity that, though perhaps
necessary as a means of dealing with and memorializ-
ing the past, can't help but miss the "ceaselessly passing
shadows." Like Auster seems to suggest at the end of
"Portrait," burying the father relies on giving birth to

him, but one can only do so from the outside. And, in giving birth, the absent father, or brother—invisible in life and in death—is appropriated, fashioned into someone or something that we can see, hold in our hands, flip through, and make sense of.

Carson admires Herodotus's approach to history for its refusal to claim authority. He makes reference to the story of the phoenix told by Hecataeus, but, as Carson tells us, introduces such passages with expressions like, "it is said," suggesting his own distance from and lack of authority on whatever information he's going to present (1.2). Taking that outsider position calls attention to the "ceaselessly passing shadows," and to the uncertainty produced by the act of questioning. According to Carson, Herodotus insists upon the strangeness of history—the human attempt to question, test, analyze, recount, and encase the past. She writes, "For often it produces no clear or helpful account, in fact people are satisfied with the most bizarre forms of answering [...]" (1.3). Carson, via Herodotus, seems to suggest that people tend to want closure, an answer in whatever form it might take. For Carson, the work of the historian remains nuanced and much less satisfying: "collecting bits of muteness" that attest to "a certain fundamental opacity of human being, which likes to show the truth by allowing it to be seen hiding" (1.3). Like Herodotus, her dealings with the past will come from the outside, aware that her best bet is to shed light on the refusal of truth—the way it hides from sight and eludes our attempts to chase it down. As she writes in "The Anthropology of Water," "Water is something you cannot hold. Like men. I have tried. Father, lover, brother, true friends, hungry ghosts, and God, one by one, all took themselves out of my hands" (117).

Carson reflections on history and the story of the phoenix frame her attempt to mourn and to portray through writing the life of her brother, Michael. She opens *Nox*:

> I wanted to fill my elegy with light of all kinds. But death makes us stingy. There is nothing more to be expended on that, we think, he's dead. Love cannot alter it. Words cannot add to it. No matter how I try to evoke the starry lad he was, it remains a plain, odd history. So I began to think about history. (1.0)

From the beginning of the text, illumination feels like a lost cause. But, perhaps, like a historian, Carson might "show the truth by allowing it to be seen hiding" (1.3). While Michael, as a "starry lad," hides, refusing to be seen, his "fundamental opacity" might take the shape of a physical object—a book that emphasizes its own materiality and hard outer casing. Like the phoenix's egg, Carson's book carries Michael's absence. *Nox* comes in a gray box, containing a continuous piece of paper folded into pages, and presenting a collage of poems, paintings, photographs, letters, transcripts of conversation, and handwritten notes. On the back of the box, Carson inscribes: "When my brother died I made an epitaph for him in the form of a book. This is a replica of it, as close as we could get." Referring to the book as an epitaph

emphasizes the physical importance of the object, something material by which she might remember Michael.
Meghan O'Rourke's, in her essay, "The Unfolding,"
notes that the replica of the original notebook "conjures
up an almost tactile sense of the handmade original. A
mourner is always searching for traces of the lost one,
and traces of that scrapbook's physicality—bits of handwriting, stamps, stains—add testimonial force." From
that perspective, Carson's emphasis on the materiality of
the book, even in its reproduction, points to her effort
to find traces of her brother's past presence, to assure
herself of his existence. Like Auster in "Portrait," the
handwritten letters, scraps of stamped envelopes, and
photographs serve that role; she collects information and
objects, an historian asking questions and testing the
evidence in an attempt to reconstruct the past. Rather
than simply writing about what she discovers, Carson
insists upon including the pieces of her investigation,
and, as O'Rourke points out, "lets Michael haunt the
work, writing into its lacunae, through the eeriness of
his handwriting, of the airmail stamps he used."

At the same time that the physicality of *Nox* allows
us to see markers of a past presence—Michael, with
his living hand, wrote *that* letter—it also undeniably
points to Michael's absence. We see that same paradox
in Barthes's relation to photographs of his mother and
Auster's collection of his father's objects. Auster call his
father's things: "tangible ghosts, condemned to survive
in a world they no longer belong to" ("Portrait" 8). The
letters, though they bear Michael's handwriting, evoke

the absent hand as much or more than they evoke the hand that wrote them. In that way, the letters and postcards, like the phoenix's egg and the hard outer casing of *Nox*, carry absence. In addition, as Sara Tanderup notes in her essay, "Nostalgic Experiments," *Nox*, as a replica of an original scrapbook, creates a "longing for capturing the past, and for restoring the original book in this work" (50). In other words, though *Nox* replicates the materiality of Carson's composition and has the reader interacting with the fragments that Carson collected and pieced together, we are always aware that what we're reading is a reproduction of an original physical object. We see, but can't feel, the physicality of crumpled pages, and therefore confront the absence of the original. Tanderup reads this as "an idealization of the book as an intimate, auratic object," which makes sense, although I would emphasize that Carson plays with the original-reproduction binary as a means of evoking loss more than an investment in conventional, binary understandings of originality (50)—partially because in the end even the "original" objects can't help but point to the absence of the individual, even before he died.

Michael, like Auster's father, navigated the world as an invisible, often anonymous man. After running away as a young man, Carson writes, "He was travelling on a false passport and living under other people's names" (2.2). While we find scraps of writing throughout *Nox*, Carson tells us that "he wrote only one letter," and that the postcards he sent were "laconic" (2.2). Carson and her mother generally didn't know of Michael's whereabouts

and had no way of contacting him. While Carson manages to track down some information after his death,
she writes, "I am looking a long time into the muteness
of my brother. It resists me" (1.3). This, as Carson has
told us, represents the work of the historian, "collecting
bits of muteness" and facing the refusal of visibility, of
illumination. The collection of physical objects in *Nox*
suggests that muteness and absence partially because
the specific objects signify the fact that Michael wasn't
around. Postcards and a letter from an unknown place
abroad demonstrate that Michael always existed elsewhere, not *here*. And while the photographs Carson
includes provide a sense of what Michael looked like as
a kid, they notably only represent his childhood, since
he disappeared as a young man and never returned. The
one photograph Carson discusses at length portrays him
underneath a treehouse, where a group of older boys had
pulled up the ladder, leaving him below. She writes, "He
is giving the camera a sideways invisible look," adding
"No one knew him" (8.2). As the photographer attempts
to capture Michael, he doesn't look away or hide from
view; instead, he returns the look sideways, *there* and *not
there* at the same time. Michael's exclusion and loneliness
perhaps appear in this photograph, but Michael doesn't;
he deflects and eludes the gaze, making him unknowable, hidden from sight.

I have not yet mentioned one of the most important
components of Carson's *Nox*: the word-by-word translation of Catullus's *Multas per gentes* (or, 101) that travels
the length of the text on the left-hand side of the fold.

Carson opens *Nox* with the poem in Latin, inscribed on a piece of yellowed paper, with smudged ink, and presumably pasted onto the first page of the original scrapbook. In addition to emphasizing the object-ness of poem, the aged, imperfect look of the paper and ink perhaps suggests the years of work Carson put into translating 101—a poem, Carson tells us, that has stumped her and left her wondering if it maybe even defies translation.[33] "I have never arrived at the translation I would have liked to do of poem 101" (7.1). Whether it is or not, the yellowy, smudged paper creates the sense that we're actually seeing the poem Carson transported from library to library, wedged in dictionaries, and left out on her desk, exposed to spills and scribbles. And it also suggests the murky work of translation—a murkiness Carson has never tried to hide, given the non-traditional, non-literal approach to translation she tends to take in her work.[34] After presenting the poem in its entirety at the beginning of *Nox*, Carson cuts it up, providing a dictionary definition of each word as it appears in Catullus's poem. As many critics have noted, Carson inserts herself into those definitions from time to time, subtly connecting the words in the poem to her search for her brother. Therefore, even at the level of the word, Carson's translation accommodates and accentuates the personal lens through which she sees the poem, never claiming her own invisibility or absence in that process. As J. Kates argues in "Catullus by Night: Anne Carson's *Nox*," Carson's excursions from a strictly literal translation allow her to explore the complexities implied in particular words and expressions. He writes, "The whole poem is rich in these multiple implications in the words, and any translation that tries to convey the movement and simplicity of the original will miss much." Of course, any translation misses, and Carson's approach to translation makes us aware of that. Because she never feels absent or invisible and instead leaves clear traces of herself in the work of translation, she draws our attention to what's necessarily lost in translation—in the sense that we see her making choices, necessitated by the fact that no "perfect" translation exists. In a translation, too, the "ceaselessly passing shadows" escape the flight forward.

The act of translation, and textual manipulation, does not only apply to the translation of the Catullus poem. Carson also translates the bits and pieces of writing and conversation left by her brother, re-framing his language by presenting it in verse, juxtaposing it with images, and conversing with it over the course of her poetic meditation on loss and grief. Carson points out the connection to translating: "Because our conversations were few (he phoned me maybe 5 times in 22 years) I study his sentences the ones I remember as if I'd been asked to translate" (8.1). Without an actual written vestige in the case of a phone conversation, Carson must rely upon her memory, reconstructing his sentences through the lens of her own experience and through the workings of her own sentences. Here, she provides an example:

Lots of crime in Copenhagen.

Danes are hardworking.

I am painting the flat.

We have a dog that's him barking.
Yes he barks in Danish.
Don't go back to the farm don't go alone.
What will you do sit on Bald Rock and look
down at the graves.
Put the past away you have to. (8.1)

The poem presumably reflects Michael's side of a conversation that he and Carson had after the death of their mother. While Carson doesn't include her own part in the conversation, we don't have to look hard to find her here. In terms of the conversation, Michael responds to the questions she poses (Does your dog bark in Danish?), and the plan she reveals to go to their parents' graves. And, in terms of the writing, Carson has fashioned her memory of the conversation into a poem, arranging the words and sentences into verse, presumably worrying less about transcribing the exact conversation than capturing the feeling of the exchange of words and silences between herself and her brother. The translation of the conversation into a poem allows Carson to emphasize certain moments of the conversation, and to frame them in a way that reflects her own interpretation of the movement, tone, and meanings of the exchange. The poem draws attention to the paradox of intimacy and foreignness that seems to characterize Carson's relation to her brother: foreign because he is a stranger, living in another country under a different name, and intimate as a result of a shared past, and shared loss. And while Carson's poem sheds light on the paradox of their relation, she remains skeptical throughout *Nox* that she can illuminate his life in any way, no matter how hard she tries. Like a poem that resists translation for decades, even when broken down into its individual words in the hopes of getting some clarity, Michael's life and his words resist, and maybe even refuse, clarification. Carson writes, "Prowling the meanings of a word, prowling the history of a person, no use expecting a flood of light" (7.1)

As Carson collects various documents, photos, and bits of information pertaining to Michael's unknown life, she laments that "there is something that facts lack." She refers to that something as "Overtakelessness," or "that which cannot be got round. Cannot be avoided or seen to the back of. And about which one collects facts—it remains beyond them" (1.3). Michael always exceeds the facts Carson collects about him; they never come together to create a portrait, nor do they seem to breathe life or voice into his ghostly, mostly silent life. Carson explains that her mother, in particular, suffered over Michael's silence—"Eventually she began to say he was dead" (4.2)—accepting his death as a fact regardless of whether or not he had actually died. Carson notes that several people she knows suggest a connection between her brother and Lazarus. Most likely, those who draw the comparison of Michael to Lazarus are suggesting his tendency to re-emerge, after years of silence, and, from his mother's perspective, presumed death. Carson provides her own reflections on the topic: "You can think of Lazarus as an example of resurrection or as a person who had to die twice. An historian will take the latter view. I don't know how Lazarus saw it" (8.4). Michael seemed to have sought his own death, in the form of a vanishing act from everyone who knew him; yet, at no point does he re-emerge from the darkness, as a symbol of re-birth. Even if he pops up after seven years of silence, he remains absent, offering little that would assure anyone he has come out of the tomb. While Michael manages to make himself disappear, and he does indeed disappear from family and friends, Carson implies that he represents an example of a person who has to die twice: despite his disappearance, he still must endure life, or that which exceeds his capacity to manufacture an end.

Coupled with Michael's inability to make himself disappear absolutely is Carson's inability to call him forth. Carson notes that in all of the Biblical passages where Lazarus appears, he remains mute—even in regards to his resurrection. The use of the word "mute" here recalls her previous explanation that this word "is regarded by linguists as an onomatopoeic formation referring not to silence but to a certain fundamental opacity of human being, which likes to show the truth by hiding it" (1.3). Thus, muteness does not translate to silence; it suggests, rather, indecipherable sound, and the resistance of human beings to come forward, to appear. In *The Infinite Conversation*, Maurice Blanchot discusses the story of Lazarus, arguing that the resurrected Lazarus hides the Lazarus who refuses to appear:

> But what does this Lazarus saved and raised
> from the dead that you hold out to me have

> to do with what is lying there and makes you
> draw back, the anonymous corruption of the
> tomb, the lost Lazarus who already smells bad
> and not the one restored to life by a force that
> is no doubt admirable, but that is precisely
> a force and that comes in this decision from
> death itself? (36)

Blanchot's reading of Lazarus points to the way that acts of revival, of illuminating what refuses our penetrating gaze, leaves the secret in the cave, further demonstrating the "fundamental opacity of human being, which likes to show the truth by hiding it" (1.3). We can only bring Lazarus forth by negating the already-dead Lazarus; we can only make him speak by silencing his muteness. After reflecting on the figure of Lazarus, Carson includes a drawing of a body lying flat like a corpse, and writes underneath: "As in some cave may lie a lightless pool" (8.4). Carson seems to land in roughly the same place as Blanchot when it comes to Lazarus and, by extension, her brother: "There is no possibility I can think my way into his muteness" (8.5). Whatever Carson manages to re-construct through her persistent questioning, collecting, and research, Michael remains unseen and mute, lying in the "lightless pool" of the cave.

Carson does arrive at a translation of the Catullus poem, but also gives herself enough room in the remaining pages of the book to cut up the translated poem and paste it in overlapping fragments, and to soak it in water so that the words become illegible—lest we conclude that she has actually arrived at anything satisfying or fixed. In her essay on *Nox*, Joan Fleming draws attention to Carson's translation of the phrase "ave atque vale," in the last line of the poem as "farewell and farewell," instead of the typical translation of the line as "hail and farewell." Fleming writes that Carson's translation works as "a repetitive form that performs a tension between finality—the double assertion of 'farewell' implying a sense of final goodbye—and a suggestion of the valediction continuing 'into forever'" (68). As Fleming suggests, in Carson's translation, the goodbye, demanded by the finality of death, opens onto the impossibility of coming to any closure, to say our goodbyes and be done with it. That inability to come to an end reflects Carson's work with 101, her composition of *Nox*, and her reckoning with Michael's life and death. In the final pages of *Nox*, she includes the end of Michael's single letter to their mother, where he writes, "Love you. Love you. Michael," mirroring the end of her translation of the Catullus poem (10.1). Coming to the end becomes the impossibility of coming to an end, of creating a letter or a scrapbook that manages to make sense of things, to transform muteness into an audible voice, or to shed light on the hidden truth that refuses it. Therefore, Carson arrives without arriving, noting, in the last line of *Nox*, "He refuses, he is in the stairwell, he disappears" (10.3).

Maggie Nelson's *Jane: A Murder*

Maggie Nelson's mixed-genre work, *Jane: A Murder*, emerges from the void of death and loss, much like "Portrait" and *Nox*. Nelson's book re-visits the life and death of her aunt, Jane, who was murdered in 1969. Though Nelson never knew her aunt, the memory of Jane maintained a haunting presence in her life, perhaps especially due to the silence surrounding the tragedy. *Jane: A Murder* responds to this silence, acknowledging the impossibility of filling it and exploring the possibility of writing in excess or outside of silence. In this way, Nelson's confrontation with a sort of doubled silence and invisibility differs from what we saw in "Portrait" and *Nox*, in the sense that it arises less from Jane's specter-like existence during her life, and more from the fact that Nelson has only ever had access to her aunt's life through whatever she can piece together, collecting evidence and prodding reticent family members. Similar to Carson, Nelson composes a book of poetry that works as a sort of collage, incorporating Jane's own writing, newspaper reports of Jane's death, and true crime narratives describing the murder. Jane's teenage journals consistently appear throughout the text, and, in this way, we feel like we have access to Jane's voice—especially since, unlike Michael's laconic postcards, Jane's writing appears to reveal rather than hide. At the same time, Jane's journals, in the absence of Jane, feel, to quote Auster, like "tangible ghosts, condemned to survive in a world they no longer belong to" ("Portrait" 8). And, perhaps for that reason, Nelson intervenes and collaborates when presenting Jane's journals, re-framing the entries in verse, appropriating and revitalizing them in the absence of their author. Nelson manages to create a conversation between Jane's journals and the other texts she includes in her work, allowing Jane implicitly to respond to those texts, and, in a sense, to have a say in the depiction of her life and death. Yet Nelson's text never feels like it's claiming to "resurrect" Jane or to bring her out of the silence imposed upon her—partially because, like Carson, she draws attention to her own participation in and even manipulation of the material. That participation paradoxically breathes life into the ghostly journals and documents, at the same time that it affirms the absence and inaccessibility of Jane's own breath and voice.

In *Jane: A Murder*, Nelson's collage-like approach emphasizes space, making us aware of the gaps between the poems and passages, and encouraging us to imagine different possibilities for assembling the pieces. After all, Jane's murder goes unsolved, and Nelson, by the end of the text, remains fully aware that her aunt, as an individual and as a story, recedes beyond her grasp. A tidy explanatory narrative would feel, at the least, disingenuous.[35] In some ways, the story has already ended, and anything that Nelson might want to add to it plays the role of a footnote or appendix, years after the fact. In one of the earliest poems in *Jane*, "Figment," Nelson's grandfather comments when she first tells him of her plans to write about Jane: "*What will it be, a figment / of your imagination?*" (23, italics in original). Her grandfather's rhetorical question, though perhaps not ill-intentioned, positions Nelson on the outside of both Jane's life and death, suggesting that her only relation to Jane is imaginary, and therefore, from his perspective, a kind of fantasy or fiction. Nelson's poem unfolds out of her grandfather's response, delving into the etymology of the word "figment," which she traces back to "*fingere,* meaning *to form*" (23)—an argument that clearly has no chance with her grandfather but begins to get at Nelson's hopes for her writing project. A figment, or a form, from that etymological perspective, is an art object—one that makes no claim to a pre-existing truth, but, rather, draws attention to the act of forming, perhaps especially when faced with the absence of a model from which one might work. Nelson's poetry arises out of the gap that separates her from Jane, and out of the oppressive silence in the family surrounding her death; in the absence of Jane, Nelson assembles a book that enjoys the freedom of its marginality, its status as a sort of afterthought. At the same time, Nelson realizes that her book, like the phoenix's egg and Carson's replicated scrapbook, carries the absence of Jane and points to the impossibility of resurrecting her. From her marginal, outsider position, she forms a portrait which asks questions and maintains silence; which favors conversation to a monologic narrative; which embraces the imaginary as a mode of shedding light, even in the absence of hard evidence and the refusal of illumination. In the prose poem following "Figment," Nelson writes, "I invent her, then, as a woman emerging from the sea" (25). Nelson "gives birth" to Jane, yet, like Auster and Carson, remains aware that the giving birth, the invention, simultaneously points to the way that activity implies and perpetuates her absence, and highlights the impenetrable darkness of the tomb.

The question of "shedding light" is important and complicated in *Jane*, since, again, Nelson seemingly wants to avoid falling into the trap of making claims to truth or resurrecting the dead. In the first "dream poem" that opens *Jane*, Nelson describes a woman who has suffered a gunshot to the head, like Jane, focusing on the bullet holes: "Sunlight shot around the circumference of each black rind, so that a long shaft of pale light cast out from the center of her forehead, and another shaft streamed behind her" (17). The woman in the dream experiences this moment of illumination as the "*light of [her] mind*," as a sort of validation of self, and wonders how she can share this light with others (17, italics in original). Yet, the poem concludes: "But in fact she was losing the light; it leaked everywhere, unstoppable" (17). This image of leaking light clearly evokes loss of life, and it also can characterize the problems of telling a story, of offering insight into a life, as the light quickly seeps out into the unimaginably dark outside. In the *Michigan Quarterly Review*, Raymond McDaniel argues that the opening dream poems of *Jane* evoke traditional elegies, yet the image of leaking light, in particular, "suggests that this text will not be easily reconciled with the

certainties of the elegiac posture." For McDaniel, Nelson
therefore gets down to the work of harnessing a quickly
disappearing moment of illumination, which must begin
with research into a life about which she, by and large,
lacks knowledge. While I agree with McDaniel's general
proposition, I'm not sure Nelson ever labors under the
illusion that she might capture the leaking light. Instead,
she begins her work with a recognition of lost light, and
dedicates herself to grappling in the dark, undercutting
the various ways others have reduced and "made sense
of" Jane's life and death. Clearly, as Nelson herself has
suggested, *Jane: A Murder* does seek to provide a portrait
of the living Jane, pushing against the tendency to define
her life in relation to her brutal death, but that portrait
continually brings attention to a nagging lack of access,
to the presence of distance and loss, to the aching, paradoxical sense of intimacy with an unknown subject.[36]

In the poem "Two Wrongs," Nelson considers the
demand, in writing about Jane, that she name the
unknown, and the way in which that name will, in some
ways, necessarily miss its mark. She describes the behavior of elephants when a member of their herd dies: "They
say elephants can recognize the bones of a dead loved
one when they stumble upon them in the wild. They
will stop and wander around the huge decaying bones,
swinging their trunks in despair" (28). The expression
"they say" simultaneously suggests the authority of *those
who know* and the uncertainty of a hypothetical statement—one that depends upon an application of what
we can know, through scientific study, to what we can't

possibly know, including, in this case, the motivations
and inner life of elephants. In the end, we lack access,
and in the absence of a shared language, we provide
explanatory narratives based on evidence. Naming the
unknown, whether we're talking about an elephant or
a deceased young woman, becomes part of the process
of trying to shed light on something that necessarily
refracts that light back to us. Nelson continues, "The
voice-over on TV might say, *The elephants know that
these are the bones of Dolly. They are mourning the loss of
Dolly.* But Dolly is our name, not theirs" (28). Naming
Dolly makes her, and the other elephants, feel accessible to us, even if the act of naming demonstrates the
language and narratives we impose, our irrecoverable
distance from that which we want to know and name.
As we saw in Blanchot's "Literature and the Right to
Death" earlier in the chapter, language, naming, negates
what we name in order to give rise to a concept: "The
word gives me the being, but gives it to me deprived of
being. The word is the absence of that being, its nothingness, what is left of it when it has lost being—the
very fact that it does not exist" (379). Nelson recognizes
the necessity of naming, and the paradox that names
seem to bring objects closer as they simultaneously push
them away. We introduce ourselves, our activity, in the
act of naming. And by the end of the poem, Nelson
points to her own activity in regards to Jane: "Her grave
has no epitaph, only a name. / I found her in the wild;
her name was Jane, plain Jane" (28). Nelson takes her
aunt out of the wild and names her, seeking closeness,

and aware of the distance and negation involved in the act of writing.

Nelson isn't making a simple statement about the way in which we anthropomorphize animals or the way in which we try to explain the unknowable; instead, she is setting the stage for her own poetic engagement with Jane's life and death. In addition to providing a site where Jane could, in a sense, tell her own story, Nelson's book deals with the act of naming others, and the projection involved in that act. In a conversation with Gaby Wood of *The Telegraph*, Nelson mentions "the excitements and perils of learning about yourself through twinning and doubling," which, she explains "can be very illuminating and bonding, but it can also be very distorting. I never knew my aunt—so it's really about me. That dance of projection and communion was compelling to me." After all, as Nelson reveals in a poem early on in *Jane*, both her grandfather and her mother seem to confound her with Jane, the former accidentally calling Nelson by Jane's name, and the latter musing that "*The spirit of Jane lives on in you*" (36, italics in original). In the poem "Slippage," Nelson herself, upon discovering her aunt's journals, at first believes they are her own: "pages / and pages of self-doubt; a relentlessly plaintive tone; / and a wanting, a raw wanting / not yet hidden in my / poems" (30). Nelson's identification with her aunt becomes a central theme of the book and puts forward her own entanglement in her representation of Jane. Perhaps for that reason, Nelson, even when presenting Jane's journals, directly intervenes, transposing them in verse and thus acting as a sort of curator for our experience of Jane's writing. This changes the context for reading Jane's teenage journal at the same time that it marks and makes us aware of Nelson's presence. In other words, as we saw with Carson, Nelson doesn't try to throw a veil over her own participation and intervention; she points to it.

One of our first experiences of Jane's writing appears in this journal entry:

Hah! Good luck.
Too bad Franny's mother
wasn't right—too bad
I don't just need
a warm bowl of soup
and a long sleep.

It's cold in here.

At this point in Nelson's book, we don't have much context for Jane's struggles and why warm soup and a good night of sleep won't do the trick. And we obviously don't have access to the original journal entry, so we can't say much about what the entry looked like before Nelson intervened.[37] I would imagine that as a two-sentence prose entry in a teenage journal, most readers, in that context, would not give it too much attention. But Nelson does, and her lineation of the entry reflects an act of reading as much as an act of writing. By that, I mean that Nelson reads the entry in a particular way and then emphasizes that reading through the arrangement of words on the page. This resembles Carson's translation of a conversation with Michael into a poem, emphasizing her interpretation of the conversation. Nelson's poem begins and ends with a declarative statement, the first mocking the idea that a physical comfort can provide solace for a metaphysical problem, and the end paradoxically affirming the physical experience of whatever the problem might be— loneliness, parental rejection, unmet dreams or desires. If nothing else, Nelson's presentation of the entry as a poem, with line breaks and white space, makes us stop and read, rather than consuming at high speed, with little contemplation. Nelson seems to ask: What if we regard this as a meaningful moment? The question both suggests the abundance of meaning, if we look for it, and also the artifice of meaning, in the sense that it's always a product of our own readings.

Nelson also arranges Jane's journal entries in a way that allows Jane to converse with those who took over her narrative, telling her story for their own exploitative purposes. While Nelson spends a significant portion of her book exploring Jane's life, integrating Jane's journals in her representation of Jane's relationships, her school life, and her ambitions, the question of Jane's death looms from the opening pages. And, once we get there, from a practical point of view, the fact of Jane's death presumably means that Jane can no longer participate in the narrative. But Nelson's book never really sticks to a chronological rendering of Jane's life and death, even if the broad strokes provide a general narrative outline. Instead, Nelson, in her assembly of the book, attempts to allow Jane's voice, through her journals, to survive beyond the moment of her death; in Nelson's book, Jane continues to speak, despite her death. For example, in the poem "The Funeral," Nelson cites a reverend, who responds to a crowd of mourners, presumably at Jane's funeral, saying, "*It is not the time to ask why these things happen, / but to have faith*" (117). On the following page, Nelson includes a journal entry from Jane: "Questioning is healthy—opinions that are unstable are great. / Pseudo-certainty is the worst crime. Nothing is absolute. / No one has all the answers. Pretense is hideous" (118). Of course, the splicing of these two poems together reveals how Nelson *would have* Jane respond to the reverend as much or more than it provides the space for Jane to respond; but that is precisely the line Nelson walks throughout the entire text. In an effort to let Jane speak, Nelson speaks. In this way, the presence of Nelson's own activity and voice affirms Jane's silence at the same time it attempts to bring that silence closer, by imagining a voice that persists beyond the grave.

In a second example, Nelson begins by providing a passage from *The Michigan Murders*, a true-crime book that details Jane's murder. Similar to Auster, Nelson sorts through a pile of newspaper articles, documents, and various types of commentary that detail and react to the murder case. In the passage from *The Michigan Murders*, the writer proposes the theory that Jane wasn't raped because she had her period and that "it was this discovery that drove [the suspect] to murderous retaliation"—a sort of repulsion for "this disgusting female impairment"

(129, 131). In the poem that follows, "Revelation,"
Nelson takes a first swipe at the true crime writer's analysis of the alleged murderer's motivations:

So what blood
is blood–
head blood, cunt blood

Black clots,
red streams.
How we've fooled ourselves,

we who've split blood
into that which pollutes,
and that which redeems. (132)

Nelson's poem provides a vitriolic response to the suggestion that Jane's menstrual blood provoked the murderer, inspiring him to "retaliate" against her—a word
that implies her complicity. Furthermore, Nelson again
brings attention to the act of naming and identifying,
which, in this case, involves the distinction and hierarchy of different types of blood. The distinction of "head
blood" and "cunt blood" reveals the desire to manage
and create boundaries, protecting the blood that marks
Jane's victimhood from contamination by the blood that
represents the alterity of her female body. But, like the
leaking light in the first dream poem, blood flows from
Jane's body, and any effort to contain it, to keep it "clean"
or "pure," ultimately fails. After "Revelation," Nelson
includes a passage from Jane's journal that begins,

"Anger is a terrible thing. / It causes hate" (133). As is
the case for many of the passages taken from Jane's journal, Nelson doesn't provide any context that would help
us to understand what, for example, inspires Jane's anger
here. Perhaps Nelson doesn't know. Regardless, Nelson's
book provides its own context; she solicits Jane's anger
as a response to the way others have told the story of her
death. In addition, Nelson blurs the boundary between
her own voice and Jane's, since, in this passage probably
more than any other, we could easily mistake Jane's journal entry for Nelson's own writing. In a sense, of course,
it *is* Nelson's own writing, since she's appropriating Jane's
journal entry to communicate her own anger and to crit-
icize the true-crime writer's dehumanizing, exploitative
telling of Jane's story.

One of the problems that arises here for Nelson
becomes how to distinguish her own interventions in and
appropriations of Jane's writing and life story from those
she criticizes for making Jane's story into a product for
mass consumption. In *The Red Parts*, a follow-up book
to *Jane* that details the re-opening of her aunt's murder
case, Nelson grapples with such questions, especially as
she hears her aunt's story told and re-told from the perspectives of various medical examiners, crime experts,
and TV producers.[38] Nelson notes the lack of shame,
the seeming lack of awareness that the body in the crime
scene photos once belonged to a living woman, and then
reflects on the possible reasons for her own shame: "[...]
I sat in the courtroom every day with a legal pad and
pen, jotting down all the gory details, no different or

better than anyone else. Details which I'm reassembling here—a live stream—for reasons that are not yet clear or justifiable to me, and may never be" (*RP* 31). Nelson depends upon *The Michigan Murders*, police records, and brutal crime scene photos—analyzing them, taking copious notes, theorizing possible explanations— just like everyone else, from the outside. In the poem "Aside," in *Jane*, Nelson refers to *The Michigan Murders* as "a book / that sickens me," adding, "Somehow I need to make it clear: / none of these details belongs to me" (141). Nelson wants to distance herself from the details upon which she depends, appropriating those details in order to cast them out, or, at least, to re-cast them in a way that rejects the narratives to which they have been tied. Beyond that, Nelson implicitly rejects the narrative mode in *Jane*—insofar as a conventional narrative seeks to connect "A" to "B," filling gaps with words, weaving together connective threads, and offering reductive explanations. As one poem in *Jane* describes, "What transpired / for five and / a half hours / between Jane / and her murderer / is a gap so black / it could eat / an entire sun / without leaving / a trace" (116). The gap persists, no matter the stories we tell; acknowledging and holding a space for that silence seems to drive Nelson's book, even as she describes crime scene photos and cites *The Michigan Murders*. Paradoxically, efforts to fill the gaps and silences of Jane's story with analysis and explanation, Nelson implies, end up silencing Jane a second time, serving our desire to have closure, in the form of a good story without loose ends.

Over the course of Nelson's book, a portrait of Jane emerges—not necessarily as a likeness, but as Nelson's own image of the aunt she never met. At the same time, Nelson refuses idealization and the tendency to turn Jane into a tragic poetic figure who can exist neatly within the borders of a well-crafted poem or book. Early in *Jane*, Nelson quotes Edgar Allan Poe, who proposed, "the death, then, of a beautiful woman, is the most poetical topic in the world" (26). After fleshing out the portrait of Jane over the course of her book, Nelson responds to Poe in one of the last poems in *Jane*, "Philosophy of Composition (Reprise)," provocatively stating, "She was not beautiful" (215). Nelson offers this comment not as a literal evaluation of Jane's beauty, but as a resistance to the appropriation of Jane as a figure of ideal beauty, and her death as "the most poetical topic in the world." The irony, of course, is that Nelson herself dedicates a book of poetry to her aunt's life and death. But, as the title to the poem indicates, Nelson doesn't reject the act of composing an image of Jane, through poetry; rather, she rejects the notion that the tragedy of Jane's story, and the value of that story to poetic composition, derives from Jane's status as a beautiful object. Nelson's poem describes a photograph of Jane:

[...] Her face and torso loom up
against a deep blue sky

a great, momentary albatross of cloud
hovering nearby. A bright block of light

bleaches out half her face, whitening
her forehead and her tough, freckled

nose. The whole picture
is beautiful. (215)

In this ekphrastic poem, Nelson emphasizes the way her
own composition depends upon other compositions—
in this case a photographic image, and at other times,
Jane's journal entries, the seldom-spoken stories that cir-
culate in the family, documents related to the crime, and
various letters and pictures kept by those close to Jane.
That dependence points to Nelson's distance from Jane,
and her struggle to find a foothold when writing about
her aunt's life and death. Nelson appreciates the photograph described in the poem because it sheds light, to
the point of over-exposure, on Jane's face and "tough,
freckled nose"; the beauty of the photo comes from the
way it illuminates Jane. In this way, Nelson distinguishes
the beauty of the picture, as a composition, from the
beauty of the photographic object. In the absence of
Jane's life and light, perhaps a beautiful composition
might still manage to illuminate. At least, that's the goal,
or "philosophy of composition."

Yet Nelson, like Auster and Carson, knows that Jane's
life exceeds the photographic composition, as well as
her own composition. The question of how she might
illuminate Jane's life, without bleaching and over-expos-
ing, remains unanswered for Nelson, especially considering the impossibility of viewing the photo without

seeing the hovering cloud, and therefore her aunt's fate. Nelson doesn't have the direct access of the camera that snaps the photo of Jane, catching a streak of light across her face; and, therefore, the photograph she describes points to the impossibility of her own composition. Like Barthes, Nelson, when looking at this photograph seems to have the dual sense that she has "found" Jane, and lost her, or at least the moment depicted in the photo. For Nelson, the hovering cloud represents Jane's death and silence, even if, at the time of the photograph, it was just a cloud in the sky; Nelson's poetry starts with the cloud, not with the light. In that way, Nelson's book explores the questions of how to depict a life in the face of death and silence; how to compose outside of, or in excess of, that silence; and how to provide space for a voice that no longer speaks, except in our own heads. Nelson composes a figment, imagining the sound of her aunt's voice and the shape of her life, as a means of recollecting a person she never knew.

CHAPTER 3:
SELF-PORTRAIT FROM THE OUTSIDE

Toward the end of Marie Redonnet's *Candy Story*, the protagonist, Mia, describes a self-portrait composed by her dying mother:

> One half of the face is the one she reveals now, which she must have painted by looking at herself in the mirror. The other half is Ma as a young girl, as she looked in a photo taken with Madame Alma. [...] The painting is signed 'Ma' in large letters painted in black so they can be clearly seen. The signature could be that of a little girl who just painted her first picture but still doesn't know how to write her name. (50)

Mia feels troubled by the portrait, though she never reveals the explicit reasons for not liking it. The description of the portrait draws attention to its three separate components—the two halves of the face and the signature—and implies a lack of unity or integration between those components. Ma's composition collapses time and space and, in doing so, paradoxically creates the sense of multiple selves, forcing the viewer to confront the impossibility of reducing the two images of Ma into one. The portrait spans most of Ma's life, therefore transcending a particular moment, yet also puts on display a sense of fractured identity that arises when trying to make sense of the passage of time. Beyond that, Ma's childlike signature situates the composition outside of language in a sense, where her self-portrait is not yet filtered through language, naming, and sense-making. Ma asserts her authorship with her signature, at the same time as the signature represents a sort of writing before or outside of writing—outside the possibility of authoring one's own story, or composing one's own portrait. As she confronts her impending death and struggles with dementia, Ma finds herself ousted from her own narrative, unfamiliar with the events of her life and the meanings she has assigned to them over time. And from that place, she composes a portrait that captures her outsidership and detachment from narrative and personal history. Her portrait tells a different kind of story, without a story, and depicts a moment of rupture, and even liberation, from imposed narratives that value integration and institutional norms and emphasize origin and telos.

Redonnet's *Candy Story*, Marie NDiaye's *Self-Portrait in Green*, and César Aira's *How I Became a Nun* all focus on first-person narrators who work to escape or break free from their own stories in a sense, rejecting the demand that self-writing illuminate rather than invent,

obscure, or turn away. The first-person perspective in
these texts paradoxically offers little insight and instead
explores the possibilities of telling one's own story from
a marginal, or outsider's, position—one that starts with
the presumption of a constantly shifting ground. Each
of the narratives can therefore be read as a reflection on
the question of writing or composing the self, generally
in a way that challenges the values of self-expression,
integration, closure, sense-making, and representability in conventional autobiographical writing. I consider "autobiography" here in terms of the plight of
the first-person narrators who try to figure out how to
compose their own stories outside or in excess of the
demands of self-expression and self-revelation—not as
a generic identifier of any of the texts, since none of
them is an autobiography according to the typical use of
that term.[39] Yet, especially in the cases of *Self-Portrait in
Green* and *How I Became a Nun*, the authors themselves
are playing with the conventions of autobiography, writing first-person narratives from the perspectives of Marie
and César respectively. In other words, in their playful
challenge to autobiographical convention, the authors
seem to suggest an inability totally to absent themselves
from their writing. For that reason, the question perhaps
becomes, at the level of both writer and protagonist,
how to shift one's relation to what we write—making
the "I" a site of multiplicity, dispersal, and outsidership,
rather than singularity and self-affirmation.

Clearly, NDiaye, Aira, and Redonnet, although they
all invoke or play with autobiographical writing in some

ways, do not abide by the "autobiographical pact" identified by Philippe Lejeune—or the author's "intention to honor his/her *signature*" (14, emphasis in original). In terms of the question of self-representation, their works more closely reflect what Serge Doubrovsky says about the problems of writing about oneself and one's life: "The meaning of one's life in certain ways escapes us, so we have to reinvent it in our writing, and that is what I personally call *autofiction*" (400). He explains that autofiction, as a genre, doesn't make the same claims as autobiography, and instead stresses its own inevitable fictionality. Beyond that, I would argue, writers like Redonnet, NDiaye, and Aira seem to make the case that fictionality—and, in particular, the way that life "escapes us," in the words of Doubrovsky—provides a fertile space for writing outside of the demand of the narrative illumination of the self. The escape, or the turning away, is the work of writing. That idea takes shape in Maurice Blanchot's discussion of the writer in "The Essential Solitude," an essay in *The Space of Literature* where he emphasizes the way that the act of writing alienates the writer from him or herself: "The writer belongs to a language which no one speaks, which is addressed to no one, which has no center, and which reveals nothing. He may believe that he affirms himself in this language, but what he affirms is altogether deprived of self" (26). In other words, writing does not enable a coming forward; instead, it inscribes a space of deferral and disappearance, where the author is nowhere to be seen.[40]

My primary focus here is to consider the question of

self-writing in *Candy Story, Self-Portrait in Green*, and *How I Became a Nun*, and how the narrators' work ultimately provides a site of turning away, of refusing to come forward and say "I." In each text, the first-person narrators respond to the demand to ground their experience and their identity in the world by a set of previously established narratives; and in each text, the first-person narrators eventually break with those demands, escaping to the outside, and inhabiting a marginal position—a space of greenness, to invoke the imagery of NDiaye's *Self-Portrait*. Redonnet, NDiaye, and Aira trouble the relationship between the "I" of the text and the subject to which the "I" refers, suggesting that, for instance, no autobiographical pact, can stabilize the relationship between the "I" and the person who writes it. Instead, the first-person narrators of Redonnet, NDiaye, and Aira's texts undermine or destabilize their own stories, refusing to affirm the status of the "I" as it emerges through storytelling.

Marie NDiaye's *Self Portrait in Green*

Marie NDiaye's *Self-Portrait in Green* plays explicitly with the notion of portraiture and what it means to compose a self-portrait. Like Ma's portrait, NDiaye's text is marked by its strangeness, and by the way in which its different components rub up against one another, disrupting its sense of continuity or integration. As many critics have noted, NDiaye's *Self-Portrait in Green* defies generic categorization, as it seems to straddle several genres. In her essay in *Contemporary French and Francophone Studies*, Marina Ortrud M. Hertrampf asks, "As in all of her texts, *Self-Portrait in Green* escapes fixed genres: is it a *récit*, a *journal intime*, a long prose poem?" (409). Hertrampf concludes that NDiaye's text, regardless of genre, represents, "the author's search for her own form of unconventional auto-fiction" (409).[41] Christopher Hogarth uses Michel Beaujour's notion of the self-portrait as a means of examining *Self-Portrait in Green*, arguing that Beaujour's misgivings about the application of the general definition of "*autoportait*" to literary texts actually point precisely to what makes that term appropriate for NDiaye's text. In other words, NDiaye's defiance of more traditional forms of literary self-representation leads to a text that feels much more like a self-portrait, Hogarth contends, even if the term has sometimes had a negative connotation: "it may be viewed as mere 'scribbling,' an attempt to encapsulate the present self in words with no clear purpose or direction" (193-4). While NDiaye's *Self-Portrait in Green* hardly equates to "mere scribbling," she clearly challenges the ideal of presenting the self, through writing, by narrating and making sense of past events, or confessing emotional truths that reveal one's inner world.[42] In addition, as Hertrampf's comment about the hybridity of the text suggests, one cannot presume that the "self-portrait" refers to NDiaye herself, nor that it excludes that possibility. In any case, in a textual world that undermines efforts to stabilize and pin down, we must remain skeptical of any singular conclusion or generic boundary. But the "self-portrait" that we read does point to its own process, demonstrating the various questions that the narrating subject must engage in order to compose her portrait. Even though the narrator of *Self-Portrait in Green* does not explicitly discuss her process of composition—unlike Mia in *Candy Story*, who, as we will see, drafts two versions of the story we are presumably reading—the text invites us to consider the narrator-writer's efforts to locate or identify a "self," and, furthermore, how she might write or compose that self, theoretically resulting in the self-portrait we read. From that perspective *Self-Portrait in Green* traces the narrator's struggle to compose her own story, and to establish her own narrative voice, in spite of her alienation from her life, her past, and her environment. It seems that in order to compose her self-portrait, the narrator must turn away from herself, inhabiting her marginal position rather than seeking to ground herself in her origin or environment.

Clearly, NDiaye's integration of photographs into the original French version of *Self-Portrait in Green* (*Autoportrait en vert*) emphasizes the visual aspect of portraiture and asks us to consider the relation between the photographs and the written text. In the critical work on *Autoportrait en vert*, most authors mention NDiaye's interview with Andrew Asibong and Shirley Jordan, where she frames the integration of the images in *Autoportrait* as a sort of afterthought, coming at the request of the publisher, *Mercure de France* (Asibong 196). Nora Cottille-Foley provides additional insight into the origin story of the photographs and considers its significance. She argues that NDiaye, in the interview, gives the photographs a narrative, and even a power, of their own, as if they resided outside of her composition of the text. Cotille-Foley concludes, "She turns the photographic object into a fantastic object. In a dual dialectical movement, because the author provides the story of the photos outside of the text, she reinscribes them in a fictional discourse while blurring the boundaries of literary creation" (550).[43] Instead of trying to compose an *hors-texte* narrative that provides a myth of integration and wholeness to her text, and to the interrelation of the photographs and writing in particular, NDiaye seems to emphasize the tenuous relation between the parts and puts into question how one might determine where a self-portrait begins and ends, and to whom it refers. In that way, the photographs' dissociation from the written text paradoxically suggests their association with some of the main concerns of the text; NDiaye's insistence on the outsidership of the photographs extends the self-portrait to the margins, off the edge of the written composition, and even altering it after the fact.

Beyond such extra-textual considerations, the photographs themselves clearly collide with any simple notion of self-portraiture or referentiality, since, at the most literal level, NDiaye appears nowhere in the images. NDiaye includes photographs by contemporary French photographer, Julie Ganzin, in addition to family photos of uncertain origin from the early twentieth-century. As Jean Duffy points out in her analysis of the figures in the photographs, "[…] Caught with their back to the camera or as they move out of the frame, radically truncated or viewed from angles that obscure their faces, they serve as *mises en abyme* drawing attention to the mobility of the concept of identity, to its resistance to circumscription and, indeed to its inextricable relationship with the liminal" (923). That sense of turning away mirrors the general movement of NDiaye's text, where individuals, including the narrator, only come partially into view, and the reader remains aware of the limits of her or his sight. While one might say that photographs often work to elucidate a text, providing a visual component that aids and interacts with the written component, NDiaye integrates images as a means of undermining those expectations, of emphasizing the impossibility of self-portraiture, and of drawing attention to the absence of self. Yes, one can perhaps locate thematic relationships between the photographs and the written text, but I would contend that imposing any additional or more specific reading on that relationship conflicts with the sense of fracture and non-integration that the photographs present, disrupting our movement through the text. As Hertrampf agrees, noting: "Photos, in NDiaye's work, no longer serve to provide proof, but are confusing, unstable, and opaque" (410). Therefore, the photographs do affirm the general sense of fogginess and unknowability that permeates the text, but they do so obliquely, above all in their resistance to integration.

Moving on to the written text, the narrator in *Self-Portrait in Green* finds herself in an often disorienting world, where she is sometimes uncertain about what she does or doesn't see, and is confused about how to identify and understand the people around her. The narrator inhabits an environment of mirror relations, patterns and repetitions, and blurred identities. While *Self-Portrait in Green* presumably concerns the portrait of the unnamed narrator, most of the narrative focuses on other characters and directly reveals little about the narrator herself. As Hogarth points out, "Throughout the text she is unnamed and the snippets of information that the reader receives about her—that she has four children, that her father lives in Africa, for example—are facts rather than psychological or emotional depictions of memories or of personality" (197). For that reason, the sparsely sketched portrait comes about indirectly, by way of the narrator's interaction with her environment and those within it—the women in green, in particular, but also her family of origin, her children, and others. And because those figures tend to shift, blur into one another, and elude the narrator's comprehension, the narrator's own sense of self, or identity, always feels tenuous and uncertain, overwhelmed by the troubling instability of the world around her. Duffy writes, "Here, as elsewhere in NDiaye, identity is a fluid, unstable and elusive phenomenon that is derived in part from, but always ready to be eclipsed by, background, whether that background takes the form of kin and community or the physical environment which one inhabits" (923). While the slipperiness and uncertainty of the environment oppresses the narrator in *Self-Portrait in Green*, it does seem that her approach to that environment evolves over the course of the text, as she considers what it might mean to sketch a self-portrait, given a world of mirrors and fog—not overcoming the multiplicity and blurriness, but putting it to use. With that in mind, she must assert a radical "I," turning away from self and toward otherness, inspired by green, and exceeding the demand for singularity, knowability, and certainty.

The first pages of *Self-Portrait of Green* describe the Garonne and the threat of the floodwaters if the river rises above the levees. The narrator explains:

> What we don't know this evening is what's coming tonight, or tomorrow—if, like last time, ten months ago. The water will stop at the top of the levees, or, as it did twenty-two years ago, spill over, submerge the streets, invade the ground floor of the houses, sometimes the second floor, sometimes the whole house. (3)

The narrator dates the first section of the text and uses the present tense, thus creating the context for the various events she recounts, in the past tense though not always chronologically, over the course of the book. The Garonne clearly works as a framing device here, providing a mood of uncertainty and anxiety, specifically over the issue of ruptured boundaries. As one would imagine, the townspeople, including the narrator, fear the flooding of their towns and homes, powerless to do anything: "We wait, we watch" (4). Without belaboring the various interpretations of the river's significance and its relation to the rest of *Self-Portrait in Green*, it seems important that the narrator opens her portrait describing a general concern about the need for things to stay in their place, within the boundaries demarcating them. If the Garonne flows over the levees, the town becomes a river and the river contains a town. How, then, can we distinguish the river and the town, and what are the consequences when such boundaries disappear?

The narrator seems to use the unpredictable, threatening ways of the Garonne as a means of introducing her own anxieties about a world where the levees often feel weak and uncertain. Those anxieties eventually point to her struggle to find grounding—to compose a self— in an unstable, endlessly shifting environment. In the first section following that on the Garonne, the narrator tells of her experiences with the woman in green under the banana tree and with her friend Cristina. Both incidences communicate the narrator's anxiety about misidentifying or misapprehending the world around her—partially because the people and objects tends to blur into one another, making it impossible to know what she is really seeing. When the narrator first notices the woman under the banana tree, she explains, "Because it was in front of her house that I saw her each day, for a long time I couldn't distinguish that green presence from her surroundings" (5). The woman in green merges with the background, putting into question the narrator's perception and pushing her to verify the presence of the green woman with her children. When the children respond, "There's nothing at all beside that banana tree," the narrator again questions herself but eventually concludes "That woman in green has always been there" (7, 9). Therefore, the narrator must confront the difference between her perception and that of her children, along with the possibility that the woman can be there and not be there at the same time, depending upon the viewer. That clearly bothers the narrator, as she emerges in this section as someone who likes to pin things down. She identifies herself as a person who "likes knowing names" and who highly values truthfulness (6, 24). The narrator eventually decides to confront the woman in green, and, after throwing herself over the balcony railing, the woman in green invites the narrator in for coffee. The woman in green, from the beginning, appears deliberately to unsettle the narrator by her unpredictability. Who knows what will follow a bizarre and dangerous dive off the balcony? At the same time, the narrator believes that the woman's strangeness and otherness also escapes the woman herself: "I sense that she's taken on the attributes of some other person, and doesn't realize it herself" (24-5). That sense of duality becomes even clearer when considering the question of the woman's name and how to identify her:

> I believe that the woman in green, who told me her name was Katia Depetiteville, is not Katia Depetiteville, and I believe that if I asked people in the village for a description of Katia Depetiteville they wouldn't describe this woman, the woman in green. They'd describe a very different person. But the woman in green doesn't know that. She sincerely and naturally believes herself to be Katia Depetiteville. (25)

Katia Depetiteville, we learn, is dead, which raises the possibility that the woman in green represents some sort of ghost, or spectral stand-in for the "real" Katia Depetiteville who once lived in the same house. The narrator never knows one way or another, nor do we. Regardless, the narrator remarks Katia's non-coincidence with herself, and the fact that no amount of information or interrogation can make the two Katias coincide. Once she realizes the impossibility of resolving the mystery of Katia, the narrator theorizes about the significance of Katia in her life: "Is it so that, at various moments in my life, I might meet up with a woman in green?" (25). The narrator seems to see Katia as a sort of opening onto a world that exceeds her ability to make sense of things and that forces her to confront the multiplicity and undecidability of her environment. After all, as the narrator realizes, "I know she'll be replaced one day by another green woman, whom I won't have chosen either" (26).

Within that same section that details the encounter with Katia, the narrator recounts an interaction with a woman on the street, whom she at first mistakes for her friend Cristina: "That's when I run into Cristina, but as soon as I see her I'm not sure it's her rather than Marie-Gabrielle or Alison. Not that her name escapes me: it's just that, among those three women, I no longer know which this one is" (14). Understandably, this sudden inability to tell her friends apart causes anxiety in the narrator: "Deep in my pocket, my fingers squeeze and shred the little lilac leaves" (14). And, from what we can tell, the narrator spends a good part of the conversation preoccupied with figuring out whether or not she is talking to Cristina, listening for certain confirming clues—that the woman does not have children, for example—that might provide the answer. The solution to the problem comes in the form of the real Cristina, who appears across the street and, logically, reveals the narrator's interlocutor as someone other than Cristina. The narrator expresses relief: "I'm grateful to [Cristina], because now I recognize her so perfectly" (20). Of course, we still don't know to whom the narrator has been talking, and the narrator's moment of solace does not last long, since Cristina makes a comment suggesting that she has children. The narrator must reassess: "And consequently, I ask myself: did I recognize her as perfectly as I thought?" (21). Much like the situation with Katia, the narrator's interaction with the women in

this scene points to the impossibility of naming, identifying, and therefore stabilizing the world around her;
something ceaselessly escapes the narrator and points
to the way that Cristina can't be counted on to cross
the street, solve the problem, and affirm the narrator's
desire to feel grounded and stable. In the end, Katia is
and is not Katia; and Cristina is and is not Cristina. In
this early section of *Self-Portrait of Green*, that fundamental, paradoxical, and strange duality causes anxiety
in the narrator, who simply wants to know what she sees
and to confirm what she knows. She wants to affirm her
perception of the world and her place in it, yet she has
no foothold.[44]

The question of "greenness" obviously arises in both
the Katia and the Cristina episodes, along with an
additional short anecdote about a mean school teacher
whom the narrator identifies as a woman in green: "Tall,
brutal, and heavyset, she promises us all a trip to prison
if we eat too slowly, if we dirty our clothes, if we don't
raise our eyes to meet hers" (11). The teacher has green
eyes and wears green clothes, although the narrator also
implies that her greenness relates to matters of behavior and personality as well. After recounting the ways
the teacher threatened and terrorized her students, the
narrator reflects: "It's true that green can't possibly be
the sole color of cruelty, just as green is by no means
inevitably the color of cruelty, but who can deny that
cruelty is particularly given to draping itself in all sorts
of greens?" (12). While the narrator advises us not to
reduce the color green to cruelty, she also suggests that

greenness and cruelty are not *un*related. The particular
cruelty of the teacher though, and the way that cruelty
might relate to greenness, perhaps comes forward a bit
more when we examine Katia, the first woman in green,
and the woman revealed as "not-Cristina," who wears
green flowered shorts. Katia, as noted above, strikes the
narrator, and most likely the reader, by her unpredictability and by the way she eludes the narrator's attempts
to identify and understand her. Not-Cristina, whether
intentionally or not, also clearly eludes the narrator,
especially since we never actually discover who she is.
"This person who might be Cristina is a young woman,
so she's wearing shorts, elastic and clinging, with a print
of green flowers against a green background. My elation
dwindles a little. It occurs to me that wariness might be
called for" (14). In response to not-Cristina's shorts, the
narrator immediately feels that she needs to keep her distance, presumably seeing the shorts as a potential indi-
cator of something threatening, untrustworthy, or just
generally unpleasant. The narrator notes that she looks
forward to the greenness of Katia, because she expects
it, and, in contrast, responds negatively to not-Cristina's
shorts because they surprised her, and are out of place in
the "first days of spring" (14). In addition, not-Cristina
presents herself in a way that seems to make the narrator
uncomfortable: "Cristina keeps her hands behind her,
pressed flat against her powerful hindquarter to display
her shorts' exuberant color as flagrantly as she can. She
stands with her legs commandingly spread, blocking
the entire width of the sidewalk" (14-5). Not-Cristina

doesn't apologize for taking up space, or for her green shorts. The narrator is now preoccupied with two things: her inability to identify her friends, and not-Cristina's "flagrant" greenness. Therefore, when the real Cristina (if indeed it is the real Cristina) interrupts the conversation, coming from across the street, the narrator almost immediately notices her "tiny pink shorts, with her graceful, jaunty gait" (19). Not only does the arrival of Cristina clear up the question of identity, but she also resolves the threat of green, with her pink shorts and a way of moving that feels light and playful, rather than determined and confrontational.

Like Katia and the often unpredictable, cruel teacher, the woman in the green shorts does seem to have some connection to uncertainty and unknowability, at least as far as the narrator is concerned. And perhaps that's the one thing we can say about the various connotations of "greenness" in the text—that the color green, like the women in green themselves, turns us away in any attempt we might make to pin it down and reduce it to a clear set of characteristics or meaning. As Warren Motte notes in his reading of *Self-Portrait of Green*, "There are very few things in *Autoportrait* upon which one can rely with certainty. One of those things may be the principle of undecidability that colors the text from first page to last, and which makes it very difficult to say anything categorical about it" (495). At the same time, the narrator does not seem to have any trouble determining the greenness of a woman, even if she can't figure out that woman's name or seemingly

simpler matters of identification. That perhaps reflect
the sense that the narrator experiences the women in
green in similar ways, even if they clearly differ from one
another; she responds to their fundamental unpredictability and opacity, and to the anxiety she experiences
when confronted with women and situations that exceed
her efforts to understand and to manage. Returning to
Motte, he writes, "Each of these women in green—
whatever else she may be—is radically *other*, and her
otherness infects the women who come into contact
with her, such that they, too, come to feel contingent
and out of place" (495). And that point brings us back
to the issue of self-portraiture; the narrator's own identity, when confronted with the women in green, is at
stake. The outsidership and otherness of the women in
green, their refusal to fit within a framework, threatens
the narrator, making her feel "contingent and out of
place." That contingency certainly causes anxiety in the
narrator throughout *Self-Portrait in Green*; and, at the
same time, I would argue, her relationship to the women
in green, to their otherness and elusiveness, evolves as
the narrator seems to explore her own possibilities for
otherness and elusiveness. The narrator of *Self-Portrait
in Green* eventually must turn to the outside, which we
might imagine to have a green hue, in order to compose
a portrait, and thus a self—one that allows for duality,
contradiction, mutability, and non-integration.

In the following section, the narrator discusses her
relationship with her father and his new spouse—the
narrator's former best friend. The narrator clearly has a

hard time making sense of that relationship, not simply because she disapproves, but because again, she must confront a certain duality that makes her uncomfortable. She explains, "My deep, longstanding friendship with this woman was over as soon as she married my father" (32). The narrator now refers to her former best friend as her stepmother, as she can't imagine how the woman could simultaneously exist as both best friend and father's wife at once. In addition, the narrator feels particularly troubled by "[...] a significant detail that has, ever since she became my stepmother, characterized this woman who was once my friend: she dresses only in green" (29). The narrator assures us that she "finds nothing at all amusing about it. I told myself: here we go again. Again the ambiguity, the groping, the unanswered questions about all this green" (29). The narrator appears to resent the way the woman's transformation— from best friend to stepmother, and from not-green to green—demonstrates the fickle, unpredictable nature of things, where one person can become another, shifting roles and colors, as if nothing at all were sacred or solid. The narrator's father, though obviously not a woman in green, creates and compounds the general environment of instability and continual change, since he is "on his fifth or sixth marriage" and has children from most of those relationships (30). The narrator knows some of those children but not others, making them simultaneously strangers and relatives, and drawing attention to the way that the narrator exists in a chain of offspring where all of the children sort of blur into one another.

That chain of seemingly substitutable individuals in a chain demonstrates what we will also see in *Candy Story*, where the repetition of slightly changed names and identities creates the sense of difference, deferral, and replicability. In *Self-Portrait in Green*, we encounter two sons who act out violently against their father, though we don't really know why. The narrator, in speaking to her father, concludes, "The problem […] is that you have too many children. If every one of your children thinks they have grounds to make you pay for something you've done and maybe forgotten, how can you hope to deal with it?" (33-4). The narrator, in empathizing with her father, again reveals her own anxiety over unpredictable situations—those which, in particular, expose an inability to identify, to tell one person from another in a chain or network of similar individuals—suggesting that the father has undermined his own security and stability in his insistence on multiplying. And, as one of the multiple children, the narrator's own security, stability, and individuality come into question.

Following a section where the narrator tells the story of her friend Jenny—and Jenny's relation to a particular woman in green—she returns to her own family, grappling with the realization that her own mother has become a woman in green.[45] She writes:

> And suddenly I discover, as I consider her briskly swaying hips, her delicate calves swathed in shimmering hose, that my mother is a kind of green woman I haven't yet come across—and what fate is it, I wonder, that

> demands that my mother herself must now
> cross my path as a green woman, to convince
> me that such is my destiny? (71)

In this passage, the narrator seems to associate greenness with sexuality and maybe even a sort of confident
swagger, but she also notes that her mother represents a
different kind of woman in green, suggesting that those
characteristics do not necessarily get at what exactly
makes her "green." The narrator does indicate, leading
up to this passage, that what confounds her about her
mother is that she "should suddenly metamorphose on
her own into a *green woman*, and one of that type's most
alien and troubling forms" especially since she has, up
until this point, "live[d] a life of stone, unchanging and
immobile" (65, 67). In other words, the narrator draws
attention to the unexpected and unpredictable change
of her mother—someone on whom, at the least, she
could count to live a bland, suburban existence, which
the narrator had come to characterize by "the inertia, the
grayness, the deadly smallness" (65). Now though, her
mother appears in different form: green, married, and
pregnant. And the narrator searches for a reason or meaning behind her mother's transformation, particularly in
terms of how it might point to her own "destiny," as her
mother's daughter. This is the first time in the text that
the narrator refers to her own potential for greenness,
therefore connecting her "study of green" with her own
evolving identity and, implicitly, the composition of her
portrait.

Similar to the situation with the narrator's father,

the one with her mother presents a world where one thing can become another, one person can shift and slip into another identity. When the narrator learns that her mother is pregnant, she admits, "This stuns me to the point of terror," later adding, "And a child? I calculate her age: forty-seven. Possible, perhaps, but not at all plausible" (68, 69). Not only does the narrator's mother become green, but she has also started a new life that totally contradicts what the narrator thought she knew about her. That new life includes a baby, the narrator's half-sister, whom the narrator's mother will be raising at the same time as the narrator raises her own children. While clearly not out of the question, that situation would seem to disrupt the more common chronology of things and again points to the interchangeability of people within a network of, in this case, familial roles (similar to the best friend becoming a stepmother). The narrator characterizes her mother as aloof, "without a word concerning her grandchildren, as if she suddenly had none, or didn't recognize them," which again mirrors the narrator's father, in that he has so many children that he potentially can't even remember them all (69). The sense that both the narrator's mother and her father manifest a world of multiplicity and slipperiness, or interchangeability, clearly troubles the narrator, especially insofar as it throws her own sense of identity and stability into question.[46] The fact that the narrator often depicts herself with one or more of her many children also suggests that she mirrors the multiplicity and reproducibility associated with her father and mother. Not only does she exist in a chain of offspring who blur into one another, but she also produces a chain of her own, suggesting an endlessly unfolding process of reproduction. In any case, the narrator's detached and distant relationship to her mother and father, and her position in a line of offspring, points to her sense of ungrounding in the world—her separation from a secure and stable origin, and the suggestion that she can be substituted or replaced by another individual in the chain. That situation seems to add to the narrator's anxiety and further emphasizes the need to compose a self-portrait outside of myths of origin or selfhood.

As I have expounded, the narrator communicates anxiety about her environment and the people therein when they challenge her attempts to identify and stabilize. And she often feels her own identity and place in the world is at stake when confronting the elusive, unpredictable women in green, and anyone or anything else that adds to the general sense of uncertainty that pervades the text. This sense of unease persists for most of the text—maybe all of it. Yet, despite her hesitations and fears, the narrator feels compelled by the women in green, ultimately regretting actions that have sent these women away: "[…] I fear I'll see myself as a senseless fool should all those women in green disappear one by one, leaving me powerless to prove their existence, my own originality" (81). That realization marks a turn in *Self-Portrait in Green*, where the narrator admits her desire to have women in green around, even if some of them are unpleasant, irrational, and even mean; she doesn't just want to keep them at a distance, but close enough for them to trouble, and for them to inspire. She continues:

> I then wonder, in my sisters' tidy kitchen, how to find bearable a life without women in green exhibiting their slippery silhouettes in the background. In order to slip serenely through these moments of stupor, of deep boredom, of crippling inertia, I need to remember they decorate my thoughts, my invisible life, I need to remember they're there, at once real beings and literary figures, without which, it seems to me, the harshness of existence scours skin and flesh down to the bone. (81-2)

Even though the narrator apparently didn't recognize women in green until relatively recently in her life, she now finds it unbearable to think of a life without them. As Motte writes, "They fire her imagination in crucial ways. They satisfy her need for the extraordinary, the exceptional, the *romanesque*" (502). To be clear, the narrator displays a fascination with the women in green throughout text, but she initially expresses a primary desire to understand them, and to identify them—in addition to anxiety when they surprise her, make her question what she sees and knows, or come too close. In the passage above, the narrator, rather than expressing anxiety over the "slippery silhouettes" of women in green, ties those spectral forms to the imaginary and to possibility. Perhaps the narrator's changing perspective allows her to compose a "self-portrait in green," where undecidability reigns and a self only emerges, if at all, as a "slippery silhouette in the background." One could argue that we see the manifestation of that approach in the self-portrait we are reading, even if the narrator does not explicitly refer to her composition of a text. From that point of view, the narrative itself becomes the evidence of the narrator's own propensity for greenness, insofar as we might relate that color to undecidability and resistance to comprehension. Like the woman in green under the banana tree, the narrator merges with her environment in *Self-Portrait in Green*, remaining as elusive as any of the women in green she identifies. And, similar to the women in the photographs occupying the margins of the text, the narrator turns away, composing a self-portrait where she largely remains in the shadows, at the edge of the narrative.

In the penultimate section of *Self-Portrait in Green*, the narrator describes a group of children, including two of her own, huddled around a "dark form, moving and anxious" (101). She runs down the stairs to intervene—though we know nothing of the threat the narrator perceives or why she feels panicked about the possibility of arriving too late—and attempts to extract her children from the situation, "as gently as possible" (102). The other children ask the narrator if she saw and can identify the mysterious, shadowy object, and the narrator replies "No, I don't know what it's called," adding "I don't think it has a name in our language" (102). She then continues, "To tell you the truth, I didn't see anything. Nothing at all. What was it?" (102). Both of the narrator's responses point to the narrator's shift towards opacity and silence, and perhaps even a recognition of the fundamental unknowability that subtends the various episodes she recounts in her narrative. Like the women in green, the black object eludes any attempt at identification—both for the narrator and for the reader; it remains unnamable, and, presumably, unknowable. Interestingly, when the black object briefly appears earlier in the text, during the conversation with the woman mistaken for Cristina, the narrator twice asks, "But what is it?", much like the children, whose primary desire is to know what exactly that thing is (20). In this case, though, the narrator not only pronounces the thing unnamable, but also adds to it a kind of refusal or denial. In Warren Motte's article, "Negative Narrative," he writes of this scene in *Self-Portrait in Green*: "One feature of the incident seems to me unavoidable: if we cannot know, it is quite simply that we have not been *told*" (65, emphasis in original). Maintaining silence, especially when faced with something that so clearly exceeds expression, characterizes the narrative approach of *Self-Portrait in Green*, and, Motte argues, represents "a singularly privileged tool in [NDiaye's] narrative repertory" (65). I do think it is important to note that the narrator, as I have established, seems to resist silence and unnamability earlier in the narrative while embracing and participating in it toward the end. To the extent that we can perceive a shift or evolution in the narrator—a sort of turn toward the greenness of her portrait—her response to the children suggests a recognition that the mysterious black object will necessarily escape our grasp and our attempts to tell. Rather than trying to rein it in, maybe it can inspire, from the outside.

In one of the passages that describes the rising Garonne and the threat that it poses to the village, the narrator wonders, "Why do so many men and so few women enjoy this tense atmosphere, this prelude to valor or heroism? Why do so many women, who've been living here forever, aspire only to move to a safe place at last, and so few men?" (38). While no one clearly wants the Garonne to flood the town, causing disaster and putting lives in danger, the narrator notes a choice: digging in one's heels, in an effort to affirm and maintain boundaries that were always at risk of rupture; or fleeing to the outside, not out of fear, but as a gesture of acceptance. Perhaps on the outside—especially for the women who presumably have less interest in maintaining the status quo and all of the boundaries that have dictated the way they have been permitted to occupy space—one doesn't have to live with the anxiety of the next big rain, or the next flood that threatens the levees. As far as we can tell, however, the people in La Réole stick around and, in the wake of the flood, they watch "the simple spectacle of water where it's not supposed to be" (103). In the end, boundaries sometimes break, reminding us that they exist to keep the world in order, and implicitly pointing to the fundamental disorder that makes the boundary necessary. Much like the people in La Réole, throughout her self-portrait, the narrator observes, with some anxiety, the fragility of boundaries and demarcations that would allow her to manage, to know, to name the things and people in her environment, including herself. And yet we read a self-portrait *in green*, suggesting that the text itself, if not the narrator, is identified with green, which perhaps also suggests that it escapes our efforts to identify or ground it. It does seem, however, that the narrator, in her self-portrait, has fled the waters of the flood to the outside, like the women of La Réole propose to do, no longer clinging on to the flimsy barriers and definitions that make an empty promise of security.

César Aira's *How I Became a Nun*

Like Marie NDiaye's *Self-Portrait in Green*, César Aira's *How I Became a Nun* explicitly plays with issues of self-representation through writing, asking us to consider the relation of the author to the first-person narrator of the same name. As noted above, NDiaye prevents us from drawing any definitive conclusions on that relation, as she crafts a "self-portrait" in which no clear self comes forward, thus eluding our attempts to name and identify. In the case of Aira's short novel, the protagonist, César, identifies as a young girl and commits herself, from the first sentence, to telling the story of how she became a nun. While her narrative in some ways feels much more revelatory or illuminating than what we saw in *Self-Portrait in Green*, fulfilling certain expectations of conventional first-person writing, the absurdity that Aira introduces from the very first sentence—and with the implied identification of the middle-aged, male author with a young girl—ensures that we take the narrative with a grain of salt. In *Las figuras paradojicas de César Aira*, Pablo Decock refers to *How I Became a Nun* as an autofiction, which takes part in a series of Airan texts that demonstrate "the author's obsession with fictionalizing, in some manner, his own life" and with "games of identification" between certain aspects of his life and those of his various first-person narrators (208).[47] The game here, I would argue, involves invoking autobiographical writing and then immediately undermining it, demonstrating an interest in the radicalization of self-representation, where the "I" marks a sort of turning away from constructions of identity—in particular, those that take shape through narratives that attempt to illuminate, normalize, and make sense of a life. César's narrative in *How I Became a Nun* enacts that turning away, as she fights to craft a narrative outside of the institutions that attempt to define and name her. Even though one can develop a convincing argument that *How I Became a Nun* represents a type of *Künstlerroman* that depicts, as Marcelo Ballvé puts it, "César Aira's beginnings as a writer," the novel itself seems to ask us, from the beginning, to favor invention over identification, absurdity over rational explanation. From that perspective, the genre of *Künstlerroman*, to the extent that it makes sense to apply that term, doesn't refer to the tale of Aira's literary origins, but to the point where a writer might escape those origins and learn how to write outside and in excess of them.[48]

One of the most striking and important aspects of the way that Aira opens his novel is to introduce the narrative as something which, at least on its face, it is not. We read, "My story, the story of 'how I became a nun,' began very early in my life; I had just turned six" (3). While one could certainly come up with some interesting theories about how César's narrative represents a sort of "taking of the veil," I am more intrigued by the unfolding of a narrative that departs from its origins, becoming something other than what it promises. We can understand that narrative departure in a number of ways—including the way it introduces the question of misidentification, or non-coincidence, between the narrative and itself, the narrator and herself, the narrator and the author; or the way that it suggests that the story begins outside of or after the story. César insists on the perfection of her memory here and elsewhere in the narrative, noting that she can "reconstruct it down to the last detail" (3)— another claim that should invite our skepticism or, at the least, demand that we reconsider what might constitute a perfect memory. Does a perfect memory align exactly with a set of objective facts about the past? Or might a perfect memory simply make a claim for its own autonomy from facts or truth, rejecting the notion that its perfection derives from its relation to "real events"? While possible answers to these questions certainly do not arise in the first paragraph of the novel, it quickly becomes apparent that the narrative perspective is much more complicated than a six-year-old relating, to the best of her ability, the memory of an event or set of events.

As César begins to recount the story of her outing with her father to get ice cream, we soon perceive many of the ways she does not fulfill the expectations of those around her, particularly her father. She perceives that her father's decision to take her out for ice cream represents an almost desperate attempt to establish some sort of commonality with her—after all, he believes, everyone likes ice cream. Therefore, when César rejects the ice cream, pronouncing it disgusting, she reflects, "Dad had already given up hope of getting any satisfaction from the outing. Sharing a pleasure and a moment

of companionship: it was too late for all that now, and
he must have been wondering how he could have been
so naïve, how he could ever have thought it possible"
(7). César's dislike of the ice cream exposes the gap separating her from her father, and the seeming impossibility of identifying with one another on any level.
While César identifies herself as a "devoted daughter,"
she also makes it clear that an ice cream outing with her
father represents a departure from more usual behavior,
and from her father's "distant, irascible nature, averse
to displays of affection" (5). Therefore, she remains
keenly aware of the disappointment that her reaction
inspires and does not seem particularly surprised by her
father's angry response: "'Everyone likes ice cream,' he
said, white with rage. The mask of patience was slipping,
and I don't know how I managed to hold back my tears.
'Everyone except you, son, because you're a moron"
(8). César's father is incensed by the fact that César,
even when it comes to ice cream, exists as an outlier, as
someone who cannot, on the most basic of levels, fit in
with everyone else. And, of course, we learn at this early
moment in the text that César's father, and everyone else
except her, identifies her as a boy. Although César never
explicitly speaks of that difference as a source of friction, it becomes another marker of misidentification and
non-coincidence. César tells her story and identifies herself in a way that conflicts with the way the world sees
and identifies her. And in this early scene, César's narrative makes it clear that she struggles with her awareness
that she profoundly disappoints her father, as a result

of her inability to assimilate to norms and expectations, and the impossibility of communicating her experience. "I wanted to say something, but I didn't know what. That I didn't like the ice cream? I had already said that. That the ice cream tasted foul? I had said that too, and it was pointless, because I couldn't get it across; it was still there inside me, impossible to convey, even after I had spoken" (11). César, retching and crying, laments her lack of access to the father—whether we see the father literally, or in symbolic or psychoanalytic terms, as a representation of stability, communicability, sameness, and even maleness.

Following her ingestion of poisonous ice cream, César has a near-death experience in the hospital, which, according to Sandra Contreras, represents a rupture, or fault line, that determines the rest of what becomes a kind of survival narrative (256). Contreras points out that César characterizes her new perspective as "disoriented," "sickly," "hypnotic," and "hyperaware of an individuality absolutely withdrawn from the general population" (256).[49] And while César eventually recovers from her hallucinatory state and leaves the hospital, as Contreras contends, her experience initiates the distinct perspective from which the story unfolds. This reading is compelling, perhaps especially insofar as it illuminates what takes place at the end of the novel and how this ending situates the entire narrative as a story of *survivre*, or going beyond, in excess of life.[50] Before we get there though, I would like to focus on the resurrected César's explicit forays into the realm of storytelling and her insistence on telling a story that deliberately upends an interpreter's attempts to tie it to an objective truth. As the doctor comes to assess César's condition, she tells us, "I was not cooperating with science. An urge, a whim or a manic obsession that not even I could explain impelled me to sabotage the doctor's work, to trick him" (34). César proceeds to explain her system of lying to the doctor about her symptoms, deviating from though not always communicating the opposite of the truth, as that would soon become too easy to unravel. She turns herself into a sort of unreadable text, refusing and subverting interpretation, no matter how well-intentioned the reader. César plays similar communication games with the nurse, pretending she has "something 'difficult' to express. I had to approach it indirectly, resorting to allegory of fiction pure and simple" (44). The "ruse," for César, involves creating the impression of a meaning, of something important, that needs expression and can only take shape in "literary" form. Aira is perhaps poking fun at and maybe even trying to preempt overdetermined readings of his novel, asking us to consider what sort of ruse he might be playing on us. At the same time, as the game with the nurse escalates into an exchange of nonsensical gestures, César admits "something snapped. [...] From that moment on I have suffered from a peculiar perceptive dysfunction: I can't understand mime; I'm deaf (or blind, I'm not sure how to put it) to the language of gestures" (44). César seems to recognize an inability to mirror others, and to express herself by way of that mirroring. It would seem that the freedom and limitlessness that allow César to indulge in whimsical, disorienting, and inventive storytelling also points to her outsidership and inability to communicate with others. We will see that telling her own story will require her to inhabit the outside—alienated from those with whom she might communicate, unable to mirror their language. Unlike *Self-Portrait in Green*, César spends the bulk of her narrative deliberately inhabiting that marginal position, largely as a result of her near-death experience.

Due to her hospitalization, César begins school three months after all her peers, and, significantly, arrives after everyone else has learned how to read. For that reason, César understands little of what takes place in the classroom. She contends, "Human beings tend to make sense of experience by imbuing it with continuity: what is happening now can be explained by what happened before" (48). Thus, in missing the "before," César must try to make sense of things in her own ways, acquiring the skills of reading and writing outside of the classroom, and thus outside of the educational institution that dictates, in many ways, one's relation to language and communication. César describes her experience at the margins of the classroom: "I was and was not involved in it; I was present but not a participant, or participating only by my refusal, like a gap in the performance, but that gap was me!" (49). Eventually, César finds herself trying to decipher the lewd bathroom scrawls of a group of neighborhood boys, copying them in her notebook, which is later found by her mother. For her, the graffiti reflects the performative language of the rough neighborhood where she lives, and she recognizes its value in terms of understanding and navigating the social dynamics of her environment. As Aaron Hillyer points out in his analysis of the novel, "This profane understanding of language as capable of tasks other than the expression of thought or predetermined meaning allows the narrator to resist the language of indoctrination as [her] class is being taught to read" (71). César's methods of learning and the source for her first interactions with language not only conflict with the propriety of the classroom space, but also with the empty recitation associated here with institutionalized learning.

When César's mother aggressively confronts the teacher after looking at César's notebook, the latter suffers a sort of breakdown—demonstrated by a breakdown of language, where her words and expressions become jumbled and unintentionally silly—and demands the loyalty of the students, and their promise to ostracize César. She tells them, "You are good, clever, sweet children. Even the ones who are naughty, or have to repeat, or get into fights all the time. You're normal, you're all the same, because you have a second mother. Aira is a moron. He might seem the same as you, but he's a moron all the same. He's a monster. He doesn't have a second mother" (58). Here we have a second adult calling César a moron, specifically because she is "not the same." In this case, the teacher feels threatened by César, painting her as a sort of orphan child who does not trace her origins— at least her educational and literary origins—back to her "second mother," the one who reproduced all of the other students as a mirror image of herself, and one another. And if César can exist, motherless, outside of an institution that values assimilation and even indoctrination, then she exposes the fragility of that institution— the possibility of surpassing or working outside of it. The desired world of the teacher, where all students perfectly reflect one another and her, resembles to oppressive world of doubling and repetition that we will see in *Candy Story*; in some sense, César's lateness in starting school saves her from being trapped in that system.

While one can imagine the difficulty of César's life circumstances—near-death experience, father in prison, completely alienated at school—her narrative tends to frame those circumstances more in terms of the ways they provide opportunities for exploration, untethered to overarching figures or systems that would dictate her experience in the world. On a bus to see her father in prison, César experiments with public performance, drawing her mother into a sort of false conversation about her father, manufacturing details and playing to an audience. "There was no stopping me now. The other passengers were already intrigued by the story, and that excited me inordinately. Because I was the owner of the story" (62). César seems to realize that the "facts" of her father's situation in no way dictate the way she can tell his story, transforming him, her mother, and herself into characters in a fabricated narrative; as the owner of the story, she has appropriated circumstances imposed upon her by transforming them into something of her own.

César's exploration of what it might mean to navigate the world and construct her own story, untethered to others' demands or institutional norms, also expresses itself in the section where she describes her fascination with the radio. In this section, César reflects on the question of transmission—on how to send a thing from here to there, whether we're talking about a message, a signal, a memory, a story, or anything else. César returns to a promise she made at the opening of the book: "Everything in this story I am telling is guaranteed by my perfect memory" (71). This time, though, César gives us a little better idea of what a "perfect memory" might suggest, especially when she explains:

> But my memory merges with the radio. Or rather: I am the radio. Thanks to the faultless perfection of my memory, I am the radio of that winter. Not the receiver, the device, but what came out of it, the broadcast, the continuity, what was being transmitted, even when we switched it off, even when I was asleep or at school. My memory contains it all, but the radio is a memory that contains itself and I am the radio. (72)

I find it interesting that in this passage César makes sure that we do not misunderstand her or what she means when she identifies herself with the radio. While the passage remains abstract in many ways, César emphasizes that she identifies with the transmission, the disembodied voices that seem to float or hang in the air, seemingly originless and untethered. And I wonder if that identification might provide a means of reading the supposed faultlessness of César's memory. If memory, for César, exists as a floating transmission, in the present, untethered to origin or destination, then perhaps perfection has little to do with an alignment with some presumably correct or accurate account of the past. Interestingly, in *The Literary Conference*, a book that Aira published several years after *How I Became a Nun*, the narrator writes about perfection: "Perfections, on the contrary, are all different: perfection in itself is the perfection or full expression of difference. This is why cultivating perfection means collaborating with what a young disciple once defined as the task we should dedicate our lives to: giving birth to the individual" (33). Aira's emphasis on difference and individuality (or singularity) in this passage seems to echo César's take on perfection, in the sense that neither narrator defines perfection in terms of a faultlessness that derives from uniformity or likeness to a set of facts. Of course, the transmission, in terms of César's narrative, claims to relate her past at some level, but, as we saw in her bus performance, she insists on the ownership over her story. In order to establish ownership—over her past, her narrative, her life—César turns away from the demand to ground herself in the world, and turns toward the possibilities that come by way of rupture. César develops a relationship of otherness with herself and her past in this way; she becomes "César," the untethered voice of the radio.

Despite César's alienation at school, she takes interest

in the practice of teaching and creates an imaginary world where she takes on the role of teacher, inventing new pedagogical approaches to the acquisition and development of reading and writing. In César's imaginary classroom, each student has a unique learning difference, preventing any standardized approach to education: "To make the game more fun, I gave them twisted, difficult, baroque personalities. Each one suffered from a different and complicated kind of dyslexia. Being the perfect teacher, I dealt with them individually, attentive to their particular needs, setting tasks adapted to their capacities" (81). Though César bases the names of the students in her imaginary class on her actual peers, she emphasizes the need to invent individual backgrounds, personalities, and modes of learning for each student, along with a specific pedagogical method that addresses their unique situations. César's vision is clearly anti-institutional and anti-assimilationist, emphasizing students' differences from one another and the possibilities for how to accommodate, and even foster, those differences, rather than trying to erase them. She admits that such an approach becomes "hellishly complicated" and impractical, given her "inflexible pedagogical principles" (82). In César's classroom, "The idea wasn't to correct each student's dyslexia, not at all. I wanted to teach them to read and write on their own terms, each according to his particular hieroglyphic system: only within that system was progress possible" (82). From that perspective, each student has his or her own language, in a sense, and César develops ways of teaching them within the system of that language. She explains, "I hadn't invented disorders so much as systems of difficulty. They weren't destined to be cured but developed" (83). One can imagine why César's own experiences in the classroom might have provoked her to invent a space that bucks uniformity and standardized learning. Beyond that, César's perspective on language, and on the practice of writing, relates to her broader concern with establishing a story of herself that resists attempts to bring her into the fold, or to identify her according to social norms. César imagines a system of language—of writing and of expressing one's experience in the world—based on difference rather than likeness, even if that system presents practical problems of communication, and maybe even prevents it. After all, César aims to tell her story in a way that resembles Ma's portrait in *Candy Story* and the narrator's portrait in *Self-Portrait in Green*—emphasizing multiplicity and defying the demand for unity and integration.

César's narrative ends with her death, trapped inside a vat of the same strawberry ice cream that causes her near-death experience at the beginning of the story. If we take her death literally, then the narrative becomes a kind of mystical tale from beyond the grave, a story that survives the death of the one who tells it. If we take César's death metaphorically, then I suppose we could go in many directions, coming up with interpretive glosses for the significance of the ice cream and the notion of death as a figure of transformation or resurrection. As Marcelo Ballvé points out, however, "Aira is concerned

not so much with verisimilitude or realism as he is with
that bewitching kernel of mystery that is at the heart of
a narrative. Aira's novels are very much like folk tales in
that they rely on paradox, disjointedness, and rupture to
carry the story forward." From this perspective, an interpretive explanation that tries to resolve the paradoxes,
mend the ruptures, and make tidy the digressive and
sometimes absurd wanderings of the narrative probably
misses the text in an effort to make sense of it. That said,
as Contreras notes, Aira clearly accentuates the framework
of the story, "pinning up the Beginning and the End,
which in Aira's novel mark the borders of the story" (257).
The novel, by returning to the incident that initiates the
narrative, creates the impression of self-containment and
tidiness, despite the logical problems of situating the narrative after we learn of the narrator's death. But that sense
of tidiness, integration, or wholeness that seems to arise
from the structure begins to fall apart once we consider
the implications of extracting César from her own narrative. César's death allows Aira to detach the story from
its origin, allowing it to float in the air, much like the
disembodied voices of the radio that fascinate César. The
story doesn't serve to illuminate and affirm the identity of the narrator, but, rather, shows that it can exist
without her—that it can survive even if she does not,
pointing to the non-coincidence or non-alignment of
narrative and narrator. Like the narrator in *Self-Portrait
in Green*, César disappears from her own composition
rather than grounding or securing it, preventing us from
identifying her through narrative.

Marie Redonnet's *Candy Story*

In *Candy Story*, Redonnet does not overtly play with autobiographical or autofictional writing, distinguishing it in some ways from *Self-Portrait in Green* and *How I Became a Nun*. Yet, in interviews and essays she has noted the autobiographical elements of her work and the way she engages her own story in her writing. In an interview with Jordan Stump, Redonnet explains:

> [Autobiography] is part of the raw material from which I create my work, without which it could never be built; but my work metamorphoses it, surpasses it, makes of it another story which is no longer only my own story. The story of the work doubles my autobiography in order to transcend it. (112)

That question of transcending one's own story—of becoming one's own double by way of writing—characterizes Mia's plight in *Candy Story*. Therefore, *Candy Story* provides an interesting metaliterary reflection on the question of writing the self and seems to reflect Redonnet's interest in engaging autobiography in order to get outside of it, releasing the story from the "I" who tells it. In this way, Mia resembles the other first-person narrators we have seen thus far and, as a writer struggling to compose a book based on her experiences, demonstrates a type of first-person writing that involves a turning away from the self.

The composition of Ma's self-portrait considered at

the opening of this chapter provides a productive lens through which we can see Mia's own efforts to write, and the relationship of that writing to self-portraiture. Interestingly, Mia dislikes Ma's portrait and eventually gives it to a guard at a nearby construction site in exchange for free passage through the closed site. The guard is in the middle of burning letters from his recently estranged wife, in order "to burn everything of hers to rid himself of the memories" (53). Perhaps Mia's handing-over of the portrait represents a similar action, especially since the portrait bears witness to Ma's foreignness, a sort of stranger to herself and to others in the last weeks of her life. Interestingly though, the guard immediately sees value in the portrait, calling it "truly a nice painting," and, Mia later discovers, sells it to a museum. When she happens upon the painting, Mia explains, "I sat on the little bench for a long time staring at Ma's self-portrait as though I were trying to figure out everything I didn't understand about her" (90). Despite Mia's initial response to the painting, and her sense that the guard scammed the museum, she seems to recognize that the portrait has something to say—that it might reveal something about Ma that could only come forward through the fractured image, through its strangeness and resistance to what Mia thought she knew about Ma. In a similar way, we see throughout *Candy Story* that Mia needs to find a way to get outside of her own story, of her memories and past, in order to inscribe a different kind of story, entering into a relation of otherness with herself. As Jean-Louis Hippolyte writes in *Fuzzy Fiction*,

Mia comes to a realization by the end of the novel: "The speaking 'I' ignores what or who she is, where she comes from and where she goes, only knowing that, to survive, she must necessarily become another, her own double, her own twin, in a game of permutations [...]" (135). Hippolyte describes that movement as "crossing into the imaginary, into her own song," suggesting that Mia's survival, and her persistence as a writer, depends upon her willingness to break with a more certain "I" that would guarantee her existence in the world (134). Like Ma, Mia must compose a portrait based on rupture, forging a space for a radical "I" that refuses "what or who she is"—insofar as that "who" or "what" pertains to the various narratives and structures that have come to identify her, to impose a history upon her rather than allowing her to write her own and, through writing, occupy the space of her double, or other.

Redonnet, in her essay, "Parcours d'une oeuvre," writes that *Candy Story*, "bears witness to the obscure and uncertain search for another voice, a desire for conversion, from one time to another, from one voice to other voices. It is situated in a painful in-between space, between a mourning that never ends and forms a block, and a desire to liberate oneself and write (hi)stories of the present" (495).[51] In order to observe how that search takes place, we can look at Mia's struggle as a writer, and how her own work might seek to manifest the "conversion" that Redonnet mentions. At the beginning of *Candy Story*, Mia has already established herself as a writer, having published a novel, *Sise Memories*, at a reputable publishing house, Boston. Mia's novel presumably has a certain degree of success, as it allows her to secure an advance for writing a second book (7-8). Perhaps more importantly, Mia often introduces herself, or is introduced by others, as the author of *Sise Memories*, which presumes a general familiarity with the novel and also demonstrates the way her identity has become tied to that piece of writing. Yet, at the onset of *Candy Story*, Mia finds herself struggling to write: "I haven't written anything all year, as if after *Sise Memories* I had nothing more to write" (11). Mia's situation evokes the "in-be-tweenness" that Redonnet describes above—a writer who identifies herself with a work that has exhausted her capacity to write. In her effort to overcome the block that keeps her from writing, Mia at first plans to write an autobiographical travelogue, much like the successful writer, Witz, but finds she has nothing to say.

We discover very little about *Sise Memories* as a work of writing, but we know that it clearly has had a stulti-fying effect on Mia and her sense of creativity. And that blockage, along with her mother's declining health and loss of memory, provides the backdrop for Mia's return to Sise, the town where she spent her childhood sum-mers with her mother. During her short time back in Sise and its surroundings, Mia engages with her past, and with the writing of that past, eventually conclud-ing: "I will never return to Sise. For me now, Sise is only *Sise Memories*" (44). While this statement clearly reflects Mia's determination to leave Sise in the past, it also reflects a turn *toward* writing. Mia rejects Sise as a locus of both geographic and historic significance in her life, instead preferring its imaginary rendering—one that captures its multiplicity, its tendency for doubling and dizziness, its transgression of limits and timelines. Mia in effect favors the version of Sise that we encounter in *Candy Story*. Similar to *Self-Portrait in Green*, the novel we read attests to the process of un-grounding or untethering that the narrators describe over the course of their respective texts.

Interestingly, Mia introduces Sise through the eyes of her mother, who looks out of her window at the Home in the Woods and mistakes it for the landscape of Sise: "Because she no longer sees clearly and confuses times and places, she thinks she has returned to Sise" (3). From the beginning of *Candy Story* Redonnet emphasizes memory and the blurring of time and space—in this instance through Ma's confusion and declining health. And while Ma's character clearly has her own plight and problems, in the novel she also serves as a double for Mia. Redonnet draws attention to this doubling from the first page, as Mia tells us, "Today, June 21, is different from any other day because Ma and I were both born on the twenty-first of June" (3). By emphasizing the doubling of Ma/Mia, Redonnet asks us to read Ma's character in excess of Ma's own individuality and to think about her character in relation to Mia. When Ma looks out the window of the home of the elderly where she lives, she sees what she imagines—a condition that presents practical problems in the world but perhaps also represents a sort of liberation from a set of limits, especially when we think about it in relation to writing and artistic production. Ma's memories of Sise, we come to learn, bring her joy; she associates it with a life before Madame Irma made "her the apprentice to a seamstress when she wanted to become a dancer," and, later, with summer vacations with her daughter (15, 32-33). In relation to Mia, Ma's entrance into the imaginary provides a kind of model for how one might break free from the constraints of the past and from the demand to see oneself and one's experiences how the world dictates, rather than allowing the imaginary to serve as a basis for entering into a different sort of relation with the past. As Hippolyte notes: "[...] history, in Redonnet, functions like a linear system, imposing its tragic teleology on the narrative" (128). Yet, for Redonnet, it seems that one might find a way to reject and challenge the "tragic teleology" while remaining engaged with her past and with the question of writing that past. When discussing her novel *Rose Mélie Rose*, Redonnet writes of the narrator's "quest to transmit [...] a new heritage, a new history" (493).

The sense of determinism that haunts Redonnet's work often creates an environment of reduced possibilities. In his discussion of Redonnet's play, *Tir & Lir*, Warren Motte describes the barren setting of the play and the obvious end towards which the four characters progress. He writes, "Its characters patently marked for death from the outset, *Tir & Lir* unfolds in a deadly, ineluctable teleology" (87). In a similar way, the reader likely never doubts the fate of the narrator, her sisters, and the hotel in *Hôtel Splendid*, as plumbing problems,

sickness, and infestation slowly submerge the hotel into
the swamp upon which it rests. While *Candy Story* feels
less restricted in some ways—partially as a result of the
vast array of characters and storylines—there are enough
characters who end up drowning by the lighthouse that
such a fate begins to emerge as one of a small hand-
ful of possible ends a character, and Mia in particular,
might experience. In this way, Redonnet's fascination
with doubling and repetition presents what feels like a
closed system, where all of the components refer back to
one another, including the beginning and the end as we
cycle through repeating histories. Yet, as Hippolyte notes,
"As long as the permutational games that Redonnet plays
endure, as long as she does not exhaust their combinatory
possibilities, her protagonists still have another shot at
escaping the fatality of closure (both formal and seman-
tic)" (131). In other words, there is another side to the
double—one that defies ends and closure, exploring the
possibility of deferral. From this perspective, Mia must,
by way of writing, tap into her own duality and tease out
the multiplicities of the world she navigates as a means
of opening up what sometimes feels like a claustropho-
bic and over-determined space.

In *Candy Story*, Redonnet expands her cast of characters compared to her previous works. Ma and Mia, while
doubling one another, also have mirror relations with
Mademoiselle Aldine, Madame Alma, and Madame Irma
(among others). Each name and character we learn in
Candy Story initiates a chain of similar names and characters, creating a series of mirror relationships that cross

paths with and incorporate one another. During Mia's last visit to her mother, she tells us, "In Ma's mind now, 'Mia' is Madame Alma, as she was known when Ma was a little girl in Sise, and Mademoiselle Aldine is Madame Alma" (83). In this particular instance, Mia finds herself caught up in a four-way mirror relation which, like Ma's portrait, collapses time and space and troubles any attempt to untangle one reflection from another. While one might reduce that scenario to Ma's dementia, in some ways her confusion mirrors the reader's experience trying to navigate *Candy Story* and perhaps provides the most accurate vision of the world depicted in the novel. And it also points to an avenue for Mia's own writing, where she might compose her self-portrait and story in a way that allows for complex mirrorings and challenges attempts to locate an origin. While Redonnet's use of doubles and repetition sometimes functions as a sort of prison of inter-referentiality, we see that it also might provide a means out of the trap—in the case of some of Redonnet's novels in particular—challenging static oppositional relationships, authoritative accounts, and teleological frameworks. Perhaps it becomes a means of inscribing a "new history," of writing outside or in excess of a closed system, breaking with myths of origin and telos. The environment in *Candy Story* recalls what we saw in *Self-Portrait in Green*, as both narrators navigate a world of mirrors and doubling, trying to find possibility within it, rather than feeling trapped by it.

In *Candy Story*, the development of Mia's relationship to her writing demonstrates an effort to subvert teleological frameworks, despite the fact that we know little about *Sise Memories*, its relation to Mia's life, or much of anything else. But what we do know about the book is worth noting. Late in *Candy Story*, Mia does eventually provide a brief description of the heroine: "a young singer from Sise hoping to obtain a contract at the Eldorado in New York" (86). While that particular storyline evokes the character of Marion far more than Mia, this doesn't stop Curtz from conflating Mia with her novel's heroine as he shows her a collection of secretly taped sexual encounters: "He wants us to act out what is playing on the screen, so that I can use the experience to write a novel for his new imprint, from which he will produce a series of videotapes" (85). Mia refuses Curtz's advances, and, offended, he vows that she will never have the opportunity to publish another novel, since she understands "nothing about America or video" (86). On top of what seems to border on assault, Curtz tries to assimilate Mia into his market-driven perspective of literature, and also assumes that Mia's heroine serves as a direct stand-in for her own wants and desires. In other words, Curtz believes Mia's fictional double represents a simple mirror image; he presumes a sort of autobiographical pact. As Ruth Cruickshank argues in *Fin de millénaire French Fiction*, "Curtz's video project dramatizes the dangers of reading fiction as reality, particularly where sexual exploitation is endemic, and is translated into celluloid images" (223). Portraying Curtz in this light, according to Cruickshank, allows Redonnet to draw attention to issues of exploitation and to "raise the question of the capacity of cultural production in general, and prose fiction in particular, to resist that pervasive seduction" (224). While that certainly makes sense, it seems important to note that Mia does indeed resist, and that, despite her initial attempt to write an autobiographical book for Curtz's imprint, ultimately goes in another direction. Her rejection of Curtz comes soon after she has written a first draft of her second novel, *Candy Story*, and therefore has already begun to free herself from the writer's block that has plagued her in the past (83).

While one might guess that *Sise Memories* does indeed bear some relationship to Mia's life and past based on the title, Curtz's assumption that Mia and her heroine form a direct mirror relation clearly doesn't hold up. Instead, as noted above, Mia's heroine seems to evoke what we learn about Marion, a woman who used to sing at the Hotel by the Sea and who serves as a sort of muse and object of adoration for a number of men in Sise and Sise City. Marion was specifically known for singing *Candy*, and the name "Candy" takes us back to Mia's story, since she tells us of several different occasions where her lovers would refer to her as "Candy," instead of her own name. Therefore, by shifting and manipulating the mirrors a bit, we can easily find reflective relationships between Mia and her book; but Curtz's sexually-motivated insistence upon singular, direct mirror relations, and his naïve belief in referentiality, misses the mark. Late in the novel, when feeling shame about her inability to write and her decision to have an affair with an Interpol agent, Mia reveals, "I'm not really crazy but

it's difficult to be Candy when I've always been Mia"
(73). Here, Mia represents Candy as a sort of ego-ideal,
lamenting the difficulty of becoming her double, and
the sense that she must get beyond "Mia" in order to
break away from her current difficulties and the static,
oppressive narratives of the past. It seems that for Mia,
the work of becoming Candy is the work of writing,
and a means of freeing her story from herself, through
writing—recalling what we saw with Redonnet's comments about the autobiographical elements of her work.
Mia's identification with Candy also resembles César's
identification with the radio in *How I Became a Nun*, as
both narrators seek a sort of untethered voice to tell, or
invent, their stories.

Interestingly, one of the men who calls Mia "Candy"
is Kell, the Interpol agent with whom she is having an
affair. After reading *Sise Memories*, Kell tells Mia that
"for the first time in his life he has met someone who is
like him" (65). While Curtz sees *Sise Memories* as a sexual invitation, Kell sees in it an opportunity for identification, perceiving a mirror relation between himself and
Mia, rather than Mia and her heroine. This difference
with Curtz in some ways makes itself clearer when Mia
reveals that later that evening Kell "made love to me so
hard, calling me Candy, that I thought I was about to
die" (66). In calling Mia "Candy," Kell recognizes Mia's
potential for difference, not only from her heroine, but
also from herself. In a sense, Mia desires her own death,
in order to become Candy. Kell's role in Mia's evolution
remains ambiguous, especially since one could interpret

his rough sexual conduct as mirroring Curtz's behavior; at the same time, he seems to provide a space in which Mia can explore her duality. Of course, Kell can't transform Mia into Candy, and, in some ways, his career and approach to narrative represents the opposite of the direction in which Mia turns in composing *Candy Story*. As an Interpol agent immersed in the criminal activities of Sise and Sise City, Kell's approach is decidedly teleological, seeking a final revelation that will make all of the pieces of the investigation fall into place. In her essay on *Candy Story* and *Nevermore*, Jeanette Gaudet describes the relationship of Kell's investigation to writing: "Conforming to the conventions of the detective story, the real perpetrators of the crime and the motives are hidden and must be brought to light" (165). Gaudet points out the entanglement of Mia and Kell's stories in the second half of *Candy Story*, and the significance of Kell's investigation to Mia's efforts to write her second book. After all, from what we can tell, Mia's *Candy Story* recounts what Kell has discovered during his investigation and clearly serves as a metafictional double for the novel we are reading. From that point of view, Mia's narrative would also presumably conform to the conventions Gaudet mentions, yet I would argue that Mia resists the teleology implicit in the process of solving a mystery—concluding her narrative with the expression, "After that I don't know," which deliberately disrupts any sense of closure (96). In addition, Mia's narrative, though incorporating and perhaps mirroring Kell's investigation, more importantly reflects her own process of becoming Candy through writing, of entering into a relation of otherness with herself and her past.

When considering the broader question of Mia's plight and the composition of her self-portrait, it is important to note the relationship between Mia's novel and her efforts to find a way to write outside of the limitations that keep her blocked. In Yvette Went-Daoust's essay on Redonnet's earlier novels, she suggests that the female protagonists are "encumbered by stand-ins and paralyzing doubles," from which they must free themselves in order to succeed, or, at the least, to avoid the fate of their mothers who were "stopped along the way in their quest for independence" (388).[52] The doubling and persistent repetitions of similar scenarios create a sense of fatalism, as we saw with *Tir & Lir* and *Hotel Splendid*, trapping the characters in an already-determined end. That same sense of entrapment appears to plague Mia in *Candy Story*, reflected in her state of immobility and stagnation: she can't write; she is waiting for her mother's condition to worsen until she dies; she finds herself re-immersed in a past she would rather leave behind; she's hung up on a guy who spent the night with her on a train and then disappeared; she feels unable to continue with her career as a school teacher. Beyond Mia's seeming inability to *move* or to *do*, she observes those around her, noting their mostly tragic and often similar fates. She recalls the story of Madame Irma, who owned the house in which Mia grew up:

> Madame Irma's depression began the year I left
> Mills-le-Pont to live with Enz in Paris. She lost

her job at the Flood Gate Bar because she was
too old to be a waitress there. She couldn't take
being alone in the house all day with And. One
day she slit her wrists and was taken to the asylum in Mills-le-Pont. She never returned, as
though she preferred the asylum to the house.
(60).

While Madame Irma avoids drowning by the lighthouse,
she represents one of the other possible fates for the
characters in *Candy Story*, suffering from mental illness
and living out her final days in a strange place, alone
and defeated. Mia adds that "Ma never forgave Madame
Irma for having made her the apprentice to a seamstress
at the age of twelve when she had wanted to be a dancer"
(60). The tyranny of the past seems to prevent the value
of moving forward, as if a past action necessarily determines a singular possibility for the future.

Immediately after telling Madame Irma's story, Mia
turns to her own life, suggesting the way that the people
around her have provided a sort of map for the future,
offering a small collection of paths leading to the same
tragic and unavoidable end:

As I waited on the platform for the RER to
Paris, I suddenly asked myself what was going
to happen to me. When Luira and I visited the
fortune-teller, the fortune-teller would always
say she couldn't read my future because it was
written in a language she didn't know. Seeing
my disappointment, the fortune-teller would
say it was proof that I had a destiny. Had I

been able to choose between a life and a destiny, I would have chosen a life. But, as the fortune-teller said, neither a destiny nor a life can
be chosen because it's all been written before,
in every language.

The fortune-teller finds Mia unreadable, using language
that suggests textuality, and implying that Mia's future
exists outside of familiar linguistic and narrative constructs. The fortune-teller concludes that Mia must have
a destiny, which seems to compound Mia's fear that she
has no choice in the way her life unfolds, destined to fulfill a narrative that has been set for her. Of course, as the
fortune-teller seems to indicate, whether we call it a "life"
or a "destiny," nothing will make Mia's life unique, as
every story has already been written, in every language,
therefore ensuring that we are all trapped by pre-existing narratives that we play out. The fortune-teller's perspective reflects the world we see in *Candy Story*, where
the constant doubling and repetition provide a sense
of entrapment. But I would like to go back to what
Hippolyte suggests in his reading of *Candy Story*—that
despite the sometimes tyrannical and fatalistic functioning of the double in Redonnet's writing, it might also
represent "an instance of emancipation in her work,"
and "announces Redonnet's primary strategy: to use the
double in a conflictual and creative dynamics in order to
subsume the fatality of the one" (130). From this perspective, rather than allowing entrapment by the double,
Mia must put the double to use—as a means to combat
the sense that the past necessarily dictates the present,

and that a singular future, or destiny, has already been written. As a writer, in particular, Mia can write outside of that system, making use of her own possibilities for doubleness and entering into a language that transgresses past narratives.

That understanding seems to resonate with what Redonnet says in an interview about the way mirror relations function in the triptych: "The narrators, through the power of their 'I,' of their radically singular voice, fight against the proliferation of the double; they try to find a name, an identity, by creating a work of their own" (110). She then adds, "[…] in my writing I start from that strangeness in order to leave it and to enter into another one, that of otherness from the world and from the other" (110). That reflection points to the two slopes of the double—the slope that entraps and that the "I" combats in order to emerge in a sort of radical singularity, and the slope that suggests a space of otherness, outside of the familiarity and narratives of the world. In *Candy Story* though, it seems that it's not enough just to write, to engage in literary production, since most of the writers depicted in the novel point to the commodification of literature and the problematic relationship of literature to confession and autobiography. Writers like Curtz, Rotz, and Witz—the last of whom is "world famous for reinventing the spy novel" (13)—depend upon the formulae of worn genres, trusting in the public desire to consume such narratives. After picking up Curtz's most recent novel in the airport, Mia notes, "The book sounds like a novel by Witz, as if Curtz were able to write only like Witz. It doesn't prevent Curtz from being very famous and successful" (15). Despite the success of these writers, they can't help but mirror one another, only able to write the same novel again and again. Perhaps even more significantly, those writers who turn to memoirs and autobiographical writing don't fare much better and, argues Cruickshank, fall into many of the same patterns as the formulaic novels: "Neither do they resist the commodification of cultural production, nor work through the legacy of the past, nor seek to find a viable narrative for negotiating the present and future" (238). The Commander's memoirs, when revealed after his death, amount to "columns of numbers and incomprehensible equations" (52); Stev's love poems to Marion don't get published during his life and feed an obsession that keeps him from functioning in the world; the memoirs of both Witz and the president of PAL result in their respective murders and never come to light; and the book containing Bobby Wick's transcendental poem ends up containing "the names and addresses of the African women he know, and in detail what he did with each one, the price he paid" (70). In trying to make sense of their lives and pasts, all of these writers fail in one way or another.

Mia clearly must distinguish herself from the many examples of writers that Redonnet's novel implicitly criticizes. In order to combat the double, to free herself from the repetition of past events, Mia must write outside of that closed system, as her own, strange double—as Candy, in effect. Rather than using writing to

order and make sense of the past, Mia composes a portrait that emphasizes the fractures and multiplicities of
the world she inhabits, and of herself. In this way, her
work resembles that of César and the narrator of *Self-
Portrait in Green*. She chooses the approach represented
by the last line of her narrative—"After that, I don't
know,"—refusing the closed system by pointing to the
uncertainty and instability that always threatens to disrupt and fracture what we think we know (96). At the
same time, Mia asserts a radical "I" in that sentence—
radical because it exists within the context of a question,
a fundamental unknowingness. In this way, Mia finds
the second slope of the double, pushing against closure
and telling her story from outside the narrative confines
of the world she depicts and inhabits—evoking what
Redonnet describes as writing "another story which is
no longer only my own story" (112).

CHAPTER 4:
WRITING THE END OF RELATION

Writing about break-ups, failed relationships, misguided affairs, or sexual encounters that demonstrate the gulf between participants rather than the possibility of union and intimacy feels like well-covered territory. From that point of view, Marguerite Duras's *The Malady of Death*, Lydia Davis's *The End of the Story*, and Maggie Nelson's *Bluets* take part in the rich narrative tradition dedicated to the grief and misery of sexual relation or, perhaps more accurately, non-relation. Yet, each writer, by taking an approach to narrative that often radically questions traditional modes of representation and writing, engages with familiar subject matter in a way that feels unfamiliar and challenging. In this chapter, I would like to use Marguerite Duras's *récit*, *The Malady of Death*, as a jumping-off point for a reading of *The End of the Story* and *Bluets*. Duras's *récit* provides a means of approaching the complex questions surrounding the end of relation—and the writing of that end—that I think interest

Davis and Nelson. *The Malady of Death* can provide an introduction to the notion of impossible relation and the way a confrontation with that impossibility might open onto a different kind of relation—one that both escapes writing and is enacted by it. Nelson's *Bluets* begins as a meditation on her love for the color blue and soon reveals itself as a work that also examines the nature of loss and the difficulty of knowing and loving another person. Lastly, in *The End of the Story* Davis focuses on the way we narrate the end of relation, sometimes before it has even happened, as a means of trying to makes sense of something that probably always eludes our grasp. By placing all three works side-by-side, we can consider how they individually and interactively point to the unbridgeable gulf that constitutes the relation between lovers and reflect upon the way writing and narrative respond to and preserve that gulf. The end of relation, or at least its eventuality, frames the lovers' relation from the start, drawing attention to the barriers to intimacy that necessarily separate the two individuals.

Marguerite Duras's *The Malady of Death*

Duras's *The Malady of Death* dramatizes a series of encounters between a man and a woman, based on a contract established by the two at the onset of the affair—a contract that implies a set beginning and end to the relation. The man proposes to pay the woman to come every night for several days, in order to "try to know" the woman, to penetrate her body in a way that provides access to what he recognizes as inaccessible (2). The man later reveals to the woman that he has never loved, desired, or even looked at a woman—a lack of experience which motivates the affair he has contracted in the text (6). Loving, desiring, and looking take on various meanings in *The Malady of Death*, however, and often represent actions that threaten violently to transgress boundaries separating self from other. While the man wants to try to know and to love, he also remains incapable of murder—penetrating the woman, actively and forcefully, and thus destroying her by collapsing the difference that protects her. Early in the text, the man looks at the woman's body and we read: "The body's completely defenseless, smooth from face to feet. It invites strangulation, rape, ill usage, insults, shouts of hatred, the unleashing of deadly and unmitigated passions" (16). Here, we see that the man does indeed look, and we see that the look is associated with appropriation and violence. According to Janine Ricouart in her study of gender and violence in Duras's novels, *Écriture feminine et violence,* the woman, by her female presence and thus her signification as giver and taker of life, allows the man to confront his fear of death. Ricouart explains, "He clings to the woman's body and his 'cannibalism' takes the form of a desire to possess the woman entirely, to appropriate for himself her knowledge, in one way or another, particularly by physical absorption (103).[53] Ricouart emphasizes the subject/object relation of the man and the woman, and the man's attempts to subjugate the woman to his will and to consume her, transgressing the distance and the boundary separating one body from another.

At the same time, if we push beyond that initial, or desired, dynamic, we see that the man, when faced with the defenseless body, says, "I can't see anything," and eventually gives up his attempts to look, even after the woman invites him to do so (17). The woman's body remains out of sight, out of reach; in its total passivity, the woman's body recedes beyond the man's grasp. Whether the man *wants* to look—to murder, to rape—remains unclear; one can conclude, though, that looking seems to prevent sight, and that any attempt to overcome the distance separating the man from the woman's body only emphasizes their difference. Maurice Blanchot's distinction of speech and sight in *The Infinite Conversation* elucidates the way that sight functions as a mode of apprehension: "To see is to make use of separation, not as mediating, but as a means of immediation, as immediating. In this sense, too, to see is to experience the continuous, and to celebrate the sun, that is, beyond the sun: the One" (28). Seeing depends upon distance in order to make use of it, and to make the object, or the other, appear in the light. For Blanchot, the unification and appropriation involved in seeing is problematic when considering the relation of the self and the other. He offers speech as a different kind of relation—one with the potential of preserving the distance. In *The Malady of Death*, the man's inability to see allows for the woman's recession and represents an alternative to appropriation and penetration. Unable to see, the man speaks to the woman, simultaneously bridging and preserving the distance between them by means of language. And their topics of conversation tend to emphasize the gulf, the inability to understand and see clearly, the difficulty of aligning their perspectives and perceptions.

According to the woman, the man suffers from "the malady of death," a condition that she can only describe in vague terms, suggesting that while she might perceive the sickness, it escapes understanding. The woman refers to the man as an unknowing "carrier" of death and seems to associate his deathly state with the fact that he has never loved, desired, or looked at a woman (Duras 34). That association creates a paradox, if we are considering the man's inaction and inexperience as a sort of passive refusal to commit murder. According to the woman, the man carries death with him, he embodies it, he contaminates others with it; at the same time, we see that he does not, and perhaps cannot, impose it. The woman recognizes as much when she says, "You think you weep because you can't love. You weep because you can't impose death" (46). The man carries death with total impotence—looking without seeing, engaging in intercourse without penetrating, trying or seeking without desiring. The man watches the woman sleep, and we read, "While she lives, she invites murder. You wonder how to kill her and who will. You don't love anything or anyone, you don't even love the difference you think you embody" (33). The man meditates upon violent action yet knows he won't commit it. His impotence, as a passive carrier of death, constitutes his relation—both the possibility and impossibility of relation—to the woman. As a carrier of death, the man brings the end of himself and the end of the woman to the relation; the malady of death allows the man to approach the woman and experience her in her inaccessibility.

As Leslie Hill notes in *Marguerite Duras: Apocalyptic Desires*, despite the man's claim never to have desired a woman and the woman's seeming indifference to the man, we should not conclude that desire does not figure into the relation of the two in the text. Hill writes:

> The infernal absence of desire is little different here from its consuming presence; like death, it has an inexhaustible circularity, and though the man and the woman are not at first sexual objects for one another, they become bound together by the same desperate necessity, for which the only name available is desire itself. (157)

If the man is propelled by his lack of desire, that lack

becomes the basis for a different desire—the desire to desire. In addition, it is only in a state of lack that desire can operate, which would mean that the perpetual distance the man experiences in relation to any potential object of love establishes the possibility for desire and for a relation that arises out of distance and difference. The woman, though coming to the affair from a different position, ultimately demonstrates her own commitment to what was originally the man's pursuit of union and intimacy. They pursue and desire the same end, which necessarily recedes their grasp and paradoxically binds them in their shared pursuit. Returning to Hill's reading, the woman's investment becomes clear as she struggles to accept the man's perception of the sea as black, when she so clearly sees it as white. In other words, the man and the woman both demonstrate a desire to overcome difference and to seek "the possibility of love and fusion for which they both yearn" (157).

As part of the contract, the man tells the woman, "she mustn't speak, like the women of her ancestors, must yield completely to [him] and [his] will, be entirely submissive like peasant women in the barns after the harvest when they're exhausted and let the men come to them while they're asleep" (4-5). While the man clearly sets the parameters for the woman's passive role, he is also ordering something that renders him powerless to achieve the goal of knowing and loving. The woman becomes a sort of ghost, drifting in and out of the man's apartment, sleeping most of the time, and passively accepting his efforts to penetrate her as she disappears into the distance separating her body from his. In Maurice Blanchot's discussion of *The Malady of Death* in his work, *The Unavowable Community*, he meditates upon the paradox of the woman's passivity: "[…] due to her very weakness, due to her very frailty, she cannot be killed, preserved as she is by the interdiction that makes her untouchable in her constant nakedness, the closest and most distant nakedness, the inaccessible intimacy of the outside" (37). Blanchot argues that the woman abandons herself so completely, so excessively— the part of her under contract, at least—that she remains ungraspable and unthreatened by murder. The woman becomes a sort of specter, carrying death herself, and pronouncing it upon the man. Through the lens of gender, the woman's frailty and passivity—demanded by the man—perpetuate problematic subject-object relations between the man and woman, which Ricouart develops in her discussion of *The Malady of Death*. But Blanchot offers another possibility for reading the woman's passivity, informed by his interest in that which might exceed relation. The woman's ghostly, ungraspable presence opens up a space of relation that defies appropriation and subjugation.[54]

Blanchot's thinking about the relation of self and other, which aligns with his notion of community based on difference, can shed light on the foundational paradox of the relation of the man and the woman in *The Malady of Death*. While Julia Kristeva, in her well-known reading of Duras's oeuvre, points to the overwhelming tone of melancholy and grief that characterizes *The Malady of*

Death and others of Duras's texts, I would argue that her insights must be pushed a step beyond what she identifies as, "this nothing, the unsignifiable of a malady that lacks tragic paroxysm or beauty, a pain that has nothing left but its tension" (140). Kristeva ties that melancholy into post-war trauma and makes some important points about the ever-present chasm separating characters who fail in their attempts to establish relation. But, the "nothing left" and the "tension" can and should be understood in terms of the way they constitute a different sort of (non-)relation. Returning to Blanchot and his notion of the ethics of relation, it's precisely the chasm that prevents murder, or the subsuming of other into self. In *The Infinite Conversation*, Blanchot describes a kind of relation "about which one must simply say: it does not tend toward unity, it is not a relation from the perspective of unity or with unity in view, not a relation of unification" (67). While the man in *The Malady of Death* contracts an affair in order to know and love the woman, thus penetrating and appropriating her, he doesn't do it. Perhaps he can't do it. And the woman, as she disappears into total, excessive passivity, recedes away from the man's grasp and affirms the chasm that constitutes their relation. For Blanchot, and I think for Duras, the melancholy and psychic pain of non-relation, if we accept Kristeva's characterization, is coupled with a sense that such non-relation affirms a different kind of relation, dependent upon the recession of both lovers beyond each other's grasp. When Blanchot remarks upon the dissymmetry of the man and the woman in

The Malady of Death, he calls it "the same dissymmetry that, according to Levinas, marks the irreciprocity of the ethical relationship between the other and
me, I whom am never equal with the Other [...]" (*The
Unavowable Community* 40). Does Duras's text offer
an ever-present melancholic chasm and the hovering,
penetrating presence of sickness and pain? Yes, but the
other, impossible side of the malady of death—the one
that suggests recession, passive escapability, protective
darkness, and the infinite recurrence of the end of relation, of life—remains an essential aspect of the relation
of the man and the woman in the text. Hill seems to
echo those thoughts when concluding her comments
on *The Malady of Death*, writing that the lovers fail in
their relation, "in order to arrive at a more radically catastrophic, purer affirmation of the sublime relationship
of non-relationship on which Duras here confers the
implicit name of love" (158).

Interestingly, the man and the woman at the end of
The Malady of Death appear to breach the gap in their
last sexual encounter. On the one hand, it seems that
the man has ultimately penetrated the woman and has
established intimacy, overcoming the distance. We read:
"She says: Look. She parts her legs, and in the hollow
between you see the dark night at last. You say: It was
there, the dark night. It's there" (50-51). The penetration of the night, "la nuit noire," suggests transgression
of the woman's bodily limits; self enters other and collapses the difference (*La Maladie de la mort* 53).[55] On
the other hand, the penetration of the night does not

suggest a sort of seeing tied to visibility or illumination, or even possibility. While the woman commands, "Look," the man sees the dark night. The woman doesn't appear to the man, as he is met with darkness. This scene in Duras's *récit* evokes Blanchot's discussion of the myth of Orpheus and Eurydice in *The Space of Literature*, where he considers the paradoxical moment of seeing the impossibility of seeing.[56] From that point of view, one might say that the man in *The Malady of Death* penetrates the darkness of Hades where Eurydice resides but confronts a darker night, and the impossibility of reaching Eurydice to bring her to the light of day. Furthermore, after this final encounter, the woman disappears, literally, becoming a "no one" out in the streets, never to be recognized again. And the man consequently questions whether or not the affair took place.

While *The Malady of Death* does not explicitly address the act of writing the possibility of relation, Yvonne Guers-Villate, in *Continuité/Discontinuité de l'oeuvre durassienne*, remarks that Duras's work often displays a sort of implicit, rather than heavy-handed, meta-fictionality, bringing our attention to the way we perceive and tell stories. Guers-Villate points to *The Ravishing of Lol Stein* as an example of a narrative that puts itself into question, since the account provided by the narrator does not originate in his own memory of Lol's past, but in his imagination, or recreation, of what took place. Guers-Villate writes, "That is why we could consider all of the reconstruction of Lol's past as a sort of metafiction" (41).[57] Similarly, *The Malady of Death*

invites reflection upon narrating and storytelling, as it
concerns the affair described in the text. We read, "The
evening after she goes, you tell the story of the affair
in a bar. At first you tell it as if it were possible to do
so, then you give up. Then you tell it laughing, as if it
were impossible for it to have happened or possible for
you to have invented it" (53). As the man attempts to
tell—and make narrative sense of—his affair with the
woman, he realizes the impossibility of recounting the
story and bringing it to light, so to speak. After giving
up, the tone of his account changes to what we might
imagine as self-deprecating laughter, and the storytelling
no longer seeks to affirm what took place, but rather it
undermines itself as a mode of truth-telling or revelation.
Furthermore, that confrontation with the impossibility
of telling puts into question the entire interaction of the
man and the woman, questioning whether or not such
an affair could have taken place—or, at least, the affair
as the man remembers and tries to make sense of it. The
affair itself, as event, disappears. But, as Leslie Hill notes:

> Much the same comments, of course, might
> be seen to apply to Duras's own text, but by
> affirming them within her own writing, as a
> set of possibilities which the text itself incor-
> porates, Duras's text outstrips or transgresses
> them too, and the result is a mode of textual-
> ity that is uncontrollably in excess of whatever
> it may itself be saying. (154)

In other words, Duras writes the story that the man
undermines and laughs off as impossible to tell, and

perhaps impossible to have happened, exceeding the limits of storytelling set within the text. This is not to say that Duras's *récit* brings to light what the man couldn't, but rather that her writing incorporates a moment that sends the writing away and announces it as excess. Yet, the story of the affair remains, in writing, perhaps in a kind of non-relation with whatever it purports to tell. Writing, in this case, resides outside of the story, in darkness and distance, in its own malady of death, passively refusing to reveal, appropriate, or apprehend what recedes beyond its grasp.

Interestingly, following the *récit*, Duras provides suggestions for how *The Malady of Death* could be staged, which, though supposedly outside of the "text proper," becomes a sort of metafictional addendum, encouraging us to think about the relations of the characters, in addition to their relation to us. Duras notes: "The young woman of the paid nights should be lying on some white sheets in the middle of the stage. [...] A man would walk back and forth around her, telling the story" (56). In this staging, the man remains separate from the dramatization of the encounter, as he recites the narrative and delivers his own lines, thus emphasizing the impossibly distant nature of his relation to the woman. That distance takes physical form, in the sense that the man never physically engages with the woman on stage, and perhaps more importantly, it creates a sort of dislocation or dispersion when considering the diegetic levels of the text, since the man is both "inside" and "outside" of the performance.

Sharon Willis, in *Marguerite Duras: Writing on the Body*, draws particular attention to the way Duras's notes at the end of the text complicate and emphasize the disorienting use of the pronoun "you" throughout *The Malady of Death*:

> [...] the male would be a narrator both address-
> ing a 'you,' and reporting his own speech—as a
> literal stand-in, a delegate. Meanwhile, simulta-
> neously and implicitly, he would play the part
> of the reader or the reading, itself staged. The
> 'you' to whom he speaks then would be spread
> across at least three sites: the absent man, the
> young woman, and the spectator, thus fractur-
> ing the separation of registers proposed by the
> text, as text or theater. (153)

Willis goes on to discuss the way this theatrical set-up dramatizes the spectator's/reader's precarious position in the play/text, incited by Duras's use of "you" in the narrative. The "you" seemingly invites us into the text by addressing us, at the same time that it casts us out by asking us to share that address with the male object to whom the narrator "speaks" (an object who remains absent in the staging of the narrative suggested by Duras). We can either identify with the man, share his pronomial position in relation to the narrative, and experience the narrative through that position; or we must confront our own exclusion from the text—a text that doesn't need us, in the sense that it incorporates and is directed at an explicit narratee. In an interview between Hélène Cixous and Michel Foucault originally published in the *Cahiers Renaud Barrault*, Cixous discusses her initial displeasure and discomfort with "the position in which [Duras] put me" (*White Ink* 159). Cixous here is referring to a linguistic position that forces an uncomfortable identification. While Cixous alludes to Duras's oeuvre in general, her comments feel particularly applicable to *The Malady of Death* and later works by Duras that engage second-person narration. According to Cixous, Duras demands a sort of absolute passivity from the reader, where our position makes us subject to the same exchange of looks that the characters experience. Interestingly, we might note that our readerly position in some ways parallels that of the man as he tells his story at the bar at the end of the *récit*. When reading Duras's final note about the staging of the piece, we can only laugh, perhaps with self-deprecation, at our mistaken sense of the place we might think we occupy in a narrative. The staging of the piece, if we imagine it as Duras describes, emphasizes the precariousness of our position and our lack of access to the narrative as a site where we might gain *insight*.

Maggie Nelson's *Bluets*

Returning to the last narrative moment in Duras's *recit*, we can observe how the man's attempt to tell his story encourages us to reflect upon the question of writing relation; that moment of closure folds back upon the entire narrative, frames it, and infuses it with self-conscious laughter and doubt. As we turn to Nelson and Davis, the question of writing explicitly preoccupies both *Bluets* and *The End of the Story*, as each writer, in a sense, enacts the scene in *The Malady of Death* where the man tries to tell the story of his affair at the bar. Self-awareness and doubt pervade *Bluets* and *The End of the Story*, as does a sense of grief over the end of relation and the possibility that relation is not, in the end, possible. And like the man in the bar, Nelson and Davis wonder if the relationships they describe might be fabrications, or, at the very least, highly dubious narrative constructions filtered through imperfect memories that displace any "real event" and respond to loss, through writing, with more loss. Nelson, who presents her book as a sort of wandering reflection on her love affair with the color blue, specifically reflects upon that concern: "I don't want to replace my memories of [specific blue things], nor embalm them, nor exalt them. In fact, I think I would like it best if my writing could empty me further of them, so that I might become a better vessel for new blue things" (7). And, since Nelson's book reveals itself not only as a meditation upon her love affair with a color, but also upon her failed affair with a lover who still haunts her thoughts, she extends her concerns to the way writing might contaminate and transform memories of her lover. Rather than displacement or transformation, Nelson seeks obliteration, a sort of blanking of the slate, through the process of inscribing what she wants to disappear.

Nelson's use of the word "vessel" makes me think of her more recent book, *The Argonauts*, which takes its title from a passage in *Roland Barthes by Roland Barthes*, where Barthes describes: "The ship *Argo* (luminous and white), each piece of which the Argonauts gradually replaced, so that they ended with an entirely new ship, without having to alter either its name or its form") (46). While the analogy here can be applied to writing in a variety of ways—especially considering the fact that Nelson refers to it in the title of a different, later book, with its own formal particularities—the image of Barthes' *Argo*, when applied to *Bluets*, suggests a way in which we might empty ourselves of a story, through the practice of a sort of writing that makes space, swapping new blue things for the old ones.[58] At some point, if all goes well, we end up in a completely new ship, even if we call it the same thing. In addition, the formal structure of *Bluets* perhaps communicates with the idea of a piecemeal *Argo*, where the fragments emphasize a certain discontinuity of the parts at the same time as they feel voyage-like, as Nelson wanders across a vast landscape of memories, reflections, and critical inquiries. In an essay on *Bluets* in *Tri-Quarterly*, Thomas Larson observes:

"*Bluets's* shape is a spiral, and the spiral, to achieve its end, must keep moving away from where it began. Its structure is built by pulling away from the core and by keeping attached to the core. The goal (if there is one) is nomadic, a sort of nomadic mosaic. As one reads, the book, despite its progression, loses its linearity and feels circular, porous, a tad unstable." That push and pull of progression and circularity, meandering and fragmentation, branching labyrinth and mosaic, characterizes Nelson's text. In an interview published in the *Los Angeles Times*, Nelson describes *Bluets* as: "explicitly interested in the fragment—both found and made— as a physical phenomenon and conceptual idea."[59] The fragmented style of *Bluets* manages to *make space*—the formal, physical space between the numbered passages and the conceptual space provided by the moments of whiteness on the page.

Regardless of Nelson's expressed hope that writing "could empty" her of memories in order to make space for new things and experiences, her book serves as a testament to the difficulty of letting go—perhaps especially because she is trying to let go of something of which she has no hold. Nelson's obsession with blue seems to have predated her love affair, but it also clearly plays a substitutional role in the wake of her break up. She opens her book, writing, "Suppose I were to begin by saying that I had fallen in love with a color," and explains that her "affinity" eventually became "more serious," and then "somehow personal" (1). Nelson goes on to introduce her love affair with the color blue in terms that feel familiar, if not normally applied to a relationship with a color: "And so I fell in love with a color—in this case, the color blue—as if falling under a spell, a spell I fought to stay under and get out from under, in turns" (1). Nelson gives herself over to her obsession, seduced and satisfied, if still aware that the spell can lead one astray. She quickly clarifies that her relation to blue is not one of yearning or longing, though we come to understand that her love of blue correlates and perhaps responds to a sense of longing and lack—a void left by a lost relationship. "I don't want to yearn for blue things, and God forbid for any 'blueness.' Above all, I want to stop missing you" (4).

As Nelson details her passion for blue, she describes it as a sort of obsession that can be fulfilled in various ways—by random sightings of blue objects that surprise her during mundane activities, by receiving blue gifts from people who know about her love, by reading reflections on color from a vast array of writers, philosophers, musicians, and artists. And that sense of fulfillment contrasts the unwanted longing that pervades her life in the wake of the end of her relationship. Nelson admits that she struggles with loneliness—a condition she describes as "solitude with a problem" (28). And then she reflects upon whether or not her relationship with blue can address that loneliness: "Can blue solve the problem, or can it at least keep me company within it?—No, not exactly. It cannot love me that way; it has no arms. But sometimes I do feel its presence to be a sort of wink—*Here you are again*, it says, *and so am I*" (21, italics in original). As far as substitutes go, blue does a pretty good job. It can't reciprocate, but it can provide a comforting presence; it can exist alongside Nelson— distant, mute, but *there* nonetheless.

And, yet, the irreciprocity nags at Nelson and pro- vokes a line of questioning that turns the substitute into a painful and annoying affirmation of loss and distance. After quoting Goethe's assertion that the color blue disturbs, rather than providing gladness or liveliness, Nelson wonders: "Is to be in love with blue, then, to be in love with a disturbance? Or is the love itself the disturbance? And what kind of madness is it anyway, to be in love with something unconstitutionally incapable of loving you back?" (15). A disturbance, here, is some- thing that troubles and unsettles, and it is also a sort of interruption or gap. A disturbance comes in between, or breaks up, something that might otherwise cohere. The inability of a color to love back presents disturbance, though Nelson also appears to invite us to extend her line of questioning to human relationships—and her failed relationship in particular. What is the point of lov- ing a color? Loving a person? Loving at all, if we consider the problem of reciprocity and the presence of distur- bance as a condition of all relations? That last question drives *The Malady of Death* and gradually becomes an implicit focus of *Bluets* as it progresses.

Part of the problem, as Nelson first notes in terms of color, has to do with the unknowability and invisibil- ity of the object of her love. "For no one really knows what color is, where it is, or even whether it is" (15).

Of course, the paradox of how we perceive color in an object is that we see the color reflected back to us by the object—the color that has not been absorbed. One might say that intrinsically—if we can even speak of color in such a way—the object's color is everything *except* what we see. Nelson takes up this line of thinking and then wonders how our misperceptions might not only apply to color: "We mainly suppose the experiential quality to be an intrinsic quality of the physical object—this is the so-called systematic illusion of color. Perhaps it is also that of love. But I am not willing to go there—not just yet. I believed in you" (20-21). We experience color subjectively, not just because individuals perceive color in different ways, but also because the object exists, with or without color, outside of our perceptions. It throws our gaze back, so to speak, and we continue to believe we have seen and held the object in its brilliant hues. And while Nelson recognizes the potential parallel with objects of love, she is not ready to admit that perhaps she loved her own experience of her lover, reflected back to her as an excessive, non-absorbed residue.

Nelson recounts a trip to a therapist who tells her, "*If he hadn't lied to you, he would have been a different person than he is*" (17, italics in original). Nelson recognizes that the therapist "is trying to get me to see that although I thought I loved this man very completely for exactly who he was, I was in fact blind to the man he actually was, or is" (17). Nelson dismisses the therapist's conclusion as formulaic and reductive, though the therapist perhaps unintentionally points us towards the possibility to which Nelson alludes when she discusses the systematic illusion of color—that love resembles the perception of color, turning us away in our attempts to see. While the therapist's formulation suggests that one can theoretically see—and that Nelson simply did not see—love, if it behaves like the perception of color, prevents sight, since the love object rebuffs our gaze, assuming that sight depends upon the perception of the supposed intrinsic qualities of an object. In any case, we return to a relation of disturbance and non-coherence, a lover's receding beyond one's ability to see. That condition of non-relation, or relation with the love object as an autonomous other who exceeds relation, resembles the one portrayed in *The Malady of Death* much more than it resembles a textbook explanation of how lying and betrayal reveals the lover's lack of sight in regards to the "truth" of the love object.

Interestingly, Nelson offers a sort of para-narrative about her relationship with a friend who recently suffered a traumatic injury that left her paralyzed. Unlike the "prince of blue," the mythic name Nelson uses from time to time to refer to her former lover, Nelson breathes narrative life into her suffering friend, detailing the contours and hues of her friend's immobile, yet terribly painful, body. Nelson's friend explains that when the nerve pain penetrates through the many drugs meant to dull her excruciating condition, she feels a barrier between herself and the rest of the world. Nelson writes, "I imagine it as an invisible jacket of burn hovering between us" (39). Nelson's lack of access to her friend's pain forges an

in-between space, an empty jacket that Nelson can't put
on and her friend can't take off. But the imaginary establishes a relation founded upon the gulf that separates
Nelson from her friend's unrelatable experience. And
the imaginary allows for empathy, though never blurring
the difference between "real" pain and associative pain:
"I do not feel my friend's pain, but when I unintentionally cause her pain I wince as if I hurt somewhere, and
I do" (39). As Nelson suffers through her break up and
the loss of a love object who was perhaps always a myth,
throwing back her gaze in a way that created the illusion
of sight, she simultaneously suffers alongside her friend,
bonded by the ever-present awareness of a distance that
prevents sight, knowledge, apprehension. That second
form of suffering takes loss and difference as foundation,
distinguishing it from the first, where loss results from a
belief in or a hoped-for union. It is what Blanchot calls
the "relation of a third kind" in *The Infinite Conversation*
and describes, as noted above, as a type of relation that
does not aim for unification (Blanchot 66).

Despite, or perhaps because of, the unbridgeable distance that separates Nelson from her friend's experience,
Nelson senses that she *sees* her friend. She refers to herself
as a "witness" to her friend and writes: "in watching her,
sitting with her, helping her, weeping with her, touching
her, and talking with her, I have seen the bright pith of
her soul. I cannot tell you what it looks like, exactly,
but I can say I have seen it" (88-89). This moment in
Nelson's text creates an interesting parallel with the final
sexual encounter of the man and the woman in *The*

Malady of Death, where he sees "the dark night" (50).
Like Duras, Nelson describes a situation that pairs sight
with invisibility. Nelson affirms that she has seen her
friend's soul, that her gaze has not been turned away, at
the same time that she qualifies that affirmation with an
equally important statement that she can't say what she
has seen—just that she *has* seen. While we might understand that Nelson is simply admitting her inability to
put what she has seen into language—probably true—I
think it also makes sense to push it further and suggest
that she doesn't know what her friend's soul looks like.
Seeing, here, does not mean apprehension; instead, for
Nelson, it signifies the act of witnessing, experiencing
something alongside another person, and thus *seeing*,
through a sort of peripheral vision, the excessive otherness of what's not her own experience, her own body,
her own soul. The act of seeing is affirmed, without the
apprehension of an object, as is the "bright pith" of her
friend's soul, in its ungraspable excess.

In the end, Nelson writes very little about her former
lover and their relationship; alongside her meditation on
the color blue, the book focuses on grief and loss, without really developing *what* once was, and *what*, therefore,
has been lost. Nelson dedicates herself to the feeling of
distance and absence provoked by the end of relation,
and the nagging thought that maybe she only had the
impression of seeing and having a relationship with her
lover. While the "prince of blue" feels abstract and barely
visible in the text in some ways, he serves an important
role in the narrative structure of the text, as interlocutor

or recipient—the "you" sometimes addressed in the text. Unlike what we saw in *The Malady of Death*, which explicitly and regularly engages a second-person perspective, the "you" of *Bluets* likely strikes us when it emerges, since most of the fragments address no one in particular, inviting us to imagine ourselves as privileged recipients of what sometimes feels like a confession-style collection of narrative and meditative pieces—or, at the least, an intimate portrayal of an internal scuffling with one's suffering and self, regardless of whether or not our presence as readers is taken into consideration. In that way, the "you" in *Bluets* displaces us as readers, but I would argue that that displacement feels central in *The Malady of Death* and sort of peripheral in *Bluets*—mostly because the address of the former lover, the "you," speaks to the absence of the lover more than it has anything to do with us, as readers.

Nelson refers to the way Leonard Cohen ends one of his songs, writing, "[…] I have always loved its final line—'Sincerely, L. Cohen'—as it makes me feel less alone in composing almost everything I write as a letter. I would even go so far as to say that I do not know how to compose otherwise, which makes writing in a prism of solitude, as I am here, a somewhat novel and painful experiment" (Nelson 41). Nelson addresses *Bluets* to her former lover, sometimes indirectly and sometimes directly, and we can imagine the text, in broad terms, as a letter to him. But Nelson's text hardly feels epistolary—perhaps mostly because there is no sense of exchange either within or hypothetically beyond the confines of the text. Nelson's "prism of solitude" might refer to the fact that the break-up has left her alone. In an interview in *The Rumpus*, Nelson notes that *Bluets* concerns "grappling with one's relation to oneself, which the painful absence of a beloved can make alarmingly possible." That grappling is certainly emphasized by the sense that she's writing a letter to no one, despite the "you" she addresses. She remembers an earlier time she wrote to her former lover: "[...] I felt no romance when you told me you carried my last letter with you, everywhere you went, for months on end, unopened" (71). While we could speculate why the former lover carried the letter around without opening it, none of it matters to Nelson, since, she explains, "I wrote it because I had something to say to you" (71). Writing, here, would seem to serve the purpose of closing the gap, to say something and to be heard. But we see how Nelson's attempts to communicate parallel her attempts to see, to understand, to love. While she apparently continues to write as if writing a letter, *Bluets* does not depend upon the willingness of a particular recipient to receive it; and it does not depend upon the sort of communication that might overcome distance. Nelson's writing speaks the distance, even if she would rather it didn't: "I want you to know, if you ever read this, there was a time when I would rather have had you by my side than any of these words; I would rather have had you by my side than all of the blue in the world" (95). She identifies her book as one of longing; her words as a poor substitute for the warm body of her lover. And, yet, the words inscribe the distance necessarily in-between Nelson and her lover—both during and after their relationship. Writing operates as a letter to no one, affirming the impossibility of relation and perhaps also the possibility of non-relation.

Lydia Davis's *The End of the Story*

While Nelson structures *Bluets* as a series of Pascalian
meditations and as a letter to someone who probably
won't read it, Lydia Davis focuses on the novel form in
The End of the Story as part of a sort of self-referential
game in which she manages to make a novel about the
novel she finds it impossible to write. Like *Bluets*, we can
see Davis's novel as an enactment of the man's attempt
to tell his story at the bar in *The Malady of Death*. In
the case of *The End of the Story*, Davis takes a recent
break-up as subject matter, although the reader usually
feels a couple steps removed from that subject, since the
bulk of Davis's novel concerns the writing process and
the narrator's struggle to craft a narrative out of faulty
memories of a relationship with a man whom she perhaps never really knew. Davis's narrator started writing
that novel before the dissolution of the relationship, and
writing her lover as a sort of character perhaps before
even conceiving of the novel. In other words, Davis's
narrator writes the relationship not in response to its
loss or failure, but as a means of crafting it while it's
happening. That's a little different from what we saw in
Bluets and *The Malady of Death*, where writing, or storytelling, comes retrospectively. In Davis's novel, writing
exists, from the start, in between the narrator and her
lover, and becomes a means of relating, of establishing
relation. Writing inscribes distance at the heart of the
relationship and the story of that relationship.

When the narrator of *The End of the Story* begins to
detail her relationship history with her lover, she notes
that she still didn't know his name several days after
they met. The man's initial strangeness and anonymity allowed the narrator to begin filling in his character
before he had a more concrete reality in her life. She
describes a dream she had about the man before knowing his name or reading his work. In the dream, the narrator finds a short piece of his writing, and the sheet of
paper has her own name and address on it. After reading
the passage on the sheet of paper, the narrator explains
that she "liked the piece and was relieved by that" (36).
Looking back on the dream now that she writes her
novel, the narrator reflects more on its significance:

> I see now that since I hadn't read anything by
> him at the time of the dream, what I was doing
> was composing something by him that I would
> like. And although this was my dream and he
> did not write what I dreamed he wrote, the
> words I remember still seem to belong to him,
> not to me. (36-37)

The dream reveals the narrator's act of composing her
lover, even as they begin to get to know one another.
The lover, as a sort of character, emerges before the narrator has identified, in the most literal sense of knowing his name, the man with whom she is developing a
relationship. The fact that the sheet of paper bears the
narrator's name, rather than the man's, reflects the narrator's authorship of his character, and the narrator's desire
that her lover fulfill a personage that has already begun

to take shape in her story. Interestingly, as the narrator explains, she starts to form his character by imagining his writing, composing a piece for him that would fit her particular idea of how she would like him to write; we have the sense that she might better identify him by writing than by knowing his name. And by the end of the passage cited above, the narrator admits that the words she composed in the dream now seem to belong to her lover, suggesting that he has or did become the character formed in her own mind—the one who takes shape through the writing of the novel.

The narrator goes on to explain that she felt shocked when she eventually did discover her lover's name—especially his last name, since it was "dense with consonants and difficult to pronounce," and thus "seemed only to belong to him" (37). But the narrator clarifies that the shock came specifically from the way that the name definitively identified the man and brought him out of the haze of anonymity. She writes:

> Knowing his name, after I had waited so many days to learn it, seemed to increase his reality. It gave him a place in the world that he had not had before, and it allowed him to belong more to the day than he had before. Until then, he had belonged to a time when I was tired and did not think as well as I did in the daytime, and did not see as well, when there was darkness on all sides of whatever light there was, and he came and went through darkness and shadow more than light. (37)

For the narrator, the man resided in darkness and obscurity, and therefore, lacking a name seemed more appropriate than having one. In addition, the man's anonymity and lack of definition allowed for his character to be written by the narrator without the limitations imposed by his reality. The narrator envisioned herself as a sort of Orphic figure, in the Blanchotian sense, descending into the depths of the night to retrieve the man she sought; like Orpheus, she sought the shadow of the man, the image of him belonging to the darkness, and felt as if she lost him once he began to appear in the light of day.[60] This again suggests that the narrator's lover began to take shape through writing, in the obscurity of that Orphic plunge into darkness, before he emerged as a speaking, breathing, identifiable person in her life. Perhaps for that reason, the narrator concludes: "But even after I knew his name, even when I had known him for weeks, I never quite lost the feeling that he was someone I had never seen in the daylight [...]" (38). All of this recalls the interactions of the man and the woman in *The Malady of Death*, and the last encounter in particular where the man penetrates the woman, seeing the impossibility of seeing, in the darkest night. And like "the prince of blue" in *Bluets*, the narrator's lover becomes mythic, in the sense that he never really emerges as a figure the reader (or the narrator) feels like she or he knows or sees in any detail. In both cases, the male lover is the subject of the narrative at the same time that he is not present; he generates narrative even as he escapes it.

Davis's novel largely concerns itself with the effort to order and make coherent the narrator's experiences with her lover. Joshua Cohen illuminates this aspect of Davis's novel in his article, "Reflexive Incomprehension: On Lydia Davis": "The novel anatomizes an affair in the light of its end, and is [...] concerned with the impossible struggle to order and shape the loss which conditions it" (510). Davis's narrator recognizes the impossibility of making narrative sense of her relationship and its failure, often with the self-deprecating tone we imagine in the man's story at the end of *The Malady of Death*. Both the man and Davis's narrator recognize the futility of constructing a narrative about an experience that escapes the demands of narrative; and yet each proceeds to tell that tale, aware of the impossibility of the gesture. In the most explicitly metafictional moments of *The End of the Story*, the narrator discusses her efforts to make narrative sense out of her experience and her various realizations about the process of translating her affair into writing. She explains:

> When I first starting working on the novel, I thought I had to keep very close to the facts about certain things, including his life, as though the point of the book would be lost if something like the Indian drums were changed and he were to play another musical instrument instead. Because I had wanted to write these things for so long, I thought I had to tell the truth about them. But the surprising thing was that after I had written them the

way they were, I found I could change them
or take them out, as though by writing them
once, I had satisfied whatever it was I had to
satisfy. (Davis 50)

The narrator describes her faithfulness to the details of
her experience and her recollection of her lover. If the
"point of the book" to which she refers here comes down
to translating her relationship with the man into a novel,
then it would make sense to provide accurate information to the extent that she can. In addition, the narrator suggests a sort of desire to purge her experience—
to replace old blue things with new blue things—and
maybe even to try to make sense of it *through* narrative. Yet, the narrator realizes that "truth-telling" might
not dictate the writing process—at least not in the way
she thought. She discovers that an initial act of writing the facts as they were seems to satisfy the demand
of "truth-telling," even if she proceeds to change those
details at a later time. The narrator can announce the
"death" of the events and details of her life with her
lover once she commits them to writing—a sort of writing that frees her to write, constructing her experiences
without the burdensome obligation to supposed facts.

That freedom, however, reveals itself as problematic in
a couple different ways. As Christopher Knight astutely
observes in his essay on *The End of the Story*, the narrator, while still in a relationship with her lover, worries
that perhaps her lover and her writing of her lover can't
exist at the same time, and that wielding the pen, so
to speak, can have drastic consequences. The narrator

explains that she filled notebooks with observations and reflections about her lover, to the extent that her writing started to replace the "reality" of her lover, to "drain him of his substance" (Davis 196). Knight notes: "if the narrator is truly participant in the creation of the past, a new worry will necessarily arise: that rather than recovering her lover from the clutches of the past, she might in fact be contributing to his erasure" (212). This represents another instance where the narrator recognizes that she has manufactured, through writing, her lover and her relation to him, not just retrospectively, but also in the midst of their engagement with one another. The act of writing seems to turn the narrator's lover into a sort of ghost, displacing him and putting into question any attempt to capture their relation through writing. Returning to Knight, he remarks, "the narrator's relation with him increasingly starts to look like a relation with herself" (212). Writing here becomes a means of erasing the man and the narrator's relation to the man, turning instead in on itself and on the narrator's own struggle to *relate*, outside of herself, through writing, with the world. This perhaps evokes the "prism of solitude" described by Nelson in *Bluets*.

The narrator's language, even when demonstrating an extreme faithfulness to the facts, seems to satisfy the truth on the one hand while completely missing it on the other. She writes:

> At times the truth seems to be enough, as long
> as I compress it and rearrange it a little. At
> other times it does not seem to be enough,

but I'm not willing to invent very much. Most
things are kept as they were. Maybe I can't
think what to put in place of truth. Maybe I
just have a poor imagination. (50)

The narrator discusses trying to "write it almost without thinking about it," perhaps seeking a hypothetical
process where the writing does not get in the way of a
straightforward communication of events and details
(50). Yet, even if she manages this—with a minimal
amount of compression and rearrangement—it does not
always satisfy or capture the experience of her relationship with her lover, or perhaps the demands of the narrative. Maggie Nelson reflects on a similar problem in
The Red Parts, a mixed-genre work in which she recounts
the 2004 trial of a man accused of murdering her aunt
in 1969. Nelson writes:

I know what I want is impossible. If I can
make my language flat enough, exact enough,
if I can rinse each sentence clean enough, like
washing a stone over and over again in river
water, if I can find the right perch or crevice
from which to record everything, if I can give
myself enough white space, maybe I could do
it. I could tell you this story while walking out
of this story. I could—it all could—just disappear. (157)

Like Davis's narrator, Nelson expresses the desire to
write without writing, in a sense. Yet, they both end up
in the same place: acutely aware that writing can't just
get out of the way or make itself transparent. Nelson

admits that writing has not been revelatory for her; and
that she can't vanish from the site of her writing. In the
case of *The End of the Story*, the narrator does not understand why relating the sparest "truth" of her lover and
their relationship seems to miss the mark, nor does she
know why she also remains unable to substitute for the
truth something more satisfying. Something eludes the
narrator, regardless of her efforts to ground the narrative in facts; it's not so much that the facts are incorrect,
but that the truth does not always reveal the truth, and
that any fabrication only emphasizes the impossibility
of writing the narrative. In some sense, any translation
of the narrator's relationship with her lover into writing
inevitably ends in mistranslation—a sort of mistranslation, or miscommunication, inscribed in the relationship
itself and played out in the act of writing. While Davis's
novel certainly explores at length the question implicitly
posited at the end of *The Malady of Death*—why is it that
such stories are impossible to tell, and maybe even experience, in a coherent way?—really it can only flesh out
the sense of impossibility and the confusion over what
remains so elusive.

As the narrator works on her novel, she simultaneously engages in her practice as a translator. Cohen
develops in his essay the way that Davis's work, including *The End of the Story*, plays on the issue of non-trans-
missibility—"what *eludes* communication" in the act of
translation, rather than what translation manages to
bring to light (503). Translation here refers to Davis's,
and sometimes her narrators', profession as a translator

of French literature and also to a more general sense of translation, which would include the way that a writer might attempt to organize and communicate an experience through narrative. As noted above, *The End of the Story* certainly reflects on the complexities of the narrator's efforts to translate her relationship with her lover into narrative and demonstrates various reasons why such a project remains more or less futile if we measure it by a standard of transmissibility. At the same time, it's important to note that translating not only serves a functional role in the narrator's life, but also manages to ground her in ways that novel writing cannot. After breaking up with her lover, the narrator describes the way that translation sometimes helps her to cope:

> A good kind of work to do was translation, and I had a short novel I was supposed to be translating. [...] It was a kind of work I could almost always do, in fact I worked better when I was unhappy, because when I was happy or excited, my mind would wander almost immediately. The more unhappy I was, the more I concentrated on those foreign words there on the page in a strange construction, a problem to solve, just hard enough to keep me busy [...]. (158)

While the narrator confesses that not all translation problems lead to a satisfying solution, she appears to take solace in the way a foreign text feels like a solvable puzzle. She is drawn to the "dry, precise voices of the editors of the dictionary offering definitions of the words [she] look[s] up," which helps her both to solve the puzzle and to distract her from the unhappiness of her break-up. The original text from which the narrator works has a material reality, and the arrangement and manipulation of its parts into a new language perhaps feels more approachable than, say, making sense of a recently dissolved relationship or attempting to communicate the experience of that relationship in a novel. On the one hand, as Cohen suggests, all of those issues—literal translating, "making sense," and writing—parallel one another and represent different kinds of translation; on the other, though, the narrator can approach her professional translation projects as a form of problem-solving—whether the solution addresses the practical need for a paycheck or the writerly need for a more concrete task.

In the end though, despite the practical value of professional translation and the narrator's tendency to see it as a relatively solvable puzzle, the work of translation points to the issue of foreignness—the narrator's outsidership in both her writing and her relationship. No matter how successfully the narrator manages the problems of any given translation, the translated text always announces itself as other than the "actual" or "original" text. The substitutional, or paratextual, position of the translated text perhaps provides one explanation for why the narrator often feels dismissed by others after revealing her profession as a translator. And it also points to the sense of dismissal that plagues the narrator in the writing of her novel. In this way, the narrator's observations about translation point to her struggle to relate the experiences of her relationship, especially since, to a certain extent, she has manufactured that relation through writing. In addition, the moments of difficulty that necessarily arise—whether in translating or novel-writing—point to the same undecidability of what the "right word" actually is. As David Winters writes in *Quarterly Conversation*, "The struggle to stabilize an object (a poetic line in a foreign language; a silhouette glimpsed through a window) intensifies its instability, leaving it blurred beyond recognition." In other words, what might in some ways feel stabilizing—the deftly translated phrase—ultimately opens onto the underlying instability revealed in moments of indecision, of knowing that the "right word" is somewhere else, if anywhere.[61]

As the novel progresses—the one we are reading and the one the narrator is writing, which might or might not be the same thing—the narrator feels she must admit that the novel seems to determine itself, at least to a certain degree, as it makes demands that reveal her lack of control over how the writing proceeds. While the narrator entertains the idea of finishing the novel and considers the options for when and how it will end, she simultaneously acknowledges the lack of choices she has had during the entire process: "many parts of the story either refused to be told or demanded to be told in only one way" (191-192). Therefore, the narrator's assertion of herself as a novelist requires her to put aside her awareness of the way the novel more or less excludes her from the decision-making we might imagine characterizes the process of a novelist. Finishing the novel appears to demand a supreme act of denial—a sort of self-imposed blindness which would allow the narrator to take on the role of an empowered Author, despite the knowledge that:

> the novel had to be just this long, leave out this much, include this much, change the facts this much, have this much description, be precise here but vague there, literal here but metaphorical there, use complete sentences her but incomplete there, an ellipsis here but none there, contracted verbs here but not there, etc.
> (192)

Such a description challenges the notion of an author as *authority*, or decision-maker, since the novel seems to scoff at the narrator's attempts to get involved. The formal demands of the writing obscure and overshadow any other concerns the narrator might have when it comes to relating the "truth" of her experience with her lover, creating a sense of distance and impenetrability that paradoxically manages to capture the gap at the heart of their relation. In this way, though the narrative style of *The End of the Story* and *The Malady of Death* differ greatly, we land in a similar place: writing means forging, even performing, the space between lovers.

In order to finish the novel, the narrator needs to find a way to re-insert herself into the writing process regardless of the ways the novel excludes her. Interestingly, she approaches that challenge not through writing, but by manipulating events in her life as a means of creating closure to the novel. She recognizes that part of the problem she confronts in trying to complete the novel concerns the fact that she "did not have good answers to [her] questions" about the way the relationship ended, which creates a sort of open-endedness that prevents her from finishing the novel (198). Therefore, the narrator can attempt, in her life, to craft the end of the story of her relationship, which would offer an avenue towards the end of the novel and allow her the means to assert her authorship—regardless of the novel's resistance to her active presence in its making. And it would also provide closure to the relationship, but that comes across as a decidedly secondary concern for the narrator:

> One reason, later, I was willing to let [my former lover] move into my garage was that it would give me an end to the story. But if he asked to live there and Madeleine [the narrator's roommate at the time] refused to consider it, it would not make a very good ending, especially since I was not even the one who did the refusing. That was what happened, so I had to look for another ending. I could have invented one, but I did not want to do that. (198)

The narrator wants and needs a concrete ending to the story—one that would establish her presence and power in the writing of the novel. Yet, not only does that concrete ending elude her, but her attempts to find one also likely strike the reader as humorous and arbitrary. The narrator eschews novelistic invention at the same time as she finds herself basing life decisions on the desire to create a proper end to the story. The need to assert authorship, to make herself into a novelist, only points to her insurmountable displacement from the novel she tries to piece together, and her displacement from the relationship which was to serve as the subject of that novel. She desires to author her novel, just as she desired to author her relationship; in both cases, which continuously blur into one another and eventually become the same thing, the narrator finds herself on the outside, powerless to close the gap and take hold of something solid.

In the final pages of *The End of the Story*, we find ourselves in a bookstore with the narrator, precisely where the novel began. As she drinks a "bitter cup of tea" in the bookstore, she decides that the cup of tea will close the novel, and she also gives two reasons for that choice (230). The narrator explains, "I think one reason the cup of tea in the bookstore seems like the end of the story even though the story went on afterward is that I did stop searching for him at that point" (230). We can, of course, understand the end of the narrator's search in a variety of ways. At the level of the story, the perpetuation of the narrative depends upon the narrator's inability to let go of her lover and the possibility that there might be more to the story. After the break-up, the narrator looks for him, thinks about him, writes about him, and imagines possible narrative paths for the future. Giving up the search, from this perspective, represents the closure of the story of the relationship as a prominent narrative arc in the narrator's life. Beyond that, the narrator shifts her approach at the level of the writing of the story; rather than trying to manufacture moments that would provide the story's ending, thus asserting her command over the writing of the novel, she chooses a moment and calls it the end. When the narrator reveals that she has stopped searching for her former lover, she points to the way in which she has also stopped searching for a moment that would provide closure and meaning to her relationship with the man and to her novel. Ironically, finishing the novel perhaps requires the narrator to admit that she will never be a novelist—that writing implies searching for something that exceeds one's reach and can only end with the acceptance of defeat. In the same vein, letting go of her relationship seems to require the narrator to acknowledge that she never really had a hold, and that the impossibility of writing is the impossibility of relation. Writing relates the gap and in doing so establishes relation by way of its own impossibility.

Davis primarily focuses on the question of writing the experience of failed relation, while Duras and Nelson's works emphasize the failure itself and the way writing might respond to that failure. In all three works, the issue of "unrelatability" applies both to the nature of the relationship between lovers and to the attempt to narrate the relationship or its loss. And that issue also pushes us to consider relation in new terms, not as a matter of recovering distance and establishing intimacy, but as a matter of speaking the distance and finding relation within it. The man in *The Malady of Death*, in his laughing attempt to tell what he soon recognizes as an impossible tale, opens us to a reading of *Bluets* and *The End of the Story* where we might see failure as foundation, impossibility as a condition for what's possible. Nelson and her paralyzed friend share "an invisible jacket of burn hovering between [them]," making it impossible to relate and paradoxically providing space for a different kind of relation on the basis and acute awareness of that impossibility (Nelson 39). And Davis's narrator, in order to finish her novel, must acknowledge that she can't—that impossibility and distance lies at the heart of her novel and the relationship she describes. In the end, the "prince of blue" never appears, nor does the woman in *The Malady of Death* or the narrator's lover in *The End of the Story*; instead, writing emerges and speaks the distance inscribed in all three relationships and any attempt to understand and narrate them.

CHAPTER 5:
APPROACHING THE END
OF THE WORLD

Apocalyptic and post-apocalyptic fiction both concern themselves with the matter of ends—how one approaches an end, what particular set of circumstances manifest an end or make it imminent, and whether or not one can think beyond an end, in excess of the destruction of all possibility and potential. Of course, when it comes to that last issue, we run into the contradictory logic of the post-apocalyptic, which points to a time that surpasses the annihilation of time. In *After the End: Representations of Post-Apocalypse*, James Berger describes post-apocalyptic representation as "a paradoxical, oxymoronic discourse that measures the incommensurable and speaks the unspeakable; a discourse that impossibly straddles the boundary between before and after some event that has obliterated what went before yet defines what will come after" (19). In the end, something always comes *after*, even though that something theoretically has no foundation upon which it builds; it starts anew, initiated by an absolute rupture with what *was*. That rupture, or world-ending destruction, can be understood at multiple levels though, and does not necessarily involve the imagined complete obliteration of all earthly things— the particular possibility that takes shape in the representations of apocalypse in Jewish and early Christian texts. Apocalypse might also denote what Berger calls "an end of something, a way of life or thinking," including past atrocities that have wiped out a group of people, or, at the least, drastically changed the way that group exists in the world (5). In that way, apocalyptic representations might imagine the final acts of history as the world ceases to exist, or they might serve as a means of framing past catastrophe, thus implying the post-apocalyptic aspects of contemporary existence.

Many contemporary critics point to the intensified interest in apocalyptic and post-apocalyptic fictions in late twentieth- and early twenty-first-century literature. That interest probably reflects a number of aesthetic, socio-political, and historical concerns, including, for instance, the looming threat of nuclear war and mass-scale environmental devastation. As Lois Parkinson Zamora puts it in *Writing the Apocalypse*, "the events of recent history, whether nuclear or ecological or demographic [...] suggest all too clearly our ample capacities for self-destruction" (1). And one might tie that modern consciousness to the proliferation of literary texts in recent decades that represent apocalyptic and post-apocalyptic

scenarios, though, as Zamora and Berger both point out,
the tradition of figuring the apocalypse and its aftermath
is nothing new. Frank Kermode emphasizes that last
point, arguing that, "It seems to be a condition attaching to the exercise of thinking about the future that one
should assume one's own time to stand in an extraordinary relation to it" (94). Of course, any study of western literature and criticism since 1945 cannot ignore
the sustained inquiry into the possibility of literature,
writing, and representation after the Holocaust, based
upon the general premise that the Holocaust constituted
an end of apocalyptic proportions, where we reached a
point of absolute inexpressibility and unrepresentability.[62] Thus, as Berger points out, much apocalyptic and
post-apocalyptic writing has a relation to trauma, and
to particular historical events that are "so overwhelming as to be fundamentally unreadable" (21). From that
perspective, when it comes to apocalyptic representation, even if we construct a narrative that provides closure—thus allowing us to look at an event or situation as
complete and reflecting, as Kermode puts it, "our deep
need for intelligible Ends" (9)—the text itself remains
unreadable. And what remains, post-apocalypse or post-
trauma, bears traces of that unreadable event despite the
inability to understand or represent it. Post-apocalyptic
texts evoke a world where we can't read, despite the
hypertextuality of the space.

That said, as Zamora points out: "Apocalypse is not
merely a vision of doom: For its original audience it was,
on the contrary, a luminous vision of the fulfillment

of God's promise of justice and communal salvation"
(2). Apocalypse, as revelation, promises to illuminate
on some level—perhaps even if a momentary flash of
light ultimately reveals the impossibility of representing or expressing the world coming to its end, acting as
a sort of illumination of the absence of light. Maurice
Blanchot, when describing Orpheus's attempt to retrieve
Eurydice from Hades, describes his look back as a "light-
ening moment," as he confronts the profound darkness
that he has called forward with his song and that simultaneously casts him out (*The Space of Literature* 172).
Orpheus's journey comes to a tragic end, the end of his
world even, at the same time that he experiences, in
revelatory fashion, his inability to do, to complete, to
understand. And, in that way, the end opens onto that
which exceeds the end. For Blanchot, that's precisely
where art begins, despite its paradoxical inability to do
so. The end represents the end of constructive negativity, or the moment when we can no longer *do* or *make*
as a means of conceptualizing and comprehending the
world—bringing it to light.[63] What do we do, then,
when we can no longer do, when the world has ended,
yet we are still here? And how might one approach writing
in such a space, bearing witness to the traces of an inexpressible end and exploring the ways that life might go
on, wandering and re-purposing what has refused to end?

César Aira's *Shantytown* and Paul Auster's *In the
Country of Last Things* meditate upon those questions within settings which, in different ways, evoke a
post-apocalyptic world. At the same time, neither book

asks us to invest in a fantasy world, or a "what if"-style dystopia that serves to warn us against the potential consequences to our short-sighted, dangerous behavior. Instead, Aira and Auster's novels rely on a sort of gritty realism to portray the survivors of catastrophe who live in a world where they have to make do with leftovers, to make a life out of others' refuse. Aira depicts the setting and inhabitants of *la villa miseria*, or shantytown, in his contemporary Buenos Aires—an environment that has existed for decades, but whose growth is often attributed to economic crises in late-twentieth and early twenty-first century Argentina.[64] In some sense, the dwellers of the shantytown have already survived the apocalypse, subsisting by means of scavenging and repurposing. Though that existence appears to be unique to the *cartoneros*, Aira's novel suggests that at some point we will all have to grapple with the moment when invention runs out, when the materials dry up, when we reach and must confront the end. While Auster's *In the Country of Last Things* generally fits within the genre of post-apocalyptic fiction, he insists that "Anna Blume walks through the twentieth century," since Anna's world does not represent a dystopic future, but, rather, points to the catastrophic ends that we have already faced and continue to face (18).[65] In addition, like Aira, Auster seems interested in the daily life of those who scavenge and have to figure out a new way to navigate a world of dwindling resources. The act of survival itself, of living after the end while simultaneously finding oneself unable to reach or achieve an end, becomes the focus of Auster's novel.

César Aira's *Shantytown*

Within the first pages of *Shantytown*, the narrator introduces us to the *cartoneros* who emerge from their makeshift living space at nightfall, looking for valuable scraps in the streets:

> The expression *cardboard collectors* was a euphemism, which everyone had adopted, and it conveyed the intended meaning clearly enough (although the less delicate *scavengers* served that purpose too). Cardboard, or paper, was only one of their specialties. They also collected glass, cans, wood . . . in fact, where there is need, there is no specialization. They had to find a way to get by and they weren't going to turn up their noses, not even at the remnants of food that they found in the garbage bags. And perhaps those borderline or spoiled leftovers were, in fact, the real objective, and all the rest—cardboard, glass, wood, tin—no more than a respectable front. (4)

The use of euphemism perhaps makes it easier for everyone outside the shantytown to avoid the bleaker reality of a group of people who, as the passage suggests, above all need something to eat. The *cartoneros* live in a situation where all is lacking, and therefore they must find a way to subsist in that environment of lack, where the possibility of starvation and death lingers around every corner. The *cartoneros* keep to themselves during the daytime and only come out after everyone else returns home for the evening; in that way they have "become invisible," and participate, afterhours, in "a social recess that most people prefer to ignore" (7). As Dánisa Bonacic explains in her discussion of *Shantytown*, "the *cartoneros* do not belong to the daily rhythm of the city (the productive part of the day), and instead subsist in the spatial and temporal periphery of city life" (369).[66] In this way the *cartoneros* live in the margins—at the outer edge of the city, after the end of the day, and off the already-used materials and foods discarded by those who prefer not to see them. They survive beyond the end of the world, making nothing, yet subsisting all the same. And that the end-of-the-world existence, we begin to see, cannot be safely cordoned-off, allowing the rest of the city to maintain its attachment to firm boundaries, stable organizing structures, and plentiful resources. The novel draws attention to the ways that the world of the shantytown, and the life of the *cartoneros*, seeps into the rest of the city and points to its fundamental instability.

Interestingly, as Pablo Decock argues, Aira's description of the *cartoneros* in the opening pages of *Shantytown*, though it emphasizes the gritty, dangerous reality of their lives, also disrupts typical modes of representation by including "a series of transgressive aesthetic recuperations that completely break with the demonizing image of the violent or upset *cartoneros* found in the mass media. Instead, the narrator insists on the dignity of the *cartoneros'* work, and highlights familial relations and the solidarity between them" (412). Thus, while the novel certainly points to the alienation and marginality of the cartoneros, it also attempts to redefine the margin. In other words, it sometimes engages in social realism, but does not necessarily stop there. The existence of the cartoneros points to what Dierdra Reber describes as "tension, aggression, and violence marked by class difference, itself measured on a gradated scale of access to consumer culture (products and technology)"; and, in addition to that realist portrayal, we see Aira's literary interest in that which exceeds assimilation or incorporation into a broader, teleological system. Both aspects of Aira's portrayal of the *cartoneros* are important and worth examining. Reber's socioeconomic and geographical reading the *Shantytown* illuminates the first, and I would like to turn to some of the aesthetic questions raised in Aira's depiction of the scavenging and repurposing of objects.

In Aira's essay, "La nueva escritura," he argues that "the 'work' [is] the process of making works, without the work." He thus emphasizes the putting-together of things, often in experimental and improvisational ways, and rejects the privileging of the literary or art product as an end or site of accomplishment. Mariano García, in *Degeneraciones textuales*, sees Aira's process-based view of writing and literature in terms of *bricolage*, connecting it to Aira's fascination with Duchamp. García describes the aesthetic and process of the *bricoleur* that takes shape in a number of Aira's novels: "Through the reconstruction of an object with prior materials, ends are transformed into means: signifieds become signifiers and vice versa"

(97).[68] Though many of Aira's *bricoleur* figures in his novels are literal artists and writers—Varamo, the various narrators named "César," Rugendas in *Portrait in the Life of a Landscape Painter*—the work of the *cartoneros* in *Shantytown* takes on artistic significance because it communicates with the aesthetic of *bricolage* and the importance of process. The narrator goes to great lengths to describe the ritualized process of the *cartoneros*—when and how they appear each night, how they navigate the different avenues, how they use their carts, and what they collect. We learn that the *cartoneros* collect materials with urgency, their lives depending on it, when traversing Avenida Rivadavia and Directorio, but then they are able to "relax and rummage in a more leisurely way through the less numerous piles of trash. There [is] always something unexpected: a little piece of furniture, a mattress, a gadget or an ornament, and curious objects whose purpose could not be guessed simply by looking at them" (10). Once their needs are met, the *cartoneros* engage with the objects in a different manner, seeing an object's potential to become something else when repurposed in an inventive or interesting way. Aira does not diminish the practical issues of survival, idealizing the *cartoneros'* work by framing it as an artistic process; yet, he allows for the *cartoneros* to demonstrate a particular aesthetic approach—one that sees an already-used object as a beginning rather than an end.

The shantytown lies at one end of Calle Bonorino, "further than anyone would choose to walk," and is "strangely illuminated, almost radiant, crowned with a halo that [shines] in the fog" (13). Despite the narrow streets and darkness leading up to the shantytown, various lighting patterns identify each street, rather than signs with names, and make visible the outer edges of the space. From that position, one can get a sense of the layout of the streets in the shantytown: "all the streets (if you could call those alleyways 'streets') led inward and were never intersected by others running crossways"; and "[the streets] ran off at an angle of forty-five degrees, all in the same direction (to the right, for someone facing inward). Which meant that none of them led to the center, or came out anywhere" (26, 28-9). Clearly, the shantytown's spatial (dis)organization prevents easy navigation and even suggests impenetrability—at least for one who doesn't already know the path and how to interpret the lighting patterns. Bonacic, applying Richard Young's discussion of mapping in Aira's novel *El sueño*, argues that the complex and seemingly illogical spatial layout of the shantytown demonstrates the "social dimension of urban spaces"—often, characteristics that one wouldn't find on a map but that organize the space for those who live in it (368). In the case of the shantytown, as Bonacic points out, the unreadability of the space protects it from outside dangers. That makes sense, although I think Aira's novel also points to the possibility that the shantytown more radically resists logic and organization, or, at the least, points to the temporality of any system that makes the space manageable. Clearly, the inhabitants of the shantytown need ways of navigating the space, but, as we later discover, they routinely swap the lighting patterns that identify the streets, disrupting any stable relation between the signifier and what it names. And, by the very end of the novel, the narrator wonders if the shantytown as a whole might have the magical ability to turn like a wheel, in order to turn away any aggressor who thinks he has figured it out: "But did that mean that the shantytown could spin? Would that be possible?" (161).[69]

The protagonist of the novel, Maxi, respects the boundaries of the shantytown, curious about the circular layers of make-shift dwellings, but as an outsider, not wanting to pose a threat in any way. Maxi, a young, middle-class man with little professional ambition or intellectual aptitude, occupies himself by helping the *cartoneros* to haul their loads of scavenged goods out of the "city proper" and back to the shantytown. Unlike the scavengers, Maxi does not himself live off the excess of others in order to piece together the materials needed to survive; instead, at least in terms of class, he represents the group who produces the excess. Yet, something compels Maxi to participate in the life of the *cartoneros*, at a moment when he feels especially alienated and uninspired by the opportunities of his own middle-class life: "His studies had languished in a slow but steady and definitive way. Looking to the future both he and his parents had come to accept that he'd never go back to being a student: he wasn't cut out for it; there was no point" (5). To be clear, Maxi encounters the *cartoneros* out of coincidence, without any intention or motivation; and, furthermore, he gives the matter little thought once he begins helping: "In any case, Maxi didn't ask himself why they were doing what they did. [...] He didn't even ask himself why he was doing what *he* did. He did it because he could, because he felt like it, because it gave his evening walk a purpose" (4). Maxi sort of falls into his heroism—not as a willful, assertive subject deliberately shaping his own life and the lives of others, but as a passive, often aloof guy with little to do.

Regardless, Maxi clearly does good in the world, and he undermines rigid class structures that determine "insiders" and "outsiders," literally transgressing geographical boundaries demarcating the two. Maxi does enjoy the feeling that the *cartoneros* come to trust him, and that his massive size can be put to use. At the same time, he seems relatively unaware of his own altruism and feels grateful to have some degree of access to a space from which others are excluded: "He felt privileged, but he didn't know why. [...] Outsiders never went there" (25). Maxi remains aware of the "squalor and desperation" within the shantytown, but that does not prevent him from observing its "halo that [shines] in the fog" (14, 13). Maxi seems to recognize that the shantytown can contain both worlds at once—lack and abundance, dark and light. Even though Maxi has some degree of access and insight into the shantytown, "his own incursions [are] limited to the outer rim [...] always within sight of the perimeter" (29). In some sense, Maxi finds himself at the edge of the edge, coming up against the limit between middle-class neighborhood and shantytown, between life and after-life. As a transporter of materials from one space to another, Maxi witnesses the transformation of trash into a means of survival, and he confronts the question of how one lives in a state of depletion, exhaustion, and lack. Again, while Maxi does not seem to reflect on broader questions of, say, socioeconomic inequity, he participates in the economy of recycling that allows the *cartoneros* to survive beyond the exhaustion of resources and to illuminate their shantytown with pirated electricity.

Inspector Cabezas, on the other hand, sees the shantytown as a haven for selling drugs and committing crimes, and wants to figure out what role Maxi plays in the drug ring responsible for a string of violent events. Of course, Maxi has nothing to do with that violence, but Cabezas feels convinced that there must be a rational explanation for the strange behavior of the young man, whom he sees coming in and out of the shantytown every night. The narrator identifies Maxi and Cabezas as "different in every way"—not just in terms of age and life experience, but also in terms of the way they move in the world, navigating and trying to make sense of the spaces they occupy (33). Maxi wanders thoughtlessly and whimsically, doing what feels right to him at any given moment. "The inspector's enterprise, by contrast, resemble[s] the deciphering of a structure" (33). The narrator links Cabezas's approach and mindset to something one would see in a detective fiction—working from the assumption that everything *means*, and it means in relation to everything else, as a part of a broader narrative. We read:

As soon as Cabezas began to take an interest
in Maxi's comings and goings, they constituted
a case in his mind. Which meant that nothing could be left unexplained, and each explanation would have to be linked to others, to
form a system, which in turn would have to be
connected to other systems, until the whole of
society was covered. (33)

While Maxi's behavior understandably strikes the
inspector as strange, and even potentially sketchy, the
irony, for the reader, immediately comes forward—since
we have already encountered Maxi and know that his
activities are improvisational and almost comically inno-
cent. Furthermore, Cabezas, in confronting behavior
that seems inexplicable, resorts to the deliberate impo-
sition of meaning—"He had to create an explanation
out of nothing, as it were" (34).

Cabezas's investigative approach to the criminal activities taking place at the outer edges of the shantytown,
and to Maxi's supposed involvement with those activities, seeks to manifest a closed system that incorporates
all of the players and events supposedly associated with
the "case." The narrator discusses Cabezas's inability to
perceive anything outside of his manufactured understanding of a situation:

He was blinkered: he couldn't see beyond the
structure and its realization. This limitation
had worked for him so far, and he had come
to believe that it always would. His mistake
was thinking that a battle is fought at a single

point in space. That is not the case. A battle
always covers a large area, and none of the participants can take it in at a glance, not even
retrospectively. Nobody can grasp the whole,
mainly because in reality there is no whole to
be grasped. (47)

Cabezas's insistence upon arriving at an overarching
understanding that integrates all of the details into a
broad system or structure ultimately blinds him to the
multiplicity of "cases" and circumstances, often unrelated, traveling in different directions. For Cabezas,
Maxi's participation in the *cartoneros'* recovery of discarded materials *must* mean something in relation to the
drug ring—even though, as the reader knows, those two
things really have nothing to do with one another outside of the relation that Cabezas manufactures. Maxi's
story and the story of Cabezas's investigation exist as
two separate trajectories in Aira's novel, only crossing
paths as a result of Cabezas's insistence on weaving them
together. After all, Maxi presumably never even knows
that he ends up as a central figure in Cabezas's interpretation of the workings of the drug ring. Yet, Aira's novel follows Cabezas on his course, making it a sort of detective
fiction, even if the reader remains aware that the detective's attempt to understand Maxi's role amounts to trying
to shove a puzzle piece into a spot where it doesn't belong.
While Cabezas's investigation propels the story forward
and unravels some aspects of the mysteries we encounter,
from the point he enters the text, his approach, which
insists on singularity and wholeness, consistently fails to

explain what is actually going on—a failure that points to the impossibility of a revelatory interpretation, at the level of detective and reader, that makes sense of everything as it comes to a close.

Interestingly, Cabezas, here, emerges as a sort of *bricoleur*, collecting information and observations, and piecing them together in inventive ways. Anything that remains excess to his system of understanding—those elements that perhaps feel related to the case but that actually have nothing to do with it—can be accommodated, with a bit of ingenuity and imagination. Similar to the *cartoneros*, Cabezas exists in his world by way of repurposing and redefining, in his case, people and events for the greater purpose of producing a unified narrative that doesn't leave any loose threads. Unlike the *cartoneros*, though, Cabezas lacks awareness of his own *bricolage*, presumably convincing himself that the narrative he has pieced together, "by pressing on and improvising," is indeed true, and that he has simply facilitated the revelation of the truth (34). As a detective, theoretically he *uncovers* rather than *makes*, engaged in a teleological quest towards a moment of total illumination. Aira plays with that end-oriented approach by "blowing up" the end of the investigation and the novel—manifesting a kind of apocalyptic scenario where the various narrative trajectories violently confront one another, largely as a result of Cabezas's manipulations. Yet, throughout the novel, Cabezas remains unaware that "the effects of his Machiavellian initiative [are] spreading like the proverbial wildfire" (47).

Returning to Maxi with Cabezas in mind, it seems that his lack of specific motivation, his willingness to experience the world from moment to moment and to act on his instincts, makes him open to the possibilities that surround him. Unlike Cabezas, Maxi has no interest in coming up with a system of understanding, or creating a narrative that would assign meaning to the world he inhabits. After falling into the rhythm of nightly excursions with the *cartoneros*, Maxi begins to give the matter some thought:

> [...] Maxi was contemplating something . . . something without a name. Action. Or silence. But no, it really didn't have a name. And then, in the depths of the inexpressible, the work that he had invented began like a melody. Was it work? A service? A way to give meaning to his strength and free time? Or was it nothing at all? (57).

Here, Maxi muses about the possibility of defining his activities, generally concluding that whatever he has been doing doesn't have a name, or even an explicit purpose. He thinks of it as "essentially, a spontaneous, unpremeditated act, almost an improvisation; in any case, not planned ahead, and impossible to integrate into a program" (57). Maxi's conceptualization of his activity, which he later frames as simultaneously improvisational and carefully deliberate, mirrors Aira's conceptualization of writing as process, as the unfolding of the continuous work (85). Aira's description in interviews of the fact that he doesn't revise his work, simply letting the process carry on in a forward movement, resembles Maxi's improvisations—of the moment, but not careless or thoughtless.[70] Even when Maxi does act in a more deliberate way, plotting to bring two shanty-town residents together and imagining the possibility of a romance, he admits, "There was no predicting what would happen later on, but they might fall in love, why not? Anything was possible" (84). Regardless, Maxi feels inspired by his work, "walking on air," and enjoying the sense of possibility, whether or not his plans succeed (84). After all, he muses, "results [are] secondary. The masterpiece [comes] first" (84). Maxi models the combination of whimsy and intention that, for Aira, guides the artistic process. While Maxi, like the *cartoneros*, is not an artist-figure in any literal way, he demonstrates an aesthetic approach to the world. That approach emphasizes the continual unfolding of the work, which necessarily exceeds efforts to contain, integrate, or plan. It is propelled forward by possibility. In that way, Maxi's work opposes what we saw with Cabezas, whose teleological approach seeks to bring the work to its end, tying all of the parts together in an effort to create a closed system.

Despite Cabezas's insistence upon the singularity of meaning within an integrated, end-oriented system, he does deliberately misidentify himself, taking on the guise and story of a man with his same name in order to trick Maxi's sister into trusting him. In other words, Cabezas muddies his own identity, playing with the propensity of language to mis-name and obscure—in this case because one name designates two very different people, therefore exceeding a singular, stable relation between signifier and signified. He gives Vanessa, Maxi's sister, a newspaper clipping written by the other Cabezas: "When he reckoned that she had reached the end, he pointed to the sender's name, and with his other hand held out his identity card, so that she could see the names were the same" (37-8). By claiming authorship over the clipping, Cabezas hopes he can get information about Maxi and the shantytown, not considering the possibility that he might not be able to control the game of doubling he has initiated. Of course, Cabezas later realizes that his purposeful misidentification of himself has spilled over into the media, producing a narrative about a corrupt policeman who seeks vengeance for the murder of his daughter, thus conflating the two men named "Ignacio Cabezas." The narrator notes, "If he'd been a better sport, he might have admitted that he had it coming because he was the one who'd started the confusion. But he wasn't in the mood for subtleties like that" (138-9). Cabezas watches the images flash across the television screen, wondering how to move forward when he has lost control of the narrative: "He looked on helplessly as the images followed one another, and the error reinforced itself and spread. He began to wonder how far it could go. Could it go all the way round and come back to bite the tail of the truth from which it had departed?" (139). While Cabezas still hopes that the "truth" will ultimately emerge, he recognizes that a misunderstanding sometimes becomes a sort of "truth," once it spreads and multiplies: "There was no point in trying to set the record straight" (139). Of course, Cabezas himself has perpetuated the spread of misinformation—not only because he misrepresents his own identity, but also because he misunderstands the relation (or non-relation) of the components of the case he investigates, creating a false narrative that has real-world consequences within the novel.

Cabezas's suspicion of Maxi, and his manipulation of the "facts," initiates a series of events that culminates in chaos, violence, and supernatural torrential rain and flooding—an end-of-the-world scenario. Cabezas himself, for most of the novel portraying the familiar type of the washed-up cop who feels displaced and exhausted, finds renewal in his decision to embrace absolute darkness and corruption: "There was one path left, and only one: evil" (114). Cabezas transforms from the role of the dirty cop into a devil-figure in the unfolding apocalypse:

> Even if confined to the meanest of forms, even if he was nothing more than a stray bundle of policeman's atoms, he could still channel the supreme powers of evil and create a new universe, a new city for himself, the hidden city, of which he would be kind and god.
>
> The heavens were bursting, their lights spinning crazily, the divine gas igniting in icy flames as the black throats let out their roars, which were echoed by a groan of exaltation exploding from the lips of Ignacio Cabezas. (115)

That description demonstrates the way that Aira's novel, as it comes to its conclusion, dramatizes with apocalyptic imagery the act of coming to an end—and, one could argue, uses hyperbole to draw attention to the artifice, and maybe even violence, of closure. Cabezas becomes evil incarnate, and, subsequently, "in a paroxysm of thunder and lightning, the rain [comes] crashing down" (118). Both Decock and Sandra Contreras note the way that many Airan novels accelerate towards catastrophe, expressing, as Contreras writes an *"urgency to arrive at the end"* (181, emphasis in original).[71] Decock argues that in *Shantytown*, Aira plays with "stereotypes of spectacle, acceleration, violence, and apocalypse," further emphasized by the media's voracious pursuit of footage and propensity for sensationalism (415). For Decock, the ludic, over-the-top ending points to Aira's broader writing project, and, as I discussed above, his aesthetic interest in a continually unfolding writing process—a perspective that, in a sense, suggests the arbitrariness of any end. Of course, a book, as a material object, will presumably need to end, and thus necessarily betrays the work.[72] Therefore, why not blow up the end, creating a sort of rupture that forces the reader to confront the problems of textual closure? Contreras also points out that Aira's tendency to manifest a sense of apocalypse at the end of his novels communicates with the broader question of how one gets to the end and still leaves space for more writing. According to Contreras, Aira manages to emphasize the end through catastrophe and trauma and also to present it as contingent, self-conscious, and aware of its shortcomings, since the failed novel is "the best method for continuing to write" (182).

The last chapters of the novel, with their end-of-the-world imagery, also circle back to the beginning, since the first several chapters detail the life of the *cartoneros*, who, in a sense, live a post-apocalyptic existence—rummaging for scraps and finding ways to survive despite the exhaustion of resources. Though the novel shifts its attention from the *cartoneros* to the unfolding plot of Cabezas's investigation, the edges of the shantytown remain important as a site where much of the action takes place, and the *cartoneros* ultimately play a central role in that plotline, since they demonstrate a set of skills that allows Maxi to elude the grasp of the murderous Cabezas. The *cartoneros* know how to manage—and to take advantage of—a continually shifting, temporary space, piecing together their existence day by day in an environment where nothing is stable. As *bricoleurs*, the *cartoneros* use their collected materials to fashion a cube-shaped shack for Maxi, which eventually serves as his hiding place from Cabezas: "It was one of a million similar cubes, juxtaposed with or without gaps, sometimes crammed together in rows or bunches, haphazardly arranged in a vast collective improvisation" (156). The narrator describes a complex scene of dwellings, passageways, and electric lines—a scene that defies rational thought and exceeds comprehension: "The electricity cables, as numerous and chaotic as the buildings they connected, reinforced the shantytown's allegiance to the world of dreams" (156). As a space that signifies life after or outside of life, the shantytown refuses incorporation into a system, existing after the end, or off the edge, of the world.

Cabezas eventually figures out the way that the *cartoneros* use temporary lighting patterns to identify streets, and, according to the detective, communicate with "buyers already circling the shantytown" where they can purchase drugs (143). While it seems that Cabezas's interpretation is generally correct, his belief that he has discovered a "complete and convincing solution to the enigma that [has] revisited him for years" again points to his desire to see a system as a self-contained whole, failing to recognize the aspects of the situation that might escape such an over-arching perspective (142). The failure makes itself apparent when he puts his theory to the test, thinking he has correctly pieced together the entire puzzle, ready to expose the participants of the drug ring in a massive bust:

> Cabezas hurled himself at the door, and the impact burst it wide open. He couldn't believe his eyes. Inside there was . . . simply nothing. There was no room. It was a door in a façade, behind which stretched a desolate scene full of rain, with other shacks, near and far, illuminated by the lightning. It was similar and different at the same time: outside, but also inside. (160)

At the moment of revelation, Cabezas confronts the impossibility of revelation, opening a door that leads nowhere. The narrator tells us that Cabezas doesn't have the opportunity to try to figure out where his calculations went astray, as the judge kills him moments after he opens the door. But even the narrator has little explanation for the last-minute shifting of the lighting patterns, wondering if the shantytown might be able to spin—if it has "only ever existed as an endless rotation" (161). We get no answer to those musings.

Regardless, the judge and media feel confident that the case is closed: "What we have seen here is the demise of one of the most dangerous criminals to have threatened our national security in recent years" (162). In other words, Cabezas did it—he got caught up in drugs, went down a path of corruption and violence, and eventually killed the judge's son, an informant who went undercover as "the Pastor." And the novel itself ends with that interpretation—from the mouth of the judge, and, presumably, representing the "official" version of the events that took place. Thus the detective plot comes to its close; yet that closure feels performative and contingent, especially since we know that the interpretation of events depends on certain misunderstandings or gaps in information. For example, as we saw above, everyone believes that there is one Ignacio Cabezas, and the narrative about what he did derives from the compounding of two individuals into one. They assign inaccurate motivations to Cabezas and know nothing of his pursuit of Maxi or involvement of Jessica and Vanessa. Regardless, the judge feels completely satisfied that she has solved the case and caught the guilty man, and she delivers a closing speech on the threat of seeking "the mother"—a term she uses to describe the drug "proxidine," and the search for meaning and truth by way of that drug. She criticizes Cabezas for choosing "the infernal path of artificial contiguity," which presumably refers to proxidine's reputation for making everything feel closer—proximate—and within reach (162, 112-3). The judge insists that "Everyone is drawn to her," to reaching "the mother," though the pursuit of the mother is a "slippery slope," and "the trajectory literally infinite" (162). In other words, the judge emphasizes the futility and open-endedness of the drug user's search for closeness, meaning, fulfillment, transcendence; that search has a single, yet unending, trajectory—in contrast, say, to a pursuit that comes to a tidy close.

To be clear, it's not that the judge criticizes the pursuit of truth or contiguity; after all, her work, and the closure she achieves at the end of this particular case, relies on establishing the proximity, or inter-relationality, of all of the elements within a system, and thus revealing the truth. She simply faults those who try to get to "the mother" artificially and suggests that they will find themselves chasing after something that will always remain out of reach. Ironically though, the judge's closing of the case clearly points to its own artifice; the revelation of truth misses its mark, and the reader knows this, even if most or all of the characters within the narrative do not. We can't help but conclude that, like the drug user seeking "the mother" with proxidine, we confront the ability of the text, as it comes to a close, to morph, "taking on every conceivable form, in an incoherent and irresponsible succession," endlessly delaying closure (162).

Paul Auster's *In the Country of Last Things*

Many critics have noted the way Auster's country of last things evokes World War II and the Holocaust, including the pervasive imagery of piled-up bodies and detailed explanations of the systems that govern matters like corpse collection and disposal. Josh Cohen, in particular, links Auster's novel to Edmond Jabès's *The Book of Questions* and Maurice Blanchot's *The Writing of Disaster*, drawing attention to the way all three writers explore the question of ends and endlessness, or the impossibility of reaching the end, even when encountering what seems to be the very end of things. While Cohen, in his insightful comparative analysis, addresses that topic in relation to the Holocaust, and looks broadly at Auster's oeuvre, I would like to develop a more detailed reading of the matter of ends and endlessness in *In the Country of Last Things*, focusing on the issue of survival—a sort of living after the end, which of course implies the impossibility of coming to the end. The country that Anna describes has all but totally collapsed, creating an atmosphere of desperation, chaos, and fear. The unstable, authoritarian government, along with thieves and murderers, present a constant threat, beyond the primary, daily concerns of staying warm and having something to eat. As Anna writes, "Life as we know it has ended, and yet no one is able to grasp what has taken place" (20). The country, which resembles no country Anna has ever known, makes no sense; and no amount of writing will help Anna to make sense of it—to the recipient of the letter or to herself. No revelation will occur; the end has already come, and now, it seems, she can simply provide an account of her attempt to continue living.

The first section of Anna's letter involves an extended description of the ways in which the inhabitants of the country navigate the continually evolving space that they occupy, and the various rules and systems that govern and restrict their navigation. Anna opens her letter by referring to the "last things"—last because, "a house is there one day, and the next day is gone. A street you walked down yesterday is no longer there today" (1). Though "life as we know it has ended," the remaining structures and people all continue to disappear as well, making the end feel like a repeated occurrence that never actually reaches a terminus (20). As a result of this constantly changing, unpredictable environment where the world slowly vanishes before one's eyes, it becomes impossible to have a foothold: "Bit by bit, the city robs you of certainty. There can never be any fixed path, and you can survive only if nothing is necessary to you. Without warning, you must be able to change, to drop what you are doing, to reverse" (6). The world looks different every day, though, generally speaking, each day represents a diminishment of resources and opportunities. According to Anna, survival requires an understanding that one cannot make plans or have expectations based upon a situation or dynamic that was true yesterday, since past experience has little bearing

on whether or not something will be true today. She
explains, "The essential thing is not to become inured.
For habits are deadly. Even if it is for the hundredth
time, you must encounter each thing as if you have
never known it before" (7). In an environment of endings, of last things, a person never knows the world she
or he attempts to navigate; paradoxically, as the world
dies, it is continually renewed, often as a grimmer, more
desolate version of itself.

Despite the bleakness of the setting, Auster's novel
draws our attention to the ingenuity of the people who
manage to stay alive, particularly Anna. The deterioration
of the country forces the inhabitants to make a life out of
less and less, until nothing remains. And for Anna, this
situation poses an intriguing question: "to see what happens when there is nothing, and whether or not we will
survive that too" (29). Anna and the other inhabitants
must depend upon recycling and re-invention, rather
than the modes of production, consumption, and disposal that typified life before the collapse. Given the
general direction of things, at some point, the country
will face a complete exhaustion of resources, yet based
on what she has seen, Anna allows for the possibility
the people might still survive nothingness. She writes:

> Utter despair can exist side by side with the
> most dazzling invention; entropy and efflo-
> rescence merge. Because there is so little left,
> almost nothing gets thrown out anymore, and
> uses have been found for materials that were
> once scorned as rubbish. It all has to do with a

new way of thinking. Scarcity bends your mind
toward novel solutions, and you discover yourself willing to entertain ideas that would never
have occurred to you before. (29)

The inhabitants of Auster's country, in their ability to
find value and usefulness in a piece of trash, often by
shifting their perspective or relation to an object, resemble the *cartoneros* of Aira's Buenos Aires shantytown.
As Anna explains, finding survival value in discarded
materials becomes a sort of intellectual exercise, born
out of necessity and desperation; those most flexible and
inventive in their thinking can presumably make more
out of less. For some, like Anna, the recycling of objects
becomes a kind of job used to support basic necessities;
"object hunters" scavenge for re-usable objects that they
can sell to "Resurrection Agents," who then re-sell the
objects (33). Since object hunters compete with one
another to find anything of value, Anna explains, "you
must be quick, you must be clever, and you must know
where to look" (33).

In addition, "[an object hunter] can never expect to
find something whole," as bits and pieces of decaying,
broken objects litter the ground, becoming an indistin-
guishable mass (36). For Anna, that reality poses onto-
logical questions—"for nothing really is itself anymore"
(35)—and requires object hunters to sift through the
muck for partially-intact objects that might fit together
with other objects and make something useful. "The
job is to zero in on these little islands of intactness, to
imagine them joined to other such islands, and those

islands to still others, and thus to create new archipela-
goes of matter" (36). Again, Anna's description emphasizes a kind of creativity of perspective and a process
of *bricolage* that re-invents the world through a clever
arrangement of otherwise unrelated scraps. Like the *cartoneros*, the inhabitants of Auster's country literally survive because they have a particular aesthetic approach
to their environment that allows them to see possibility
in waste, and lack as a starting place for re-imagining
the world. Of course, none of that negates the deterioration of the conditions in which they live and the reality
that ingenuity, too, can only go so far. And, yet, as far
as Anna can tell, the survivors persist, deferring the end
by re-inventing and re-defining the last things, and thus
the space they inhabit. Like the shantytown, Auster's
country continually changes, its occupants always in
the process of reconstructing it in order to meet the
basic needs for survival and extending their *bricolage*
to the space of the city as a whole. Tim Woods agrees,
noting in his essay about the novel, "People are shown
to be never simply fixed within a locale, but are active,
space-producing *bricoleurs*" (110-11).

Turning specifically to the character of Anna, much
like the country and the objects of that country, she
undergoes a continual process of destruction and renewal.
She originally goes to the country in order to find her
brother, a journalist who disappeared after he went to
report on the collapse. While Anna has brief periods
of relative stability, the reader remains aware, as does
Anna, that every situation is temporary and that one

risks losing everything at any given moment. In a review of Auster's novel in *The Quarterly Conversation*, we read that, after Anna's preliminary descriptions of the setting and survivors, "the rest of *In the Country of Last Things* consists of the protagonist's experiences in the city as she builds herself out of nothing several times, only to always be demolished." In that way, Anna develops an intimate relation with her own death, coming up against it again and again, and having to re-invent her life multiple times after the one she has been living comes to an end. Anna reveals early in the letter her philosophy that in order to remain alive, "you need to make yourself die" (20). Since "life as we know it has ended," and all of the new lives she pieces together out of the rubble also come to an end, Anna must extinguish her humanness, becoming an adaptable survivor who can persist in a world without humanity, after the end of life (20). Several times throughout the text, Anna alludes to her former self, and to her relationship with "you," the intended recipient of the letter. In the first instance, she emphasizes her imagination and love of storytelling:

> You remember what a playful little girl I was. You could never get enough of my stories, of the worlds I used to make up for us to play inside of. The Castle of No Return, the Land of Sadness, the Forest of Forgotten Words. Do you remember them? How I loved to tell you lies, to trick you into believing my stories, and to watch your face turn serious as I led you from one outlandish scene to the next. (11)

It is hard to believe that Anna wouldn't recognize the irony of the titles of her stories—given that she currently finds herself navigating a Kafkaesque castle full of sad people who, she tells us, forget the words for objects that no longer exist—but perhaps it comes down to the way that she has changed, not allowing herself to think beyond the most literal facts of her existence. "Now I am all common sense and hard calculation. I don't want to be like the others. I see what their imaginings do to them, and I won't let it happen to me" (11). Anna refuses what she calls "the language of ghosts," or a wishful and imaginary way of the thinking by which people escape the realities of their environment, eventually losing their hold on the world and slowly disappearing until they die (10). Anna vows, "I cannot let myself go. I will not allow it. I am going to hold on as long as I can, even if it kills me" (11).

Yet Anna relies on imaginative thinking in order to survive. Though she generally remains practically-minded and realistic throughout the novel, as we saw above, her ingenuity and creativity become a survival tool—despite her fear that anything other than hard calculation might threaten her hold on the world. As an object hunter, Anna has to imagine used, broken objects as something other than they appear. Elizabeth Wesseling notes in her discussion of Auster's novel, "Significantly, Anna describes scavenging as an imaginative endeavor" (499). Beyond that, Anna's discovery of the library and Samuel Farr allow her to exist, at least temporarily, within a space where storytelling and creativity have value, maybe even survival value. Sam reveals as much when he describes his massive book project about the country to Anna: "I can't stop. The book is the only thing that keeps me going. It prevents me from thinking about myself and getting sucked up into my own life. If I ever stopped working on it, I'd be lost. I don't think I'd make it through another day" (104). Sam recognizes that his project in some ways remains beyond his reach—"it's impossible for one person to tell [the story]" (104)—but the endlessness of his work results in the deferral of his own end. Anna soon finds herself offering to share her resources with Sam in exchange for shelter; as a result, the two become intimately involved, and Anna joins Sam in his efforts to write his book. She writes:

> Those were the best days for me. Not just here you understand, but anywhere—the best days of my life. It's odd that I could have been so happy during that awful time, but living with Sam made all the difference. Outwardly, things did not change much. The same struggles still existed, the same problems still had to be confronted every day, but now I had been given the possibility of hope, and I began to believe that sooner or later our troubles were going to end. (107)

Anna connects her "best days" to a feeling of hope and to the sense that, at some time, the last things will make way for first things, that the prolonged and painful process of ending will itself come to an end.

The library itself becomes an important space for Anna on a number of different levels. As Clara Sarmento explains in her analysis, "Safety and comfort are only allowed indoors. And the library [...] is a very special inner space, surrounded by chaos, devoted solely to books, the sole sheltering harbor in the collective drifting of this society" (149). The library represents a space of fantasy—one that Anna and Sam indulge while they can, despite their awareness, as they throw tomes into the fire for warmth, that "the world [books] had belonged to was finished" (116). Anna becomes invested in Sam's writing project and, at least on some level, engages with a part of herself she has repressed in favor of hard calculation and practicality. While the library ultimately becomes a "last thing," as well as Sam's manuscript and Anna's "best days," Anna's experiences there introduce the notion that the writing or telling of one's experience has a relation to survival, or to a sort of endless deferral. Sam collects and records the experience of survivors, and, as long as people and their stories remain, his project will presumably not reach its end; the perpetuation of the book attests to the perpetuation of people who somehow manage to stay alive in an environment that offers little more than death. And as evidenced by the letter we read, Anna eventually picks up the pen herself, trying to extend her own life by writing a letter about her inexpressible experiences.

In addition to writing and storytelling, the library reconnects Anna with other aspects of her life before the collapse. Anna happens upon a rabbi and his followers

in an inner room of the library, and she ends up developing a relationship with the rabbi. She reflects, "Perhaps
he reminded me of how things had been when I was
very young, back in the dark ages when I still believed
in what fathers and teachers said to me. I can't say for
sure, but the fact was that I felt on solid ground with
him, and I knew that he was someone I could trust"
(96). Anna's description suggests a rediscovery of a self
that died in the country of last things—one who trusts
others and has a sense of security in the world. The child
she describes here is the same child who loved to tell
stories and to engage in imaginative play, and the rabbi
seems to inspire Anna to return, even if momentarily,
to that self. Even if Anna now lives in a world where she
feels she can't indulge in the imaginary, which, as Anna
tells the rabbi, includes belief in God, he encourages
her to consider her fight for survival in the broader context of her Jewish heritage: "Every Jew, he said, believes
that he belongs to the last generation of Jews. We are
always at the end, always standing on the brink of the
last moment, and why should we expect things to be any
different now?" (112). In some sense, the rabbi suggests,
the Jewish people have already faced the apocalypse, or,
at the very least, have lived at its edge for centuries,
continually facing the threat of annihilation. The rabbi's thoughts recall Aira's depiction of the *cartoneros* in
Shantytown, who have already suffered the end of the
world and now work to piece together an existence from
the remnants. In both cases, the end does not represent
a moment of completion or totality, but a "brink," as

the rabbi says, where one simultaneously surpasses the end and remains unable to reach it. Josh Cohen ties the rabbi's comments to Blanchot's notion of the measureless end, which, he argues is not "the apocalyptic end which completes history, but the spectral end which keeps it open, which fastens the ties of destruction and survival, of 'waiting' and 'wearing out,' at the heart of 'Judaism' and 'writing'" (106). Anna's experience of continually coming up against her end, in a country of ruins and death, links her plight to the broader plight of the Jewish people— something that the rabbi appears to suggest, and perhaps intends as a means of prodding her forward, despite the inexpressible loss that characterizes life in the country of last things.

Anna eventually loses everything she has at the library and ends up at the Woburn House after crashing through the window of a building and inexplicably surviving the fall. Those attending her at the Woburn House conclude that Anna's survival is "less a recovery than a resurrection, an absolute rising up out of nothingness" (126). The language here again emphasizes the sense that Anna lives after or beyond life, in excess of the end and also unable to reach it. When Anna regains consciousness, her caretakers marvel at the fact that she has survived, but Anna quickly realizes the extent of her losses, which include her life in the library, her pregnancy, Sam, and Sam's book. As her body heals, she continues to suffer from despair: "I knew that everything from now on would be aftermath—a dreadful, posthumous sort of life, a life that would go on happening to me, even though it was finished" (137). Anna's "living on" seems to strike her as a curse here, since she has lost any connection to meaningfulness and purpose. She eventually finds herself immersed in the daily rhythms of Woburn House, an environment of relative luxury where one, at least temporarily, does not have to fight and scavenge for food and shelter. Anna explains, "By any standard, Woburn House was a haven, an idyllic refuge from the misery and squalor around it" (139). Yet, much like the library, Woburn House's security depends upon a set of highly permeable borders that will only hold up for so long—especially considering the depletion of the house's resources and the eventuality that the house will merge with its context, no longer able to sustain a different sort of life. Anna's job at Woburn House involves interviewing hopeful residents, and thus requires that she listen to others' stories of desperation and tragedy: "It was too gruesome, too unrelenting, and it was all I could do to hide behind the mask of the job" (144). Perhaps even more than misery, for Anna, the stories communicate "an essential randomness in their design: this then that, and because of that, this" (144). Listening to others' stories, Anna must endure the constant reminder of the contingency and senselessness of life in the country of last things; she must suffer in her awareness that stories offer very little when up against an excruciating, stark sense of randomness.

When Sam later shows up at Woburn House, Victoria Woburn assigns him to the role of doctor, mostly because she believes that having a fake doctor will give people more hope and strength than not having one at all. Anna objects on the basis that such a "masquerade" serves to cover the truth of the world in which they live—that Victoria is exchanging "her straightforwardness, the clarity of her motives" for something much darker, ungrounded, and imaginary (166). Anna's "common sense and hard calculation" tells her that such fantasies lead people astray, inviting them to speak the "language of ghosts" and thus walk towards their death (11). Despite his skepticism that it will do any good, Sam agrees to play the role of doctor and ultimately finds himself in a position similar to Anna's, listening to stories of suffering and tragedy. Unlike Anna, however, Sam feels fulfilled by the stories he hears: "His interior world grew larger, sturdier, more able to absorb the things that were put into it" (168). Matti Hyvärinen, in her essay about the novel, argues, "By contrast to Anna, he has his training as a journalist and he has his white coat and the fake title as doctor to keep himself within the confines of a role. He is thus better equipped to protect himself against the overflowing, transferential trauma" (14). Listening to others' stories allows Sam to put his own suffering to the side and to gain strength by collecting the stories of those who have survived, in some ways, I would argue, revitalizing his lost book project. Compiling the stories one by one, putting them side by side so that they can exist collectively, enables Sam to situate his own story and experience, since he no longer has to grapple with his own story directly, alienated from the experience of others. He tells Anna, "As it is, I have a way to listen to them now, to put them where they belong—next to my own story, next to the story of the self I no longer have to be as long as I am listening to them" (168). While the collected stories, including Sam's own, will not form any sort of meaningful whole, they combat the alienating experience of a random, senseless world where individuals must fight each other to survive; they emphasize collective experience and the way that stories bears witness to survival, to the deferral of the end.

Throughout the novel, Anna vacillates between her determination to stay grounded and practical, and her desire to imagine a different world, where the end might not actually be the end. For the most part, however, she values "common sense and hard calculation" and, as we have seen, remains wary of flights of the imagination or wishful thinking that cause individuals to lose sight of the task at hand: staying alive in a world of starvation, hopelessness, and death. In every relatively stable situation, Anna eventually confronts the problem of waning resources and thus the problem of framing survival as a matter of staving off the end. In a conversation with Boris, an eccentric man who helps Victoria sell off objects from Woburn House, Anna takes a jab at his sentimentality, and Boris responds: "We all speak our own language of ghosts, I'm afraid. I've read the handwriting on the wall, and none of it encourages me. The Woburn House funds will run out. [...] Unless we begin to look ahead, there won't be much future for any of us" (155). Here, Boris implies that survival demands imaginary and wishful thinking, as it propels us forward when there is no other direction in which to go. Survival, from that perspective, becomes a question of how one might surpass the end and arrive somewhere else—a possibility that one can only imagine, since it doesn't exist in the present moment. And as Boris predicts, the occupants of Woburn House realize they will soon have to face the end: "Little by little, the distinction between Woburn House and the rest of the city was growing smaller. We were being swallowed up, and not one of us knew how to prevent it" (171).

For Anna and the other remaining residents of Woburn House, the end of life at the house means that they will seek a life beyond the country of last things, by attempting to escape across one of the borders. The outer edges of the country, much like Aira's shantytown, represent a space that resists logic and masterful navigation. It seems that everything can shift at any given moment, meaning that a possible exit one day might not exist the next. While Sam ventures out to survey the situation along the borders of the country and Boris lingers around municipal buildings trying to overhear any helpful bit of information, they uncover more questions than answers, partially because whatever they observe or hear "is too muddled and discordant to be of any concrete value" (186). And beyond the uncertainty of the situation at the borders, Anna notes that the actual crossing of the border is also in question, given the possible fraudulence of the travel permits they purchased: "They could be forged, in which case we stand to be arrested at the moment we present them to the Exit Supervisor.

Or he could confiscate them for no reason at all and tell us to turn back. Such things have been known to happen, and we must be prepared for every contingency" (186). That preparation demands information, along with common sense and hard calculation, at the same time the uncertainty of the situation and the space resists such an approach. In some sense, Anna, and the others, must have one foot in the world, observing and calculating, and one foot in the imaginary, thinking beyond the confines of their experience and collected knowledge.

While Anna has generally judged negatively any behavior that is not grounded in the objective realities of life in the country of last things, we can observe a shift in perspective at the end of the book. Her discovery of Isabel's notebook does seem to provoke a kind of revelation, or, at the least, a significant insight into the demand to survive the end. In Jesús Lerate's article in *Revista de Estudios Norteamericanos*, he describes the moment that Anna uncovers Isabel's notes: "This experience turns into an epiphany for Anna as it reveals to her and the reader that even in the depleted country of the last things, disinterested goodness, friendship and love—as exercised by Isabel, Sam or Victoria Woburn— are enough for sustaining one's will to live endlessly" (126). Lerate's reading points to Anna's rediscovery of humanity in a world where even that feels like a waning, almost exhausted resource. I would also add, however, that Anna's encounter with Isabel's notebook points specifically to the value of inscribing one's experience of darkness, as an act of survival. She writes:

> The first several pages were covered with her
> messages, the short notes she had written to me
> during the last days of her illness. Most of the
> messages were quite simple—things like "thank
> you" or "water" or "my darling Anna"—but
> when I saw that frail, overlarge handwriting
> on the page and remembered how hard she
> had struggled to make the words clear, those
> simple messages no longer seemed very simple
> at all. A thousand things came rushing back to
> me at once. (182)

During Isabel's last days, the notebook serves the purpose of communicating what she could no longer say, as
her voice became "an incoherent sputter, an awful noise
that sounded like chaos itself" (78). When Anna redis-
covers the notebook, however, she seems to see more;
the minimal or "simple" notes attest to Isabel's fight to
survive and to express her experience of the end, even as
her actual voice disintegrates and mirrors the chaos of her
environment. And the material qualities of the inscription
leave a trace of Isabel's strength and suffering, despite the
brevity and seeming mundanity of the actual messages.
The notebook provokes a flurry of thoughts and feelings
within Anna and inspires her to inscribe her own experience, considering the possibility that Isabel's end might
open onto something else, as long as she, Anna, begins
writing: "If Isabel had not lost her voice, none of these
words would exist. Because she had no more words, these
other words have come out of me. I want you to remember that. If not for Isabel, there would be nothing now.

I never would have begun" (79). Anna re-purposes the notebook with Isabel's written inscription of survival, seeing its value despite its brokenness, and appropriating it in order to inscribe her own story.

Anna explains to the letter's recipient that she intended simply to provide the basics of her situation, but that she has now found herself at the end of the notebook feeling as if she has barely even started to write her experience in the country of last things. She writes:

> That explains why my handwriting has become smaller and smaller as I've progressed. I've been trying to fit everything in, trying to get to the end before it's too late, but I see now how badly I've deceived myself. Words do not allow such things. The closer you come to the end, the more there is to say. The end is only imaginary, a destination you invent to keep yourself going, but a point comes when you realize you will never get there. You might have to stop, but that is only because you have run out of time. You stop, but that does not mean you have come to the end. (186)

Up against the final page, while simultaneously up against the end of life in the country, Anna realizes the inevitability of open-endedness, the impossibility of achieving closure. Rather than offering a path to an outer limit that would complete her progress through the notebook, words work to defer the end, always leaving just a little more room to continue—even if they are so small that we must imagine what they say, knowing that they rattle on, no matter our ability to see them inscribed on the page. Anna is a survivor of ends in a country of last things; but those ends and last things produce a sort of remainder or excess, meaning we can only imagine something more absolute—closure, comprehension, wholeness. In that way, the end of Auster's novel, though quite different in tone from Aira's high-speed, apocalyptic finale, comes to a similar conclusion: the end is imagined; it propels us forward as it recedes beyond our grasp.

The act of writing her experience becomes an act of survival for Anna, much as it does for Isabel; but unlike the elderly and infirm Isabel, Anna does not write in response to a loss of voice, seeking an alternate means for uttering her last words. Instead, the end of Anna's letter attests to an excess of words, piling up in the remaining space of the notebook, each one refusing to become a last word, to surrender as a last thing. Writing creates an opening here, largely because it resists closure, inspiring Anna to vow that she will keep producing words, in an unknowable, imaginary future: "Once we get to where we are going, I will try to write to you again, I promise" (188). When Boris playfully constructs ridiculous fantasies about life after their flight from the country, rather than rebuffing him for straying from the hard facts of the world, Anna plays along. She reflects, "Considering what we have to look forward to, it is pleasant to dream of these absurdities" (187). Anna remains aware of the difficulties the group will face as they try to escape, at the same time that she allows herself to indulge in the sense of possibility, even if represented absurdly, in a life where one steps off the edge of the country to some other place that can't be imagined. "I cannot even begin to think what will happen to us out there. Anything is possible, and that is almost the same as nothing, almost the same as being born into a world that has never existed before" (187-8). Despite an inability to imagine a world after the end, or off the edge—to name or identify anything specific—Anna imagines all the same. She imagines, more simply, an "out there," and the possibility of a world that does not yet exist and that she cannot bring into existence, as the one she knows comes to a close.

WORKS CITED

Aira, César. *How I Became a Nun*. Trans. Chris Andrews. New York: New Directions, 2007.

—. *The Literary Conference*. Trans. Katherine Silver. New York: New Directions, 2010.

—. "La nueva escritura." *Centro de Estudios de Teoría y Crítica Literaria* 8 (2000), 165-170.

—. *Shantytown*. Trans. Chris Andrews. New York: New Directions, 2013.

Asibong, Andrew. *Marie NDiaye*. Liverpool: U of Liverpool P, 2013.

Auster, Paul. *In the Country of Last Things*. New York: Penguin, 1987.

—. *The Invention of Solitude*. New York: Penguin, 2007.

—. "Pages for Kafka." *The Art of Hunger*. New York: Penguin, 1993, 23-25.

Ballvé, Marcelo. "The Literary Alchemy of César Aira." *The Quarterly Conversation*. The Quarterly Conversation n.d. Web. 5 July 2018.

Barone, Dennis. "Introduction: Auster and the Postmodern Novel." *Beyond the Red Notebook: Essays on Paul Auster.* Philadelphia: University of Pennsylvania Press, 1995, 1-26.

Barrette, Laura. "Framing the Past: Photography and Memory in *Housekeeping* and *The Invention of Solitude.*" *South Atlantic Review* 74.1 (Winter 2009): 87-109.

Barth, John. "The Literature of Exhaustion." *Surfiction.* Ed. Raymond Federman. Chicago: Swallow Press, 1975. 19-33.

Barthes, Roland. *Camera Lucida.* New York: Hill and Wang, 2010.

—. "The Death of the Author." *Image-Music-Text.* Trans. Stephen Heath. New York: Hill and Wang, 1978.

—. *The Grain of the Voice.* Trans. Linda Coverdale. Berkeley: U of California Press, 1991.

—. *Mourning Diary.* Trans. Richard Howard. New York: Hill and Wang, 2012.

—. *Roland Barthes by Roland Barthes.* Trans. Richard Howard. New York: Hill and Wang, 2010.

—. *S/Z.* Trans. Richard Miller. New York: Hill and Wang, 1974.

Beaujour, Michel. *Poetics of the Literary Self-Portrait.* New York: NYU Press, 1992.

Berger, James. *After the End: Representations of Post-Apocalypse.* Minneapolis: U of Minnesota P, 1999.

Blanchot, Maurice. *The Infinite Conversation.* Trans. Susan Hanson. Minneapolis: U of Minnesota P, 2003.

—. "Literature and the Right to Death." Trans. Lydia Davis. *The Blanchot Reader.* New York: Station Hill Press, 1999. 359-399

—. *The Space of Literature*. Trans. Ann Smock. Lincoln: U of Nebraska P, 1989.

—. *The Unavowable Community*. Trans. Pierre Joris. New York: Station Hill P, 1988.

Bonacic, Dánisa. "Espacio urbano, crisis y convivencia en *La villa* de César Aira." *Revista de Crítica Literaria Latinoamericana*, 40.79 (2014), 359-376.

Borges, Jorge Luis. "The Aleph." *Collected Fictions*. Trans. Andrew Hurley. New York: Penguin, 1998. 274-288.

—. "The Garden of Forking Paths." *Collected Fictions*. Trans. Andrew Hurley. New York: Penguin, 1998. 119-128.

—. *Selected Non-Fictions*. Trans. Esther Allen, Suzanne Jill Levine, and Eliot Weinberger. Ed. Eliot Weinberger. New York: Penguin Books, 1999.

Brooks, Peter. *Reading for the Plot: Design and Intention in Narrative*. Cambridge: Harvard UP, 1992.

Bronfen, Elisabeth and Sarah Webster Goodwin. "Introduction." *Death and Representation*. Baltimore: The Johns Hopkins University Press, 1993. 3-25.

Bruckner, Pascal. "Paul Auster, or the Heir Intestate." *Beyond the Red Notebook: Essays on Paul Auster*. Philadephia: University of Pennsylvania Press, 1995. 27-33.

Carson, Anne. *Autobiography of Red*. New York: Vintage, 1998.

—. *Eros the Bittersweet*. Champaign: Dalkey Archive Press, 1998.

—. *Nox*. New York: New Directions, 2010.

—. *Plainwater: Essays and Poetry*. New York: Vintage, 2000.

Chambers, Ross. *Loiterature*. Lincoln: U of Nebraska P, 1999.

Cixous, Hélène and Michel Foucault. "On Marguerite Duras." *White Ink: Interviews on Sex, Text, and Politics*. Ed. Susan Sellers. Trans. Suzanne Dow. New York: Columbia UP, 2008, 157-165.

Cohen, Josh. "Desertions: Paul Auster, Edmond Jabès, and the Writing of Auschwitz." *The Journal of the Midwest Modern Language Association* 34.1 (2001), 94-107.

—. Cohen, Joshua. "Reflexive Incomprehension: On Lydia Davis." *Textual Practice* 24.3 (2010).

Contat, Michel. "The Manuscript in a Book: A Conversation." Interview with Paul Auster. Trans. Alyson Waters. *Yale French Studies* 89 (1996): 160-187.

Contreras, Sandra. *Las vueltas de César Aira*. Rosario, Argentina: Beatriz Viterbo Editora, 2002.

Cruickshank, Ruth. Fin de millénaire *French Fiction*. London: Oxford UP, 2009.

Culler, Jonathan. *The Pursuit of Signs*. Ithaca: Cornell UP, 2002.

—. *Framing the Sign*. Hoboken, NJ: Blackwell Publishing, 1988.

D'Agata, John. "A ____ with Anne Carson." *Iowa Review* 27.2 (1997): 1-22.

Davis, Lydia. *The End of Story*. New York: Picador, 2004., 501-516.

Decock, Pablo. "Big Bang y aporías del final en el barrio de César Aira." *Los imaginarios apocalypticos en la literature hispanoamericana contemporánea*. New York: Peter Lang, 2010, 399-419.

—. *Las figuras paradojicas de César Aira*. New York: Peter Lang, 2014.

De Man, Paul. *Allegories of Reading: Figural Language in Rousseau, Nietzsche, Rilke, and Proust.* New Haven: Yale UP, 1982.

Derrida, Jacques. "No Apocalypse, Not Now (Full Speed Ahead, Seven Missiles, Seven Missives)." *Diacritics.* Trans. Catherine Porter and Philip Lewis 14.2 (1984), 20-31.

—. "Structure, Sign, and Play in the Discourse of the Human Sciences." *Writing and Difference.* Trans. Alan Bass. Chicago: U of Chicago P, 1978, 278-294.

—. *The Truth in Painting.* Trans. Geoff Bennington and Ian McLeod. Chicago: U of Chicago P, 1987.

Dick, Jennifer K. "The Pilgrim and the Anthropologist." *Anne Carson: Ecstatic Lyre.* Ed. Joshua Wilkinson. Ann Arbor: U of Michigan P, 2015. 63-68.

Doubrovsky, Serge. Interview with Roger Célestin. *The Journal of Twentieth-Century/Contemporary French Studies* 1.2 (2008): 397-405.

Dow, William. "Paul Auster's *The Invention of Solitude*: Glimmers in a Reach to Authenticity." *Critique: Studies in Contemporary Fiction.* 39.3 (1998): 272-281.

Duras, Marguerite. *La Maladie de la mort.* Paris: Editions de Minuit, 1982.

—. *The Malady of Death.* Trans. Barbara Bray. New York: Grove P, 1994.

Felicelli, Anita. Review of *The Story of My Teeth*, by Valeria Luiselli. *The Rumpus.* 29 Sept 2015. Web. 15 January 2016.

Fleming, Joan. "'Talk (Why?) With Mute Ash': Anne Carson's *Nox* as Therapeutic Biography." *Biography* 39.1 (Winter 2016): 64-78.

García, Mariano. *Degeneraciones textuales*. Buenos Aires: Beatriz Viterbo Editoria, 2000.

Gaudet, Jeanette. "Between a Rock and a Hard Place: Marie Redonnet's *Candy Story* and *Nevermore*." *Disguise, Deception, Trompe-l'oeil*. Ed. Leslie Boldt-Irons, Corrado Federici, and Ernesto Virgulti. New York: Peter Lang, 2009. 163-76.

Genette, Gerard. Paratexts: *Thresholds of Interpretation*. Trans. Jane E. Lewin. Cambridge: Cambridge UP, 1997.

—. *Palimpsests*. Trans. Claude Doubinsky and Channa Newman. Lincoln: U of Nebraska P, 1997.

Goffman, Erving. *Frame Analysis*. New York: Harper, 1974.

Guers-Villate, Yvonne. *Continuité/Discontinuité de l'oeuvre durassienne*. Brussels: Editions de l'Université de Bruxelles, 1985.

Hall, Edith. "The Autobiography of the Western Subject: Carson's Geryon." *Living Classics*. Ed. S.J. Harrison. New York: Oxford UP, 2009. 218-237.

Handke, Peter. *A Sorrow Beyond Dreams*. New York: Farrar, Straus and Giroux, 2012.

Haviland, Beverley. "Missed Connections." *Partisan Review* 56.1 (1989) 160.

Hejinian, Lyn. "The Rejection of Closure." *The Language of Inquiry*. Berkeley: U of California P, 2000.

Hertrampf, Marina Ortrud. "Traces littéraires et photographiques: enjeux esthétiques dans 'l'écriture de la trace' de Marie NDiaye." *Contemporary French and Francophone Studies* 18.4 (2014): 407-15.

Hill, Leslie. *Marguerite Duras: Apocalyptic Desires*. New York: Routledge, 1993.

Hillyer, Aaron. *The Disappearance of Literature*. New York: Bloomsbury, 2013.

Hippolyte, Jean-Louis. *Fuzzy Fiction*. Lincoln: U of Nebraska P, 2006.

Hogarth, Christopher. "The Image of Self-Effacement: The Revindication of the Autonomous Author in Marie NDiaye's *Autoportrait en vert.*" *Framing French Culture*. Eds. Natalie Edwards, Ben McCann, and Peter Poiana. Adelaide, South Australia: Adelaide University Press, 2015.

Hutcheon, Linda. *A Poetics of Postmodernism*. New York: Routledge, 1988.

Hyvärinen, Matti. "Acting, Thinking, and Telling: Anna Blume's Dilemma in Paul Auster's *In the Country of Last Things.*" *Partial Answers* 4.2 (2006), 1-19.

Jameson, Fredric. *Postmodernism: Or, the Cultural Logic of Late Capitalism*. Durham, NC: Duke UP, 1991.

Jennings, Chris. "The Erotic Poetics of Anne Carson." *University of Toronto Quarterly* 70.4 (2001): 923-936.

Kabat, Jennifer. Interview with Valeria Luiselli. *BOMB Magazine*. 129 (2014): n.p.

Kates, J. "Catullus By Night: Anne Carson's *Nox.*" *Harvard Review Online* 23 July 2011. Web. 1 Feb. 2018.

Kermode, Frank. *The Sense of an Ending*. Oxford: Oxford UP, 1968.

Knight, Christopher. "Lydia Davis's Own Philosophical Investigation: *The End of the Story.*" *Journal of Narrative Theory* 38.2 (2008), 198-228.

Kristeva, Julia. "The Pain of Sorrow in the Modern World: The Works of Marguerite Duras." *PMLA* 102.2 (1987), 138-152.

—. *Revolution in Poetic Language.* Trans. Margaret Walter. New York: Columbia University Press, 1994.

Larson, Thomas. "Now Where Was I? On Maggie Nelson's *Bluets.*" *Tri-Quarterly.* Northwestern University 24 January 2011. Web. 8 September 2016.

Lejeune, Philippe. *On Autobiography.* Trans. Katherine Leary. Minneapolis: U of Minnesota P, 1989.

Lerate, Jesús. "The Apocalyptic Urban Landscape in Paul Auster's *In the Country of Last Things.*" *Revista de Estudios Norteamericanos* 4 (1996), 121-127.

Luiselli, Valeria. *Faces in the Crowd.* Trans. Christina MacSweeney. Minneapolis: Coffee House Press, 2014.

—. *Sidewalks.* Trans. Christina MacSweeney. Minneapolis: Coffee House Press, 2014.

—. *The Story of My Teeth.* Trans. Christina MacSweeney. Minneapolis: Coffee House Press, 2015.

Lyotard, Jean-François. *The Postmodern Condition.* Trans. Geoff Bennington and Brian Massumi. Minneapolis: U of Minnesota P, 1984.

MacCallum, E.L. "Toward a Photography of Love." *Postmodern Culture* 17.3 (2007): n.p.

McConnell, Anne. *Approaching Disappearance.* McLean, IL: Dalkey Archive Press, 2013.

McDaniel, Raymond. "Narrative and Crime." *Michigan Quarterly Review* 44.4 (Fall 2005): n.p. Web. 7 Dec. 2017.

McElroy, Alex. "The Textured Narratives of Valeria Luiselli's *The Story of My Teeth.*" *3: AM Magazine.* 17 Sept 2015. Web. 15 Jan 2016.

McHale, Brian. *The Obligation Toward the Difficult Whole.* Tuscaloosa: U of Alabama P: 2004.

—. *Postmodernist Fiction*. New York: Routledge, 1987.

Merivale, Patricia and Susan Elizabeth Sweeney. "The Game's Afoot: On the Trail of the Metaphysical Detective Story." *Detecting Texts*. Philadelphia: University of Pennsylvania Press, 1999. 1-24.

Miller, Geordie. "Shifting Ground: Breaking from Baudrillard's 'Code" in *Autobiography of Red.*" *Canadian Literature* 210/211 (2011): 152-167.

Montalbetti, Christine and Nathalie Piégay-Gros. *La Digression dans le récit*. Paris: Bertrand-Lacoste, 2000.

Motte, Warren. *Fiction Now*. McClean, IL: Dalkey Archive Press, 2017.

—. "The Greening of Marie NDiaye." *French Review* 85.3 (2012): 489-505.

—. "Negative Narrative." *"L'esprit createur* 53.2 (2013): 56-66.

—. *Small Worlds*. Lincoln: U of Nebraska P, 1999.

Moudiléno, Lydie. "Marie NDiaye's Discombobulated Subject." *SubStance* 111.35.3 (2006): 83-94.

Murray, Stuart J. "The Autobiographical Self: Phenomenology and the Limits of Narrative Self-Possession in Anne Carson's *Autobiography of Red.*" *English Studies in Canada* 31.4 (2005): 101-122.

Nealon, Jeffrey T. *Post-postmodernism: Or, the Cultural Logic of Just-in-time Capitalism*. Stanford: Stanford UP, 2012.

Nelson, Maggie. *Argonauts*. Seattle: Graywolf Press, 2015.

—. *Bluets*. Seattle: Wave Books, 1989.

—. Interview with Darcey Steinke. *The Rumpus*. The Rumpus 6 March 2015. Web. 8 September 2016.

—. Interview with Sasha Frere-Jones. *The Los Angeles Times*. The Los Angeles Times 8 March 2016. Web. 8 September 2016.

—. *Jane: A Murder*. Berkeley: Soft Skull Press, 2005.

—. *The Red Parts*. Seattle: Graywolf Press, 2016.

O'Rourke, Meghan. "The Unfolding: Anne Carson's *Nox*." *The New Yorker* 12 July 2010. Web. 1 Feb. 2018.

Phillips, Adam. "Fickle Contracts: The Poetry of Anne Carson." *Raritan: A Quarterly Review* 16.2 (2002) 112-119.

Rae, Ian. "Dazzling Hybrids." *Canadian Literature* 16 (2000): 17-41.

Review of *In the Country of Last Things* by Paul Auster. The Quarterly Conversation n.d. Web. 1 Sept. 2018.

Reber, Deirdra. "Cure for the Capitalist Headache: Affect and Fantastic Consumption in César Aira's Argentine 'Baghdad.'" *MLN* 122.2 (2007), 371-399.

Redonnet, Marie. *Candy Story*. Trans. Alexandra Quinn. Lincoln: U of Nebraska P, 1995.

—. *Hôtel Splendid*. Trans. Jordan Stump. Lincoln: U of Nebraska P, 1994.

—. Interview with Jordan Stump. *Nevermore*. Trans. Jordan Stump. Lincoln: U of Nebraska P, 1994.

—. "Parcours d'une oeuvre." *Contemporary French and Francophone Studies* 12.4 (2008): 487-98.

Ricouart, Janine. *Ecriture féminine et violence*. Birmingham, AL: Summa Publications, 1991.

Saramento, Clara. "The Angel in a Country of Last Things: Delillo, Auster, and the Post-human Landscape." *Arcadia* 41.1 (2006), 147-59.

Smith, Barbara Hernnstein. *Poetic Closure: A Study of How Poems End.* Chicago: U of Chicago P, 1968.

Sparks, Stephen. Review of *The Story of My Teeth,* by Valeria Luiselli. *The White Review.* October 2015. Web. 15 Jan 2016.

Tanderup, Sara. "Nostalgic Experiments: Memory in Anne Carson's *Nox* and Doug Dorst and J.J. Abrams' *S.*" *Image [&] Narrative* 17.3 (2016): 46-56.

Tshofen, Monika. "First I Must Tell About Seeing: (De)monstrations of Visuality and the Dynamics of Metaphor in Anne Carson's *Autobiography of Red." Canadian Literature* 180 (2004): 31-51.

Villanueva, Graciela. "El 'enfrente del enfrente': circuitos urbanos en las novelas de César Aira." *Las ciudades y el fin del siglo XX en América Latina: Literatures, culturas, representaciones.* Ed. Teresa Orecchia Havas. Bern: Peter Lang SA, 2007.

Went-Daoust, Yvette. "Ecrire le conte de fees: l'œuvre de Marie Redonnet." *Neophilologus* 77 (1993): 387-94.

Wesseling, Elisabeth. *"In the Country of Last Things*: Paul Auster's Parable of the Apocalypse." *Neophilogus* 75 (1991), 496-504.

Willis, Sharon. *Marguerite Duras: Writing on the Body.* Chicago: University of Illinois Press, 1987.

Winters, David. "Like Sugar Dissolving: On Lydia Davis's *The End of the Story." The Quarterly Conversation* 35 (2014).

Wood, Gaby. "Murder is Red, Heartbreak is Blue: How Maggie Nelson Found a New Way to Write About Trauma." *The Telegraph.* 27 May 2017. Web. 15 Jan. 2018.

Woods, Tim. "'Looking for Signs in the Air': Urban Space and the Post-modern in *In the Country of Last Things." Beyond the Red Notebook*. Ed. Dennis Barone. Philadelphia: U of Pennsylvania P, 1995.

Zamora, Lois Parkinson. *Writing the Apocalypse: Historical Vision in Contemporary U.S. and Latin American Fiction*. Cambridge: Cambridge UP, 1989.

ENDNOTES

[1] The term "contestation" appears most often in the work of a number of French writers, most notably Maurice Blanchot and Georges Bataille, and in the work of critics who have discussed those writers for the last several decades. Unfortunately, the term in English is rather awkward and opaque—but it really has no synonym. Contestation, as I will use it here in the Introduction, refers to a moment or point where everything comes together and falls apart at the same time. It is a moment or point of closure that confronts the impossibility of closure.

[2] In 1974, not long after the publication of Kermode and Smith's books, Erving Goffman published *Frame Analysis*, which also relates to questions of closure and boundaries. In the book, he analyzes the way we frame our experiences, as a mode of organization and understanding, suggesting that external apparatuses necessarily affect the way we perceive and define our everyday lives. Kermode focuses on the broader issue of conceptual frameworks—rather than something more specific to art and literature—but his book, specifically the chapter, "The Frame Analysis of Talk," can

be seen as an influence on contextual analyses of literature, including Jonathan Culler's *Framing the Sign*, which I discuss · later in the Introduction.

[3] See Derrida's *The Truth in Painting*.

[4] See De Man's *Allegories of Reading*.

[5] See Nealon's P*ost-postmodernism: Or, the Cultural Logic of Just-in-Time Capitalism*. Nealon's title and essay clearly play upon Frederic Jameson's identification of postmodernism as the "cultural logic of late capitalism." Jameson agrees that postmodernism concerns itself with endings, arguing that "premonitions of the future, catastrophic or redemptive, have been replaced by senses of the end of this or that (the end of ideology, art, or social class; the 'crisis' of Leninism, social democracy, or the welfare state, etc., etc.)" (Jameson 1). For Jameson, that emphasis on the end of things produces a kind of disconnect with the past, with history.

[6] Many of the essays collected in *Supplanting the Postmodern* challenge certain hallmarks of postmodernism in an attempt to return to a more humanist perspective, highlighting, for example, authenticity and sincerity, in contrast to postmodern irony. In other words, many of the writers of those essays do not frame the newer trends in literature as an extension of postmodernism, but as a rejection of it. Therefore, notions of exhaustion and excess, the question of what comes after the aftermath, are not necessarily a part of, for example, "renewalism." On the other hand, other critics see contemporary literary trends as emerging out of and reflecting many of the interests of postmodernism. My work here, though not particularly interested in defining texts in terms of literary movement, presumes a continuity between the earlier texts I have chosen from the 1980's to the most recent texts,

from the last five or ten years. The particular texts in this study all demonstrate an interest in issues of excess, marginality, and exhaustion—whether we call them "postmodern," "post-postmodern," or anything else.

[7] Barth's notion of exhausted possibility resembles Maurice Blanchot's discussion of Hegel's pronouncement that art is a "thing of the past" (Blanchot, *The Book to Come* 195)— because, with the advent of aestheticism, it no longer belongs to the realm of history and truth. Rather than disputing Hegel's claim, Blanchot embraces it, discussing the way that art begins precisely at the point where it can no longer begin—unable to bring anything to light, or to make anything available for comprehension. Like Barth, Blanchot suggests that the exhaustion of possibility, the end of doing and making, does not represent an absolute end or moment of closure.

[8] Eshelman's description of "performatism" is only one example of the various attempts to identify what follows postmodernism. A number of the essays collected in *Supplanting the Postmodern*, do share his sense of the reader's/viewer's desire to get back to more solid ground, through a contemporary form of realism, even if we accept the continuing influence of postmodern skepticism. See, for example, John Toth's description of "renewalism" (Stavris and Rudrum 209-249).

[9] Eshelman argues that "performatist" works coerce the reader into a singular reading the text, providing a construct that leads us to a particular interpretive conclusion. Even though we are aware of the artifice, we choose to go with it, contented with the "positive aesthetic identification" (118).

[10] "The Anthropology of Water" appears in *Plainwater*. In different reviews and analyses of most of Carson's work, one

sees the terms "speaker," "narrator," and "Carson" used to refer to the "I" of the text—generally due to the difficulty of defining the genre of her work. I have chosen to use the term "speaker" here for lack of a better term; the suggestion, of course, is that we can "The Anthropology of Water" as a prose poem.

[11] Translation is mine.

[12] I refer here to Gerard Genette's definition of "paratext" (2-3).

[13] This recalls Ross Chambers's discussion of footnotes and endnotes as digressive, in the sense that they implicitly point to the possibility of more footnotes and endnotes, or the extension of the text further beyond its end. See Introduction.

[14] See, for example, Karl Miller, "International Books of the Year—and the Milleneum," *London Times Literary Supplement*, 3 Dec. 1999, 6, where he argues that the extra-textual material in *Autobiography of Red* is more or less unnecessary.

[15] I will refer to the speaker of the proemium, "Red Meat: What Difference Did Stesichoros Make?", as "Carson," though I do not necessarily mean to conflate the speaker's voice with that of the author. One could easily argue that the "I" of the proemium is a sort of academic persona— especially since the question of writing the "I," and autobiographical writing, are at issue in the text. In addition, my own paper's claim that a boundary marking "inside" from "outside" is problematic and impossible to locate suggests that we can't pin down the status of the "I" in this section. Regardless, I will refer to that speaker as "Carson," with the understanding that the first-person pronoun in this supposed "pre-text" cannot be reduced to the author.

[16] I am alluding here to the discussion of Carson's *Plainwater* from the Introduction, and her invitation to "step off the edge" of the text.

[17] One need only glance at the translated fragments of the *Geryoneis* to see that, in addition to inserting modern elements, Carson deliberately refuses to provide an "easy" poetic line that would create a sense fluidity between the ancient and modern texts. I would refer the reader to Rae's brief comparative analysis of Carson's translations next to more traditional translations of Stesichoros's poetry (24).

[18] "The Only Secret People Keep," along with the title of this photograph chapter refer us back to the epigraph, Emily Dickinson's poem, #1748. In the poem, immortality is the secret, which has a direct application to the legend, since the ones who came back were said to be immortal.

[19] Ian Rae develops a convincing reading of the interview wherein he argues that the "S" represents Stein and affirms the shift away from Stesichoros's "master text."

[20] Genette notes, "[Paratexts] provide the text with a (variable) setting and sometimes a commentary, official or not, which even the purists among readers, those least inclined to external erudition, cannot always disregard as easily as they would like and as they claim to do" (3). Luiselli, of course, explicitly challenges attempts to identify and disregard the "external."

[21] See, for example, the interview in *BOMB Magazine*.

[22] See Introduction for discussion of Hejinian's "open text."

[23] In Luiselli's first novel, *Faces in the Crowd*, she writes, "A horizontal novel, told vertically. A novel that has to be told from the outside in order to be read from within" (61). That

description, to me, evokes, her discussion of layering in the afterword to *The Story of My Teeth*. While the horizontal novel comes to an end—considering the novel as a linear progression from first page to last—the vertical novel remains, open to additional layers.

[24] See Nelson's "Preface to the Paperback Edition," in *The Red Parts*, and Auster's interview with Michel Contat in *Yale French Studies*.

[25] I have developed a lengthy reading of Blanchot's understanding of negativity in *Approaching Disappearance* (Champaign: Dalkey, 2013), to which I refer the reader.

[26] "Portrait of an Invisible Man" is the first part of two in *The Invention of Solitude*, which appears in the Works Cited. Most critics have dealt with the text as a whole, partially because the two parts seem to communicate with one another in various ways. I have chosen to focus on "Portrait of an Invisible Man" in this chapter because it specifically concerns Auster's efforts to depict his distant father, and therefore relates to my discussion of *Nox* and *Jane: A Murder*. It is perhaps relevant to note that Auster originally wrote "Portrait of an Invisible Man" as a stand-alone piece and later merged it with "The Book of Memory" to compose *The Invention of Solitude*. See Michel Contat's interview with Auster in *Yale French Studies*.

[27] Throughout the chapter, I will refer to the first-person narrative voice in "Portrait of an Invisible Man" as "Auster," though I make no claims to an equivalency between Paul Auster, the writer, and the "I" of the text. Clearly, "Portrait" takes the shape of a personal essay, but Auster encourages us throughout his work to approach the "I" and the stories "I tell" with a degree of skepticism. I like the way that William Dow presents the "I" of "Portrait": "The self (i.e. Auster's

self) then is defined in the diaristic form of *Invention* as a position, a locus where the discourse between Auster and his father intersect" (275).

[28] See "The Book of the Dead" in *The Art of Hunger* (New York: Penguin, 1993, 107-114) on the writing of Edmond Jabès.

[29] In *Detecting Texts*, Merivale and Sweeney discuss Auster's detective fiction and identify the postmodern detective-writer thusly: "Rather than definitively solving a crime, then, the sleuth finds himself confronting the insoluble mysteries of his own interpretation and his own identity" (2). While "Portrait" doesn't fit into the genre of detective fiction, as I have suggested in the language of my analysis, Auster seems to present himself as a sort of detective figure when digging through the relics of his father's past.

[30] Auster's citation of Blanchot's *Arrêt de mort* also throw us back to an earlier passage in "Portrait" where he uses language that echoes the one he later cites by Blanchot: "For the past few days, in fact, I have begun to feel that the story I am trying to tell is somehow incompatible with language, that the degree to which it resists language is an exact measure of how closely I have come to saying something important, and that when the moment arrives for me to say the one truly important thing (assuming it exists), I will not be able to say it" ("Portrait" 30).

[31] Hecataeus, Carson explains, was an Ancient Greek historian who lived before Herodotus, "the author of that role," and therefore can't really be called a historian (1.1).

[32] Similar to the disclaimer I made about the "I" in "Portrait," I would like to note that I will refer to the first-person voice in *Nox* as "Carson"—again, not as a way to identify

the narrative or poetic "I" of the text unproblematically to Carson herself, but, in this particular case, because the first-person voice in *Nox* takes on multiple forms over the course of the text, given the continually changing genre and media. Therefore, I use the identification "Carson" in my discussion of *Nox* with quotation marks implied. That rationale also applied to my use of "Nelson" to refer to the speaker in *Jane: A Murder*.

[33] An earlier translation of the poem does appear in Carson's book *Men in the Off Hours* (Vintage, 2001).

[34] I develop Carson's approach to translation at greater length in my discussion of *Autobiography of Red*.

[35] In *The Red Parts*, Nelson voices her disdain for comments about the "human needs for storytelling," or about the say stories help us by making sense out of our lives. She writes, "I became a poet in part because I didn't want to tell stories. As far as I could tell, stories may enable us to live, but they also trap us, bring us spectacular pain. In their scramble to make sense of nonsensical things, they distort, codify, blame, aggrandize, restrict, omit, betray mythologize, you name it" (155).

[36] Something with Nelson saying she wants to tell about Jane's life.

[37] Nelson does tell us she doesn't change major stuff

[38] While *The Red Parts* serves as a "sequel" to *Jane* in terms of the subject matter, in terms of genre and approach, it differs significantly. *The Red Parts* resembles Auster's "Portrait" more than *Jane* or *Nox*, as a self-consciously autobiographical prose piece, rather than a book of poetry—though Auster, Nelson, and Carson have all expressed and demonstrated a playful skepticism in regards to generic definitions.

[39] For instance, Philippe Lejeune defines autobiography as: "*Retrospective prose narrative written by a real person concerning his own existence, where the focus is his individual life, in particular the story of this personality*" (4, emphasis in original). There is no indication in any of these texts that the "I" of the narrative corresponds to the author, as a "real person," or to his or her individual life.

[40] I have developed Blanchot's notion to the author's disappearance at length in the first chapter of *Approaching Disappearance* (Champaign: Dalkey Archive Press, 2013).

[41] Translations of Hertrampf are mine.

[42] Michel Beaujour, contrasting autobiography with self-portraiture, simultaneously disparages and employs the term "self-portrait" as a means of identifying non-narrative self-writing the presents itself as a sort of sketch, without beginning or end, or any claim to wholeness or coherence. "Self-portraitists make self-portraits without knowing what they are doing. This 'genre' proffers no 'horizon of expectation'. Each self-portrait is written as if it is the only text of its kind" (3). Those characteristics also fit well with NDiaye's text.

[43] Translation is mine.

[44] In an essay on NDiaye's novel *Rosie Carpe*, Lydie Moudileno describes the protagonist as a "discombobulated subject," arguing that the novel demonstrates "the condition of a contemporary subject ill-equipped to interpret a reality whose logic always seems to escape her" (84). Though the narrator of *Self-Portrait in Green* differs from Rosie Carpe in many ways, I would argue that Moudileno's characterization of Rosie applies to the narrator of *Self-Portrait* as well—in the sense that we have a subject who struggles with the way

that the world escapes her, no matter how hard she tries to understand and manage her environment.

[45] In this middle section of *Self-Portrait in Green*, the narrator turns most obviously away from herself, remaining at a distance from the story Jenny tells, since it doesn't implicate her and has no concrete effect on her life—unlike her encounters with other green women whom, as we have seen, trouble the narrator's grasp on the world and confront her with uncertainty and multiplicity. Perhaps for that reason, the narrator consumes Jenny's story freely and voraciously, based on her intense fascination with the woman in green. From that point of view, the narrator's distance from the story allows her to observe the workings of greenness, of a particular woman in green, without feeling threatened by the situation.

[46] See Asibong, "Little Tar Baby: Framing the Invisible Child" in *Marie NDiaye*, 142-167. Asibong argues that both the narrator and her parents demonstrate a kind of parenting that makes the child invisible or anonymous, and emphasizes the differences in perception between children and their parents in the text.

[47] Translation is mine.

[48] In an interview with Maria Moreno, Aira insists, "Autobiographical material runs out. [...] In that sense I have no trouble, because in my work everything is invented, and I can go on inventing indefinitely."

[49] Translation is mine.

[50] I am thinking here of Jacques Derrida's engagement with the term *survivre*, in particular in his essay on Maurice Blanchot's *L'arrêt de mort*.

[51] Translation is mine.

[52] Translation is mine.

[53] Translation is mine.

[54] My purpose here is not to dismiss the question of gender and subject/object relations, but to use a Blanchotian lens to consider the woman's "passivity" in another light. I would actually argue, though I don't have the space here to do it, that the woman's outsidership and ungraspability in *The Malady of Death* evoke what Hélène Cixous describes in "The Laugh of the Medusa," when she argues that woman escapes the controlling reach of the phallus, which allows her to write outside the system.

[55] I have included the expression from the original French here, as it emphasizes the absolute darkness of the night.

[56] *The Space of Literature*, 171-6.

[57] Translation is mine.

[58] In *The Argonauts*, Nelson refers specifically to Barthes' comparison of *The Argo* with the subject who says "I love you," in that the task of the expression, while formally the same, is to bear new meaning with each use (5). While the application of Barthes' *Argo* is a little different here, one can understand that difference in terms of the way *Bluets* and *The Argonauts* differ, thematically and structurally.

[59] Maggie Nelson, interviewed by Sasha Frere-Jones, *The Los Angeles Times*, Los Angeles Times, March 8, 2016. Interestingly, in this interview, Nelson resists the suggestion of structural similarity between *Bluets* and *The Argonauts*, explaining that she doesn't see the latter as having an interest in fragmentation. From that perspective, the application of Barthes' *Argo* would work differently than the one I have suggested for *Bluets*.

[60] Here, again, I make reference to Blanchot's "Orpheus's Gaze," in *The Space of Literature*. Like Duras, Davis converses with Blanchot's thought, often using language that evokes the French writer. While I wouldn't want to belabor the significance of Blanchot's role in Davis's work simply due to the fact that she has translated several of his essays, noting that connection feels fruitful when following certain trains of thought through Davis's novel and short stories.

[61] In her review of *Break it Down*, Beverly Haviland remarks on that sense of anxiety as a characteristic of Davis's work, which she describes as a "program of writing adhered to by one perhaps fearful of the consequences of a slight error" (160).

[62] I am thinking, for instance, about Maurice Blanchot's *The Writing of the Disaster* (Trans. Ann Smock. Lincoln: U of Nebraska P, 2015) and Theodor Adorno's essay, "Cultural Criticism in Society," where he introduces the notion of "barbaric writing" (*Prisms*. Trans. Shierry Weber Nicholsen and Samuel Weber. Boston: MIT Press, 1983, p.17-34).

[63] Blanchot discusses constructive negativity, often in reference to Hegel, in many places, including his essay, "Literature and the Right to Death" (*The Blanchot Reader*. Trans. Lydia Davis. New York: Station Hill P, p.359-400). I would also refer you to *Approaching Disappearance*, where I have a chapter on Blanchot's understanding of negativity and death, in relation to poetry and art (Dalkey Archive Press, 2013, p.17-49).

[64] See the opening of Bonacic's essay, where she discusses the socio-economic environment of Buenos Aires around the turn of the century, and also refers the reader to Eduardo Anguita's book, *Cartoneros, recuperadores de desechos ye causa perdidas* (Bogotá: Grupo Editorial Norma, 2003).

[65] While some critics identify Auster's novel as apocalyptic, others see it as post-apocalyptic. Elisabeth Wesseling and Jesús Lerate both read the novel as a sort of fight against the end, seeing the apocalypse as an absolute end that can only be imagined—at least partially inspired by Jacques Derrida's discussion of the way that nuclear annihilation can only exist textually, or as "signified referent," since the actual event represents the literal end of the world, and thus any discussion about it (Derrida 23). From this perspective, the post-apocalyptic can't exist. In my reading of the text, I choose to see Auster's novel as post-apocalyptic, more along the lines of Berger's consideration of catastrophic ends and their aftermath. Though we don't know much about the collapse of Auster's country of last things, we do know that the remaining inhabitants live in a post-traumatic environment of scavenging, chaos, and constant danger, where they first and foremost must figure out how to survive each day. In other words, the people survive the end and also struggle to stave off the end, which captures the paradoxical threat that the apocalypse will recur.

[66] All translations of Bonacic are mine.

[67] All translations of Decock are mine. Decock also includes page numbers to exemplify those characteristics of the *cartoneros* in the novel.

[68] Translation is mine.

[69] In Graciela Villaneuva's article, "El 'enfrente del enfrente': circuitos urbanos en las novelas de César Aira," she points out that the urban space that Aira composes in many of his novels becomes a literary space, labyrinthine and circuitous. She mentions *Las noches de Flores*, where the pizza delivery people wind through the streets of Buenos Aires on

motorcycles (Barcelona: Literatura Random House, 2016). Clearly, *Shantytown* explores the space of Buenos Aires as well, although it is specifically interested in examining and interrogating the border between middle-class neighborhood and shantytown. And, as I have mentioned, Aira points to the aesthetic aspects of the *cartoneros* construction and navigation of space.

[70] See Aira's interview with Carlos Alfieri in *Conversaciones: Entrevistas a César Aira, Guillermo Cabrera Infante, Roger Chartier, Antonio Muñoz Molina, Ricardo Piglia, y Fernando Savater* (Katz, 2008), p. 25-6.

[71] All translations of Contreras are mine.

[72] Blanchot discusses the relation of the book and the work in *The Space of Literature* and elsewhere in his oeuvre. He writes, "The writer belongs to the work, but what belongs to him is only a book, a mute collection of sterile words, the most insignificant thing in the world" (23).

ACKNOWLEDGEMENTS

I would like to thank West Virginia State University for supporting the writing and publication of this book. I would also like to thank the West Virginia Humanities Council, which provided a research grant for this project. Lastly, I would like to express gratitude to Warren Motte, who offered his time, insight, and encouragement as I wrote this book.

This project is presented with financial assistance from the West Virginia Humanities Council, a state affiliate of the National Endowment for the Humanities. Any views, findings, conclusions or recommendations do not necessarily represent those the West Virginia Humanities Council or the National Endowment for the Humanities.

MICHAL AJVAZ, *The Golden Age.*
The Other City.
PIERRE ALBERT-BIROT, *Grabinoulor.*
YUZ ALESHKOVSKY, *Kangaroo.*
FELIPE ALFAU, *Chromos.*
Locos.
JOE AMATO, *Samuel Taylor's Last Night.*
IVAN ÂNGELO, *The Celebration.*
The Tower of Glass.
ANTÓNIO LOBO ANTUNES, *Knowledge of Hell.*
The Splendor of Portugal.
ALAIN ARIAS-MISSON, *Theatre of Incest.*
JOHN ASHBERY & JAMES SCHUYLER, *A Nest of Ninnies.*
ROBERT ASHLEY, *Perfect Lives.*
GABRIELA AVIGUR-ROTEM, *Heatwave and Crazy Birds.*
DJUNA BARNES, *Ladies Almanack.*
Ryder.
JOHN BARTH, *Letters.*
Sabbatical.
DONALD BARTHELME, *The King.*
Paradise.
SVETISLAV BASARA, *Chinese Letter.*
MIQUEL BAUÇÀ, *The Siege in the Room.*
RENÉ BELLETTO, *Dying.*
MAREK BIENCZYK, *Transparency.*
ANDREI BITOV, *Pushkin House.*
ANDREJ BLATNIK, *You Do Understand.*
Law of Desire.
LOUIS PAUL BOON, *Chapel Road.*
My Little War.
Summer in Termuren.
ROGER BOYLAN, *Killoyle.*
IGNÁCIO DE LOYOLA BRANDÃO, *Anonymous Celebrity.*
Zero.
BONNIE BREMSER, *Troia: Mexican Memoirs.*
CHRISTINE BROOKE-ROSE, *Amalgamemnon.*
BRIGID BROPHY, *In Transit.*
The Prancing Novelist.

GERALD L. BRUNS,
Modern Poetry and the Idea of Language.
GABRIELLE BURTON, *Heartbreak Hotel.*
MICHEL BUTOR, *Degrees.*
Mobile.
G. CABRERA INFANTE, *Infante's Inferno.*
Three Trapped Tigers.
JULIETA CAMPOS, *The Fear of Losing Eurydice.*
ANNE CARSON, *Eros the Bittersweet.*
ORLY CASTEL-BLOOM, *Dolly City.*
LOUIS-FERDINAND CÉLINE, *North.*
Conversations with Professor Y.
London Bridge.
MARIE CHAIX, *The Laurels of Lake Constance.*
HUGO CHARTERIS, *The Tide Is Right.*
ERIC CHEVILLARD, *Demolishing Nisard.*
The Author and Me.
MARC CHOLODENKO, *Mordechai Schamz.*
JOSHUA COHEN, *Witz.*
EMILY HOLMES COLEMAN, *The Shutter of Snow.*
ERIC CHEVILLARD, *The Author and Me.*
ROBERT COOVER, *A Night at the Movies.*
STANLEY CRAWFORD, *Log of the S.S.*
The Mrs Unguentine.
Some Instructions to My Wife.
RENÉ CREVEL, *Putting My Foot in It.*
RALPH CUSACK, *Cadenza.*
NICHOLAS DELBANCO, *Sherbrookes.*
The Count of Concord.
NIGEL DENNIS, *Cards of Identity.*
PETER DIMOCK, *A Short Rhetoric for Leaving the Family.*
ARIEL DORFMAN, *Konfidenz.*
COLEMAN DOWELL, *Island People.*
Too Much Flesh and Jabez.
ARKADII DRAGOMOSHCHENKO, *Dust.*
RIKKI DUCORNET, *Phosphor in Dreamland.*
The Complete Butcher's Tales.

RIKKI DUCORNET (cont.), *The Jade Cabinet.*
The Fountains of Neptune.

WILLIAM EASTLAKE, *The Bamboo Bed.*
Castle Keep.
Lyric of the Circle Heart.

JEAN ECHENOZ, *Chopin's Move.*

STANLEY ELKIN, *A Bad Man.*
Criers and Kibitzers, Kibitzers and Criers.
The Dick Gibson Show.
The Franchiser.
The Living End.
Mrs. Ted Bliss.

FRANÇOIS EMMANUEL, *Invitation to a Voyage.*

PAUL EMOND, *The Dance of a Sham.*

SALVADOR ESPRIU, *Ariadne in the Grotesque Labyrinth.*

LESLIE A. FIEDLER, *Love and Death in the American Novel.*

JUAN FILLOY, *Op Oloop.*

ANDY FITCH, *Pop Poetics.*

GUSTAVE FLAUBERT, *Bouvard and Pécuchet.*

KASS FLEISHER, *Talking out of School.*

JON FOSSE, *Aliss at the Fire.*
Melancholy.

FORD MADOX FORD, *The March of Literature.*

MAX FRISCH, *I'm Not Stiller.*
Man in the Holocene.

CARLOS FUENTES, *Christopher Unborn.*
Distant Relations.
Terra Nostra.
Where the Air Is Clear.

TAKEHIKO FUKUNAGA, *Flowers of Grass.*

WILLIAM GADDIS, JR., *The Recognitions.*

JANICE GALLOWAY, *Foreign Parts.*
The Trick Is to Keep Breathing.

WILLIAM H. GASS, *Life Sentences.*
The Tunnel.
The World Within the Word.
Willie Masters' Lonesome Wife.

GÉRARD GAVARRY, *Hoppla! 1 2 3.*

ETIENNE GILSON, *The Arts of the Beautiful.*
Forms and Substances in the Arts.

C. S. GISCOMBE, *Giscome Road.*
Here.

DOUGLAS GLOVER, *Bad News of the Heart.*

WITOLD GOMBROWICZ, *A Kind of Testament.*

PAULO EMÍLIO SALES GOMES, *P's Three Women.*

GEORGI GOSPODINOV, *Natural Novel.*

JUAN GOYTISOLO, *Count Julian.*
Juan the Landless.
Makbara.
Marks of Identity.

HENRY GREEN, *Blindness.*
Concluding.
Doting.
Nothing.

JACK GREEN, *Fire the Bastards!*

JIŘÍ GRUŠA, *The Questionnaire.*

MELA HARTWIG, *Am I a Redundant Human Being?*

JOHN HAWKES, *The Passion Artist.*
Whistlejacket.

ELIZABETH HEIGHWAY, ED., *Contemporary Georgian Fiction.*

AIDAN HIGGINS, *Balcony of Europe.*
Blind Man's Bluff.
Bornholm Night-Ferry.
Langrishe, Go Down.
Scenes from a Receding Past.

KEIZO HINO, *Isle of Dreams.*

KAZUSHI HOSAKA, *Plainsong.*

ALDOUS HUXLEY, *Antic Hay.*
Point Counter Point.
Those Barren Leaves.
Time Must Have a Stop.

NAOYUKI II, *The Shadow of a Blue Cat.*

DRAGO JANČAR, *The Tree with No Name.*

MIKHEIL JAVAKHISHVILI, *Kvachi.*

GERT JONKE, *The Distant Sound.*
Homage to Czerny.
The System of Vienna.

FOR A FULL LIST OF PUBLICATIONS, VISIT: www.dalkeyarchive.com

JACQUES JOUET, *Mountain R.*
Savage.
Upstaged.

MIEKO KANAI, *The Word Book.*

YORAM KANIUK, *Life on Sandpaper.*

ZURAB KARUMIDZE, *Dagny.*

JOHN KELLY, *From Out of the City.*

HUGH KENNER, *Flaubert, Joyce and Beckett: The Stoic Comedians.*
Joyce's Voices.

DANILO KIŠ, *The Attic.*
The Lute and the Scars.
Psalm 44.
A Tomb for Boris Davidovich.

ANITA KONKKA, *A Fool's Paradise.*

GEORGE KONRÁD, *The City Builder.*

TADEUSZ KONWICKI, *A Minor Apocalypse.*
The Polish Complex.

ANNA KORDZAIA-SAMADASHVILI, *Me, Margarita.*

MENIS KOUMANDAREAS, *Koula.*

ELAINE KRAF, *The Princess of 72nd Street.*

JIM KRUSOE, *Iceland.*

AYSE KULIN, *Farewell: A Mansion in Occupied Istanbul.*

EMILIO LASCANO TEGUI, *On Elegance While Sleeping.*

ERIC LAURRENT, *Do Not Touch.*

VIOLETTE LEDUC, *La Bâtarde.*

EDOUARD LEVÉ, *Autoportrait.*
Newspaper.
Suicide.
Works.

MARIO LEVI, *Istanbul Was a Fairy Tale.*

DEBORAH LEVY, *Billy and Girl.*

JOSÉ LEZAMA LIMA, *Paradiso.*

ROSA LIKSOM, *Dark Paradise.*

OSMAN LINS, *Avalovara.*
The Queen of the Prisons of Greece.

FLORIAN LIPUŠ, *The Errors of Young Tjaž.*

GORDON LISH, *Peru.*

ALF MACLOCHLAINN, *Out of Focus.*
Past Habitual.

The Corpus in the Library.

RON LOEWINSOHN, *Magnetic Field(s).*

YURI LOTMAN, *Non-Memoirs.*

D. KEITH MANO, *Take Five.*

MINA LOY, *Stories and Essays of Mina Loy.*

MICHELINE AHARONIAN MARCOM, *A Brief History of Yes.*
The Mirror in the Well.

BEN MARCUS, *The Age of Wire and String.*

WALLACE MARKFIELD, *Teitlebaum's Window.*

DAVID MARKSON, *Reader's Block.*
Wittgenstein's Mistress.

CAROLE MASO, *AVA.*

HISAKI MATSUURA, *Triangle.*

LADISLAV MATEJKA & KRYSTYNA POMORSKA, EDS., *Readings in Russian Poetics: Formalist & Structuralist Views.*

HARRY MATHEWS, *Cigarettes.*
The Conversions.
The Human Country.
The Journalist.
My Life in CIA.
Singular Pleasures.
The Sinking of the Odradek.
Stadium.
Tlooth.

HISAKI MATSUURA, *Triangle.*

DONAL MCLAUGHLIN, *beheading the virgin mary, and other stories.*

JOSEPH MCELROY, *Night Soul and Other Stories.*

ABDELWAHAB MEDDEB, *Talismano.*

GERHARD MEIER, *Isle of the Dead.*

HERMAN MELVILLE, *The Confidence-Man.*

AMANDA MICHALOPOULOU, *I'd Like.*

STEVEN MILLHAUSER, *The Barnum Museum.*
In the Penny Arcade.

RALPH J. MILLS, JR., *Essays on Poetry.*

MOMUS, *The Book of Jokes.*

CHRISTINE MONTALBETTI, *The Origin of Man.*
Western.

NICHOLAS MOSLEY, *Accident.*
Assassins.
Catastrophe Practice.
A Garden of Trees.
Hopeful Monsters.
Imago Bird.
Inventing God.
Look at the Dark.
Metamorphosis.
Natalie Natalia.
Serpent.

WARREN MOTTE, *Fables of the Novel:*
French Fiction since 1990.
Fiction Now: The French Novel in the
21st Century.
Mirror Gazing.
Oulipo: A Primer of Potential Literature.

GERALD MURNANE, *Barley Patch.*
Inland.

YVES NAVARRE, *Our Share of Time.*
Sweet Tooth.

DOROTHY NELSON, *In Night's City.*
Tar and Feathers.

ESHKOL NEVO, *Homesick.*

WILFRIDO D. NOLLEDO, *But for*
the Lovers.

BORIS A. NOVAK, *The Master of*
Insomnia.

FLANN O'BRIEN, *At Swim-Two-Birds.*
The Best of Myles.
The Dalkey Archive.
The Hard Life.
The Poor Mouth.
The Third Policeman.

CLAUDE OLLIER, *The Mise-en-Scène.*
Wert and the Life Without End.

PATRIK OUŘEDNÍK, *Europeana.*
The Opportune Moment, 1855.

BORIS PAHOR, *Necropolis.*

FERNANDO DEL PASO, *News from*
the Empire.
Palinuro of Mexico.

ROBERT PINGET, *The Inquisitory.*
Mahu or The Material.
Trio.

MANUEL PUIG, *Betrayed by Rita*
Hayworth.

The Buenos Aires Affair.
Heartbreak Tango.

RAYMOND QUENEAU, *The Last Days.*
Odile.
Pierrot Mon Ami.
Saint Glinglin.

ANN QUIN, *Berg.*
Passages.
Three.
Tripticks.

ISHMAEL REED, *The Free-Lance*
Pallbearers.
The Last Days of Louisiana Red.
Ishmael Reed: The Plays.
Juice!
The Terrible Threes.
The Terrible Twos.
Yellow Back Radio Broke-Down.

JASIA REICHARDT, *15 Journeys Warsaw*
to London.

JOÃO UBALDO RIBEIRO, *House of the*
Fortunate Buddhas.

JEAN RICARDOU, *Place Names.*

RAINER MARIA RILKE,
The Notebooks of Malte Laurids Brigge.

JULIÁN RÍOS, *The House of Ulysses.*
Larva: A Midsummer Night's Babel.
Poundemonium.

ALAIN ROBBE-GRILLET, *Project for a*
Revolution in New York.
A Sentimental Novel.

AUGUSTO ROA BASTOS, *I the Supreme.*

DANIËL ROBBERECHTS, *Arriving in*
Avignon.

JEAN ROLIN, *The Explosion of the*
Radiator Hose.

OLIVIER ROLIN, *Hotel Crystal.*

ALIX CLEO ROUBAUD, *Alix's Journal.*

JACQUES ROUBAUD, *The Form of*
a City Changes Faster, Alas, Than the
Human Heart.
The Great Fire of London.
Hortense in Exile.
Hortense Is Abducted.
Mathematics: The Plurality of Worlds of
Lewis.
Some Thing Black.

RAYMOND ROUSSEL, *Impressions of Africa.*

VEDRANA RUDAN, *Night.*

PABLO M. RUIZ, *Four Cold Chapters on the Possibility of Literature.*

GERMAN SADULAEV, *The Maya Pill.*

TOMAŽ ŠALAMUN, *Soy Realidad.*

LYDIE SALVAYRE, *The Company of Ghosts.*
The Lecture.
The Power of Flies.

LUIS RAFAEL SÁNCHEZ, *Macho Camacho's Beat.*

SEVERO SARDUY, *Cobra & Maitreya.*

NATHALIE SARRAUTE, *Do You Hear Them?*
Martereau.
The Planetarium.

STIG SÆTERBAKKEN, *Siamese.*
Self-Control.
Through the Night.

ARNO SCHMIDT, *Collected Novellas.*
Collected Stories.
Nobodaddy's Children.
Two Novels.

ASAF SCHURR, *Motti.*

GAIL SCOTT, *My Paris.*

DAMION SEARLS, *What We Were Doing and Where We Were Going.*

JUNE AKERS SEESE,
Is This What Other Women Feel Too?

BERNARD SHARE, *Inish.*
Transit.

VIKTOR SHKLOVSKY, *Bowstring.*
Literature and Cinematography.
Theory of Prose.
Third Factory.
Zoo, or Letters Not about Love.

PIERRE SINIAC, *The Collaborators.*

KJERSTI A. SKOMSVOLD,
The Faster I Walk, the Smaller I Am.

JOSEF ŠKVORECKÝ, *The Engineer of Human Souls.*

GILBERT SORRENTINO, *Aberration of Starlight.*
Blue Pastoral.
Crystal Vision.

Imaginative Qualities of Actual Things.
Mulligan Stew. Red the Fiend.
Steelwork.
Under the Shadow.

MARKO SOSIČ, *Ballerina, Ballerina.*

ANDRZEJ STASIUK, *Dukla.*
Fado.

GERTRUDE STEIN, *The Making of Americans.*
A Novel of Thank You.

LARS SVENDSEN, *A Philosophy of Evil.*

PIOTR SZEWC, *Annihilation.*

GONÇALO M. TAVARES, *A Man: Klaus Klump.*
Jerusalem.
Learning to Pray in the Age of Technique.

LUCIAN DAN TEODOROVICI,
Our Circus Presents . . .

NIKANOR TERATOLOGEN, *Assisted Living.*

STEFAN THEMERSON, *Hobson's Island.*
The Mystery of the Sardine.
Tom Harris.

TAEKO TOMIOKA, *Building Waves.*

JOHN TOOMEY, *Sleepwalker.*

DUMITRU TSEPENEAG, *Hotel Europa.*
The Necessary Marriage.
Pigeon Post.
Vain Art of the Fugue.

ESTHER TUSQUETS, *Stranded.*

DUBRAVKA UGRESIC, *Lend Me Your Character.*
Thank You for Not Reading.

TOR ULVEN, *Replacement.*

MATI UNT, *Brecht at Night.*
Diary of a Blood Donor.
Things in the Night.

ÁLVARO URIBE & OLIVIA SEARS, EDS.,
Best of Contemporary Mexican Fiction.

ELOY URROZ, *Friction.*
The Obstacles.

LUISA VALENZUELA, *Dark Desires and the Others.*
He Who Searches.

PAUL VERHAEGHEN, *Omega Minor.*

BORIS VIAN, *Heartsnatcher.*

LLORENÇ VILLALONGA, *The Dolls'*
Room.

TOOMAS VINT, *An Unending Landscape.*

ORNELA VORPSI, *The Country Where No*
One Ever Dies.

AUSTRYN WAINHOUSE, *Hedyphagetica.*

CURTIS WHITE, *America's Magic*
Mountain.
The Idea of Home.
Memories of My Father Watching TV.
Requiem.

DIANE WILLIAMS,
Excitability: Selected Stories.
Romancer Erector.

DOUGLAS WOOLF, *Wall to Wall.*
Ya! & John-Juan.

JAY WRIGHT, *Polynomials and Pollen.*
The Presentable Art of Reading Absence.

PHILIP WYLIE, *Generation of Vipers.*

MARGUERITE YOUNG, *Angel in the*
Forest.
Miss MacIntosh, My Darling.

REYOUNG, *Unbabbling.*

VLADO ŽABOT, *The Succubus.*

ZORAN ŽIVKOVIĆ , *Hidden Camera.*

LOUIS ZUKOFSKY, *Collected Fiction.*

VITOMIL ZUPAN, *Minuet for Guitar.*

SCOTT ZWIREN, *God Head.*

AND MORE . . .